America's First Cuisines

AMERICA'S FIRST CUISINES

Sophie D. Coe

 University of Texas Press   Austin

Fifth paperback printing, 2005

Requests for permission to reproduce material from this
work should be sent to Permissions, University of Texas
Press, Box 7819, Austin, TX 78713-7819.

www.utexas.edu/utpress/about/bpermission.html

♾ The paper used in this publication meets the minimum
requirements of American National Standard for
Information Sciences—Permanence of Paper for Printed
Library Materials, ANSI Z39.48-1984.

Library of Congress Cataloging-in-Publication Data

Coe, Sophie D. (Sophie Dobzhansky), date
America's first cuisines / Sophie D. Coe. — 1st ed.
p.   cm.
Includes bibliographical references and index.
ISBN 978-0-292-71159-4
1. Aztecs—Food.   2. Mayas—Food.   3. Incas—
Food.   I. Title.
F1219.76.F67C64   1994
394.1'2'08997—dc20   93-8836

Cover illustration:
Underworld throne scene from a Maya vase
in the Princeton University Art Museum.
Drawing by Diane Griffiths Peck.
Courtesy Michael D. Coe.

Contents

ILLUSTRATIONS

Preface

To begin with a metaphor appropriate to a book about food: If this book is the fruit of much reading, eating, traveling, and studying, then the core of the fruit consists of the six articles, three on Aztec food and three on Inca food, that I published in shorter versions in *Petits Propos Culinaires* between 1985 and 1991. But the tree that produced the fruit was planted long before that by an extremely gracious letter that I received from the editor of *Petits Propos Culinaires,* Alan Davidson, in return for what was the most banal of letters subscribing to his then newly founded journal. That directed me from the interest and concern common, one hopes, to all competent family cooks toward a more historical and scientific focus for my efforts. For his friendship and encouragement over the years, I cannot thank Alan enough.

Once the project had taken root, the kindness of many libraries helped it to grow. First and foremost I must thank the library system of Yale University, whose amazing resources never seem to come to an end and which endangers researchers by exposing them to too much material and too many paths to explore, rather than too little and too few. The tolerance and helpfulness of the staff is as boundless as the resources, and I am grateful to them all.

Other libraries that I have consulted must also be acknowledged, including the Biblioteca Marciana in Venice, which allowed two total strangers who wandered in off the Piazzetta to read the world's only surviving copy of the *Littera mādata della insula de Cuba de Indie.* The Biblioteca Urbaniana, the library of the British Academy, and the

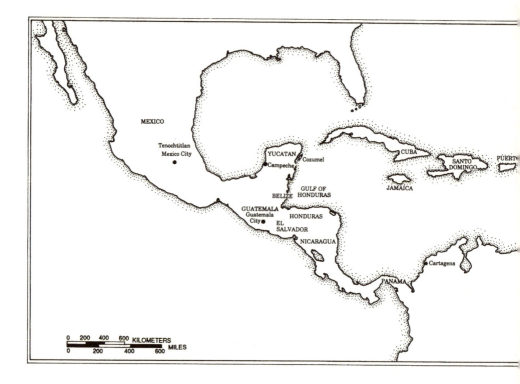

North and Central America. Map by Jean Blackburn.

Instituto Italo–Latino Americano, all in Rome, introduced me to many of the sources.

Many individuals also aided me with advice and comments. From the anthropology department of Yale University they include Floyd Lounsbury, Harold Conklin, and Richard and Lucy Burger. José Arrom, professor emeritus of Spanish, was also a great help. R. S. MacNeish and Charles Remington gave advice in their fields of specialization. From other parts of the world David Pendergast, Robert Laughlin, my Harvard thesis advisor Evon Vogt, Payson Sheets, Dennis and Barbara Tedlock, Steve Houston, Karl Taube, Arturo Gómez-Pompa, and Justin and Barbara Kerr all aided my efforts to discover more about the food of the Classic Maya. Doris Heyden and Louise Burkhardt did the same for the Aztecs, and special gratitude is

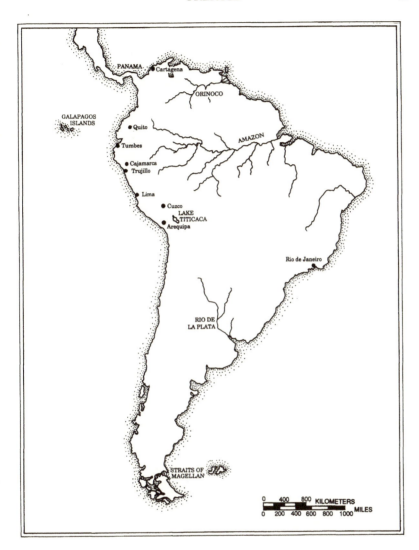

South America. Map by Jean Blackburn.

due to Lawrence Kaplan for laying to rest the myth about Pierio Valerio and the beans of Lamon.

Many people from other fields added to my knowledge. Jane Buikstra edified me as to the difference between the menu and the ingredients, which I hope will be evident in the pages that follow. My colleagues in the amorphous ranks of food historians also encouraged me with their insights. They are too numerous to mention, but I thank them all.

The translations in the pages that follow are my own, and I am of course responsible for any errors. The only exceptions are the translations by others from Nahuatl, which were checked by my resident Nahuatlato, Michael Coe, and corrected if he thought it necessary. The botanical names have been checked with Mabberley (1989).

And the first shall be the last. More than anyone else, I must thank my husband, Michael Coe, who over the years has seen his treasured library ravaged, his dinners disrupted, and his wife either absent or absent-minded. To him, for all his interest, encouragement, and every other possible sort of assistance, this book is dedicated.

America's First Cuisines

Introduction

This is a book written to celebrate the contribution made by the original inhabitants of the New World, the American Indians, Native Americans, or whatever you wish to call them, to the food of the contemporary world. Their gifts, like this book, can be divided into two parts. The first part of the book deals with the contributions of the New World, the ingredients which the original inhabitants gathered, domesticated, and ate for many millennia before Europeans ever laid eyes on them. This section touches the disciplines of botany and zoology, as it explores the wild flora and fauna from which New World plants and animals were selected for the ultimate benefit of all humanity. There are brief "biographies" of some of the more important New World crop plants, sketching, insofar as is known, the history of their adoption by small groups of ancient gatherers, then tracing their expansion over climatically suitable areas of this continent and their eventual conquest of the entire globe.

The second portion of the American contribution constitutes the second half of the book. This is concerned with the uses to which these ingredients were put, both the major ones that got the biographies in the first part and the vast gamut of minor actors that had only more local distinction. In other words, I move from the ingredients to the menus in which they were employed. Where data are available, I try to expand the scope of investigation to cover the whole constellation of beliefs, manners, and customs with which all human beings surround their nourishment.

To do this I must use the contemporary accounts of the first meetings of the Europeans with the three high cultures of aboriginal America, the Aztec, the Maya, and the Inca, and try to winnow from them something about the food these people ate. The reason for the choice of these three is simple: that is where the information is. For these people there are available descriptions of food preparation techniques, methods of preservation, and even the ever-elusive recipes, as well as the manner of serving the food and the etiquette of eating it. Unfortunately, and probably due in large part to the absence of female writers, this evidence can also be sparse and scattered, although there were luckily some male writers who were sufficiently concerned with food matters to record them for us.

As a conclusion I give a similar description of the food of the Spaniards in the New World, during the first few decades following the conquests. That earliest infancy of the hybrid cuisine of the modern world, with its attendant loss and tragedy as well as victory and profit, will stand for the mixture of good and evil that the discovery of the New World brought to the world.

ONE

Domestication

The accusation is often made that the American Indian did not really make much of a contribution as far as the domestication of animals and plants went. The animals—the dog, llama, alpaca, turkey, muscovy duck, guinea pig, and cochineal insect—are not considered important enough to merit more than a sneer in passing. As for the plants, it is implied that American Indians loafed in their hammocks, with tropical produce effortlessly dropping into their laps, and it was up to the Europeans to take the crops they found growing, presumably spontaneously, and make something truly important and edible out of them. The fact that many millennia of patient observations, considered economic decisions, and hard physical work were necessary to assemble the New World crop inventory was brushed aside.

Domestication is no quick and simple matter. Rather, it is a lengthy and continuous process, beginning with the first forager who burned off a stretch of vegetation, or deliberately left some scraps of roots in the soil, so that the plant that was being gathered could survive and produce more foodstuffs to be gathered, and ending with intensive factory farming, where the plant cannot survive without the farmer, and the farmer cannot live without the plant. Actual domestication, that is to say the propagation and maintenance of genetically different plants and animals, many of which could not survive or reproduce in the wild, comes fairly late in the sequence and leads to the practice of agriculture, that is to say the cultivation and tending of plants and animals that are now genetically different from their wild ancestors.

The process is definitely a reversible one. Many a wild plant was cultivated and may have been well on the way to domestication, only to slip back into the wild as tastes changed or newer and better foods appeared. Who now remembers foxtail millet (*Setaria geniculata*), an early foodstuff important in northeastern Mexico (Callen 1967), which was discarded around 2200 B.C. when maize was introduced, or sumpweed (*Iva annua*), a staple in the southeastern United States, which became obsolete at roughly the same time and for the same reason (Heiser 1985)?

The reader may well ask at this point how one can tell a domesticated plant or animal from a wild one. Dictionary definitions telling us that a domesticated plant or animal is one which has its genetic development under the control of human beings, or the mirror-image definition which has the human beings' genetic development under the control of the animal or plant, are no help when the archaeologist or food specialist is confronted with a handful of charred seeds, a few splinters of bone, or a couple of squash peduncles.

Domesticated plant and animal species generally exhibit more visible variation than wild ones, although the wild ones obviously possess hidden genetic reserves that make the varieties of their cultivated descendants possible. Consider the endless named sorts of apples pictured in nineteenth-century pomologies, or picture in your mind's eye a tiny shaggy brown Highland cow next to a gigantic sleek grey Zebu—yet wild ancestral apples and ancestral cows were probably all pretty much alike to the eye.

This is not to say that noticeable differences do not occur within wild species. They do, and they were exploited by the American Indians as they were by all early foragers. In fact, this may well have led to some of the first steps toward domestication, when a particularly favored tree, let us say an oak that produced acorns that were less bitter than others of the same species, would be tended by the local gatherers and its acorns transported farther, perhaps to sprout, beyond the places that they would ordinarily have had a chance to fall and take root. Modern berry pickers exercise the same sort of freedom of choice when they pick the bushes producing the fat juicy berries and avoid the ones producing lean seedy fruit.

Another way of distinguishing the domesticated from the wild is to notice if the portions of the organism that are of the greatest interest to the domesticators, in our case the portions that are edible, have increased in size and quantity. One grain of modern domesticated maize contains more nourishment than the entire cigarette-butt-sized ear of the earliest domesticated maize. Domesticated plants are also at least partially denuded of their physical defenses against the enemies which attack them in the wild and prevent them from producing further generations. Such defenses include bristles, irritating hairs, thorns, spines, and impermeable shells, all of which are undesirable for plants which are going to be growing for the benefit of humans.

There are also the chemical defenses with which plants are armed. Put bluntly, many wild plants taste bad if they do not make the eaters sick or kill them. Domestication is one factor that makes food taste better, although there are others, as we shall see. Let no one imagine that such matters are of no interest to non-Europeans, even if they are living on the subsistence level. Our contemporaries express amazement that the Aymara of Peru and Bolivia can discriminate among their hundreds of kinds of potatoes by taste, while they take the gustatory feats of European wine tasters and tea samplers for granted. Let us hope that this attitude is due to sheer thoughtlessness, not to the sort of racism that many of the early authors on the New World were guilty of.

That all human beings are interested in the taste of their food may be confirmed by looking into those absolutely invaluable sources for early culinary history, the dictionaries compiled by the first travelers and missionaries. Priests, who were instructed to have as little to do with the female sex as possible, and secular writers, who would not otherwise pay the least attention to matters culinary, would gladly stoop to including food terminology, and sometimes even rudimentary recipes, in the quest for a lengthy and therefore impressive compilation. Not one of the dictionaries lacks an extensive vocabulary having to do with food and taste, words meaning savory, well-cooked, and tasty and their opposites like insipid, tasteless, and burned.

To return to the consequences of domestication: Domesticated animals and plants quite often lose the capacity to reproduce without human assistance. Some cultivated plants produce no seeds at all, like the banana (*Musa* spp.), which is an Old World domesticate, but one that spread so rapidly over the tropical New World that some of even the earliest chroniclers mistook it for a native. Bananas are propagated by planting the suckers that form at the base of the mother stalk, and these suckers must have been among the earliest cargoes routed to the New World. Manioc (*Manihot esculenta*) is a New World domesticate that has no seeds and must be multiplied by means of stem cuttings. Other plants can reproduce both sexually, that is to say by seed, and vegetatively, that is to say by planting portions of the plant, as is the case with many potatoes. Plants of this nature are a blessing to observant gardeners, giving them a chance to produce plants identical to their predecessors by vegetative reproduction or to get new varieties by using the seeds. These new varieties may or may not be superior to the parents, but they will certainly be different from them. Still other plants, as a consequence of domestication, lose their capacity to distribute their seeds efficiently, because efficient seed distribution often means easily shattering stems and pods or even explosive seed containers. Obviously this is a trait any domesticator seeks to eliminate— the last thing a person intent on gathering seeds wants is for the plants bearing them to have the capacity to shoot them all over the landscape. The husk of the modern ear of maize is an example of this. It is an effective guardian of the calories it contains, but if left to its own devices maize would soon die out, because that same husk prevents the seed from dispersal and germination.

The most modern and sophisticated domesticated plant varieties are extremely uniform, as uniformity is desirable when planting, cultivating, and harvesting by machine. A modern field crop should ripen all at once, so that one pass of the harvester can do the job. For nonindustrial farming conditions a crop that ripens gradually is preferable, because it spreads the labor of harvest, transport, and preparation for storage over a period of time, rather than having it come in an overwhelming avalanche. A crop that germinates, grows, and ripens unevenly is also a form of insurance, guaranteeing that even if some seedlings or fruit are destroyed by drought or rain or predators, others will survive to be harvested.

But it is not all that simple. Some of the toxic compounds and protective mechanisms that it would seem should be immediately gotten rid of defend the domesticated plant from its enemies just as efficiently as they defended the wild ancestor of that domesticated plant. The hydrocyanic acid content of bitter manioc (*Manihot esculenta*) makes necessary a whole battery of processing techniques to make it into something that can be eaten without fatal consequences, but it also protects the plant from the swarming pests in the tropical lowlands where it grows. If sweet manioc, which contains no hydrocyanic acid, were planted in these areas, it would not survive to produce a crop. In the same fashion, the hard horny outsides of flint maize kernels made it difficult for the women who had to transform them into something edible, but they protected the grains against weevils and insect larvae in the granary. Such complex interactions of benefits and draw-backs make one respect the nameless domesticators who are ultimately responsible for the produce heaped up in our supermarkets.

Plant food, wild or domesticated, could not be a major part of human diet without processing by fire, that is to say cooking. Too much vegetable food contained poisonous or nasty-tasting substances and excess nutritionless fiber (however much we may value it today), or was just too hard and tough to chew. Application of heat made these substances usable by humans. Another reason to cook the food was that it made it taste better. A nineteenth-century French doctor doing biochemical work at the University of Nancy proved that roasting, baking, or frying produced a browning caused by turning the starches into sugars, now called for its discoverer the Maillard effect. This makes flavors more complicated, more interesting, and in every way superior to the original raw material. The only foods found in nature that approach the subtlety of flavor of baked, broiled, or fried food are fully ripe fruits (McGee 1990).

Foods cooked by boiling do not profit from the flavor-enhancing Maillard effect and probably came later, because of the necessity of having containers in which to do the boiling. Before the invention of pottery either skins or baskets could be used, with the water being heated by stone boiling, where stones hot from the fire were dropped into the liquid with a pair of tongs. It is interesting in this connection that the bottle gourd (*Lagenaria siceraria*), a plant which originated in Africa but apparently managed to bob its way over the ocean in time to be picked up by the early inhabitants of both Mexico and Peru, is the earliest domesticated plant so far found in the New World. Its primary use was almost certainly as a container, but here again the users would have had to be discriminating, because some bottle gourds impart intense bitterness to any liquid they hold, while others leave their contents untainted.

Cooking was but one of the many methods used to tame recalcitrant foodstuffs. Not that any particular substance received only one treatment—far from it. In many cases intricate sequences of techniques were used, so complex that one wonders however such processes could have been invented, and how the time and energy could be spared to implement them.

These other methods of food processing conferred different flavors and textures on the raw materials, as well as making them easier for human beings to assimilate. They included making the substance into smaller pieces by cracking, pounding, grating, or grinding it. Before or after the particles were made smaller the foods could be soaked in water, or leached. Finally, to round out the four basic methods of food treatment, that is to say cooking, grinding, and soaking, we have fermentation, which opens up vast new possibilities for changes in flavor and texture as well as the potential for the production of alcohol, a substance which was of as much interest to the inhabitants of the New World as it was to the dwellers in the Old.

Different treatments applied in different sequences change not only the flavor, texture, and digestibility of the food but the nutritional value as well. It is amazing to read ignorant archaeologists building up elaborate hypotheses about the nutritional value of the plant and animal remains found in dry caves and establishing "carrying capacities" for that particular environment without once stopping to ask themselves how the foods could have been prepared and consumed. Presumably they think that it does not make a difference. It does make a difference, and, as we shall see, sometimes it is a big one.

Some of these food-value-enhancing techniques will be touched on in the chapters to come, but this is not a nutritional treatise and does not pretend to be one. The goal of this book is to describe the complex and highly developed culinary traditions of the New World, which are now part of the world's culinary heritage. I will begin by sketching the history of some of the major foodstuffs of the New World and their initial impact on the Old World. Having become familiar with some of the ingredients important either in pre-Columbian times, or our own times, or both, we can go on to investigate the whole constellations of culinary practices, customs, and beliefs which constituted the cuisines of the three major New World civilizations: the Aztecs of Mexico; the Maya of Mexico, Belize, Guatemala and Honduras; and the Inca of Peru, Ecuador, and Bolivia. A brief section on the foodways of the Europeans in the New World during the early period of their settlement will point out the striking similarities between their food and the food of the peoples they conquered, as well as the differences. Finally, the food of all four of these culinary cultures will be contrasted to our own, the food of the industrialized world during the last decade of the twentieth century.

TWO

New World Staples

MAIZE

In the beginning the gods made people out of wood. The stick figures did not give satisfaction, and the gods destroyed them. Only when the gods made people out of maize dough were true human beings created. This picture of the central role played by maize in the civilization of the New World is given to us by the Maya bible, the *Popul Vuh* (Tedlock 1985), but the Aztecs and the Inca would agree that maize was the life blood of New World civilizations. Even the arriving Europeans instantly identified maize as the equivalent to their own principal carbohydrate staple, wheat, and classified it as *pan,* or bread, with all the religious and social connotations that that word implied.

This reverence for or, indeed, worship of bread is strange to us, being accustomed to a post-industrial diet which is unique in lacking a basic carbohydrate staple. To the Aztecs, the Maya, the Inca, and the Europeans of the sixteenth century bread was the all-important carbohydrate source the lack of which meant famine and the presence of which, even alone, meant that one was fed and contented. Bread did not have to be solid, or baked; it could be formless, like the maize grains cooked in water called *mote* by the Inca, which Acosta (1954: 109) compared to the rice of the Chinese and the Japanese, defining them both as bread. Modern ignorance of this concept of the basic carbohydrate staple has led to numerous misinterpretations of the sources which would have been impossible had the reader been brought up in a society which depended on a single staff of life.

As examples of the reverence for bread and the identical attitude toward it in both the Old World and the New, one can quote a few Old World customs that lasted into the twentieth century and compare them with the Aztec treatment of maize. In Eastern Europe there are places where a piece of bread fallen on the floor is kissed, to expiate the carelessness of dropping it. Quite commonly bread is disposed of in a special way, as befits a sacred object. If at all possible it is reused, as bread crumbs, or bread pudding, or the Spanish *migas*. If inedible by human beings, if it is moldy, or the dog got it, it is put out for the birds. Never, under any circumstances, should bread be consigned to that realm of the unclean, the garbage. The Aztec man who paid a forfeit if he spilled a bit of maize gruel and the Aztec woman who breathed on the maize as she put it in the pot so that it would not fear the fire and who picked up the grains of maize scattered on the floor for fear the grains should complain to their lord and she would starve—both of them would understand the European peasant completely.

Why not call maize, the bread of the Indies, corn? Because corn is a generic term for a staple grain that has been used for different plants in different countries at different times. Maize is a New World name, derived from a word that the Europeans picked up in the Antilles and then, after an acquaintance of some thirty years, imposed upon the Mexicans, who had domesticated the plant and then lived with it, and depended on it, for millennia. Maize is an indigenous name for this one particular plant, *Zea mays,* and nothing else. Admittedly popped maize sounds ridiculous to the American ear, but we will have to put up with this for the sake of precision.

The origin and history of maize have been the subject of academic debate of unparalleled ferocity. It is easy to see why. Maize is the third most important crop in the world, following wheat and rice, even though much of this enormous production goes for animal feed rather than directly for human food. More than the satisfaction of mere scholarly curiosity could ride on an innovation like perennial maize, seeing that fortunes were made when hybrid maize revolutionized farming, and fortunes could be made again.

At the moment some people think that the ancestor of maize was maize. This hypothesis has been with us for a long time, although for a while it was submerged in a sea of other scenarios, and it now seems to be surfacing again. Pollen dating to eighty thousand years ago was found in a core taken under the Bellas Artes concert hall in downtown Mexico City, long before any possible human occupation. The next time we find maize, either wild or in the early stages of domestication, is in the dry caves of the Tehuacan valley of southern Puebla and northern Oaxaca in Mexico, at a date of about 5000 B.C. (Mangelsdorf, MacNeish, and Galinat 1964). Not that maize was necessarily domesticated in the Tehuacan valley, but a happy combination of preservation and a perceptive archaeologist led to the finding of the earliest examples of domesticated maize there. The domestication of maize was probably a gradual and widespread process, taking place over a sizable portion of Mexico and Guatemala, where we find the greatest number of cultivated maize varieties growing today. The maize cultivated in Peru during preconquest times was so different that a separate domestication is sometimes suggested. Wild maize does not exist today.

The source of much of the controversy and debate on the ancestry of maize has been *teosinte*. This is a colloquial name applied to all sorts of plants in Mexico and Central America, but the ones we are interested in were considered by many people to have been possible ancestors of maize, or at any rate to have been involved in the development of cultivated maize. One variety of *teosinte* is perennial (*Zea diploperennis*), which makes the question one of potential practical significance. The annual variety is now relegated to being a subspecies of maize (*Zea mays mexicana*); it used to be considered a separate genus (*Euchlaena*). It is postulated that through a series of complex mutations *Euchlaena* might have developed the arrangement of a male flower, or tassel, at a distance from the ear and silk, the female portions. This is an arrangement unheard of among other members of the grass family but characteristic of maize.

Part of the debate as to whether the ancestor of maize was maize or *teosinte* was carried on in culinary terms. Mangelsdorf, the main proponent of the ancestor of maize is maize hypothesis, assured his readers that *teosinte*, which has a hard horny seedcoat, was fundamentally inedible (Mangelsdorf 1974). Beadle, a supporter of the *teosinte* ancestry of maize, discovered that it was possible to pop it and that the horny mature grains if soaked could be chewed, as could the immature spikes (Beadle 1980). He claimed that motivated by sufficient hunger a single person in a day could process, by grinding and flotation, enough *teosinte* seeds to feed a small family for a day or more. How it could have been prepared, or whether anyone would care to eat it, is not taken into account. Nor is it mentioned that it has never been found in archaeological food debris. The taste of this grain of necessity is mentioned in the vaguest of terms. Yet that was what Columbus noticed when he first ate maize. He said, "It tasted very good" (Colón 1749, 1: 24).

There have been modern efforts to eat *teosinte*. During the great spurt of interest in *teosinte* in the 1880s, when an effort was being made to combine the perennial character of *teosinte* with the productivity of maize, Thomas Murrey published a little book called *Salads and Sauces,* in which he recommended the use of young shoots of *teosinte* as a salad green (1884: 259). Alas, his book, which smells more of the library than the kitchen, could not overcome the fact that *teosinte* is adapted to growing in the short days of the tropics, does not do well in the long days of a temperate summer, and will not set seed here. *Teosinte* as a salad ingredient remained in the salad book, not the salad bowl.

Another flurry of interest in the edibility of *teosinte* came during the twenties, when Oliver La Farge, traveling in Guatemala, had a bowl of soup at the Finca Chanquejelvé. The maize had just been planted, but there was something in his soup which looked like a young ear of maize, "having the unmistakeable flavor of corn [sic]" (Nuttall 1930: 219). He thought it was *teosinte.* Some years later two agronomists involved in maize studies tracked down the lady who had made La Farge's soup and published the result of their investigation. No matter what it had looked like and tasted like to La Farge, the soup ingredient was not even remotely related to maize or *teosinte,* being the fruiting body of the aroid *Spathiphyllum friedrichsthalli,* commonly called *güisnay* (Kempton and Popenoe 1937).

In the 1950s it was the turn of the *teosinte* seed. Despite the usual claims that it was much higher in protein than wheat, rice, oats, maize, or rye, despite making it into muffins and baking-powder bread as well as tortillas and tamales, which were hard to shape unless they used half maize flour and half *teosinte,* the investigators at Iowa State College had to admit that it did not taste like cracked wheat or maize. In fact, all that they could find to say about the flavor was that it was mildly nutty, and the texture was described as somewhat grainy, unlike any other cereal (Melhus and Chamberlain 1953). The contribution of the palate to the maize-versus-*teosinte* debate must be that *teosinte* is not very good to eat, and maize is.

The flavor of maize might well have been the first reason for the early hunters and gatherers to bring it home in their collecting baskets. After they accidentally spilled a few seeds on the fertile black soil of the trash heap outside, it would not have taken them long to discover the many other virtues hidden within the husk. European observers were struck by the fact that maize could be eaten at many stages of its development, thus shortening the hungry period preceding the harvest. The dry caves that give us so much information about the early development of maize also give us physical evidence of one of the earliest uses of maize, both in the sense of early in time and in the sense of early in the growing season. There we find preserved many quids, the fibrous remnants of very young maize ears chewed up husk, silk, cob, and all. Consumed this way Mangelsdorf says that maize is tender, succulent, and sweet (Mangelsdorf, MacNeish, and Galinat 1956).

A wait of a few weeks is rewarded by one of the earth's greatest delicacies—green maize, either roasted in the husk or boiled. The appearance of ears in this stage of development was often greeted with religious ceremonies of thanks and rejoicing, and anyone who has had the pleasure of biting into an ear at the peak of condition, rushed to the pot from the garden, and then to the table after the briefest of boiling, can understand why.

From then until the stage of total maturity the grains could be used in any number of different ways, depending on the particular variety of maize and the desire of the user. Other parts of the plant could also be eaten. The tassels were eaten during famines, and a sweet juice, not to be confused with modern "corn syrup," could be extracted from the green stalks. This was done by removing the nascent ears so that the sugars accumulated in the stalk. Peter Kalm, who traveled in North America in 1748, said that it was a "clear water . . . as sweet as sugar" (Kalm 1974: 112) and that people had failed in their efforts to make syrup out of it. They did better farther south, because Cortés mentions maize stalk syrup as being among the sweetenings he saw for sale in the great market of the Aztecs in their capital, Tenochtitlan (Cortés 1986: 104).

Misreading a passage by José de Acosta, a seventeenth-century Jesuit missionary to Peru, has caused several authors to say that the aboriginal inhabitants of Peru knew how to extract vegetable oil from maize. What Acosta actually said was that "Pigs fattened on maize are very fat, and they are used for lard to replace oil; so that for livestock and for people, for bread and wine and oil, they use maize in the Indies" (Acosta 1954: 110). Maize made many contributions to the pre-Columbian larder, but our modern "corn syrup," "corn starch," and

THESE PRODUCTS ARE FROM MODERN ENGINEERING

"corn oil" are not among them. They are made from maize by means of a process invented in the late nineteenth century and described as "a triumph of mechanical and chemical engineering" (Hosking 1948).

One of the distinguishing traits of cultivated plants is extreme variability within the species, and maize is no exception. There are five major groups: dent, flint, flour, sweet, and pop. They differ in their contents of sugar and starch and the hardness of the stored mixture. Add to this the different colors of the plants and the kernels, the different length of time necessary to ripen a crop, from the maize that produces an admittedly skimpy harvest in forty days to that which takes the better part of a year to ripen its ears, plus varying endowments of resistance to drought, heat, insects, and diseases, and one can begin to visualize the number of varieties of maize.

There was a maize for every need. Some varieties could dye maize beer a fine red color, others had broad husks to use for wrapping tamales, still others provided the best roasting ears. Whichever wild plant the ancient inhabitants of the New World began with, they transformed it into the cereal most efficient in converting air, water, and sunlight into human food.

game changer: nixtamalization

It was not enough, however, merely to domesticate maize. It was another discovery that made it a truly superior foodstuff, and that discovery was of the process of nixtamalization. Nixtamalization is the complex process that starts with soaking the ripe maize grains and then cooking them with lime or wood ashes. This enables the transparent skin on the grain, the pericarp, to be removed, and of course makes the grain easier to grind. But the major contribution of nixtamalization is that it much enhances the protein value of the maize for human beings (Katz, Hediger, and Valleroy 1974). So superior is nixtamalized maize to the unprocessed kind that it is tempting to see the rise of Mesoamerican civilization as a consequence of this invention, without which the peoples of Mexico and their southern neighbors would have remained forever on the village level. When and where this discovery was made is unknown, but typical household equipment for making nixtamal out of maize is known on the south coast of Guatemala at dates between 1500 and 1200 B.C.

The Europeans accepted maize immediately, but unfortunately for them they accepted it as another grain, to be used like European grains, that is to say ground and then made into mush or bread. They ignored nixtamalization, probably thinking it unnecessary with their more powerful and efficient mills. Because of this, maize-dependent

Nixtamalization. Original caption: "Method of Making Bread.
(1) Woman peeling the grain, (2) Woman grinding it,
(3) Woman forming and cooking the bread."
From Clavigero 1780, vol. 2, following p. 218.

cultures away from the New World suffer from dietary deficiencies
like pellagra and kwashiorkor, which do not exist where nixtamalization is used. Nor did the Europeans take back home with them the nutritionally superior combination of maize and New World beans, although the two ingredients made the trip separately.

Maize was probably introduced to the Old World by Columbus on
his return from his first voyage, because it was being grown in Spain by
1498, which means that there was a considerable supply of seed available. Giovanni Battista Ramusio, who might be called the Italian Hakluyt, except that he was publishing the accounts of travelers in the
New World while Hakluyt was still a squalling infant, spotted the new
plant growing in Venetian fields in 1554. Venice at that period was
finding its trade routes to the East closed off by Muslim expansion and
was therefore particularly open to planting this productive novelty on

its mainland fields. The mush of sorghum or millet that the peasants called *polenta* was replaced by a bright yellow new *polenta* made of ground maize. Eighteenth-century Italian writers gave the American plant credit for the fact that there had been no universal famines or plagues since its introduction, but because nixtamalization was not introduced with the maize, nutritional deficiency diseases replaced the plagues.

Spain and Italy were not the only ones to welcome the newcomer. By 1560 the Portuguese were growing it in the Congo, and Rauwolf collected it along the Euphrates in 1574. Although maize is a day-length-neutral plant, being able to produce seeds during short tropical days or long temperate summer ones, it took much longer for its virtues to be recognized in Northern Europe, where it is still looked on with suspicion in certain quarters. Fortunately for the inhabitants of the northern Old World there were other New World plants more adapted to their climates and ready for their embrace.

MANIOC

Maize was more comprehensible to the Europeans than the other staple plants that they were to discover. It was, after all, that familiar thing, a grain-producing grass. You planted a seed, which grew and produced more seeds. You saved some seeds to plant and ground the rest into flour to make your "bread." Calling it the wheat of the Indies placed it to everybody's satisfaction. Other plants were much more difficult to categorize.

No root crops in temperate Europe before 1492 were a major source of calories. Carrots, parsnips, radishes, beets, and turnips were none of them of any great importance, all belonging to the humble and despised category of vegetables. The discovery of manioc changed the low esteem accorded to root crops, at any rate for the tropics. In some ways the role of manioc during the earliest portion of the conquest, before 1521, was more important than that of maize. It was a major supplier of calories in the West Indies, and could be prepared in a way that was storable for a long time, and therefore superbly suitable for military rations.

It used to be thought that there were two species of manioc, the bitter or poisonous one, *Manihot utilissima,* which contains enough hydrocyanic acid to make it deadly if consumed without processing, and the innocuous sweet species, *Manihot dulcis.* Because these two species intergrade, they have now been combined to form one variable species known as *Manihot esculenta*. It is mostly used in humid lowland tropics, which means that the archaeological record is sparse, but it may have been domesticated in northeastern Brazil, where there are still many wild species. There is a secondary cluster of wild species in Mexico, and some think the sweet variety was domesticated there and the bitter one in Brazil. Since it is so far unfortunately impossible to distinguish sweet from bitter manioc in vegetable matter found archaeologically, one must rely on finding artifacts such as the stone chips for graters, which are associated with the processing of bitter manioc, to know which of the two was being cultivated. Using this sort of evidence we can say that bitter manioc was apparently being grown in the lowlands of Venezuela and Colombia by about 3000 B.C., and sweet manioc was probably being planted on the coast of Peru by about 2000 B.C.

Why did anyone grow the stuff? In the first place, it was very easy to grow. It was not propagated by seed or even by a piece of the edible portion, the root, but by stem cuttings. Early European writers never tired of repeating descriptions of how pieces of the stem could be inserted into heaps of earth, and in less than a year great roots the size of a man's leg would be ready to lift out. Once removed they did not keep well, but they could stay in the ground for several years, after which they finally became inedibly woody.

Sweet manioc, which was always a crop of secondary importance, was mainly grown as an adjunct to maize. It was easy to prepare: All you needed to do was to take a fresh root, harvested that same day, and put it either in the embers of the fire or on a rack of green sticks, a *barbacoa*, over them. You turned the root from time to time, and when it emitted a strong and agreeable odor, you removed it, peeled it, and ate it.

It was far harder to convert the bitter manioc into something edible. The root had to be grated, either on a grater painstakingly constructed out of stone chips or perhaps on a sharkskin. The still poisonous grated matter was treated by putting it in a diagonally woven tube and then hanging the tube somewhere and inserting a weighted pole in a loop at the lower end. This caused the manioc mass to be squeezed and the poisonous juice to be expelled. This juice contained the hydrocyanic acid, and when the inhabitants of the West Indies were seeking every possible route to escape from their new masters, many of them chose to commit suicide by drinking it. The Europeans, already baffled to find what seemed to be the same plant poisonous in some places but not in others, were absolutely dumbfounded when they discovered that this deadly liquid could be boiled down to become a very tasty sweet-sour sauce, which I have tried myself and lived to tell the tale.

The dry matter left in the tube was almost pure starch. It could be baked into great cakes on a flat clay griddle over the fire, the thickness of the cakes ranging from collision mats two fingers thick, made of coarsely grated manioc for the commoners, to exquisite thin white cakes made of super finely grated manioc for the top people. The Europeans quickly discovered the virtues of this bread. The plants were easy to grow, it was cheap and simple to prepare in large quantities, and, best of all, it would keep, dry, for several years, making it ideal military and naval rations. Unlike maize tortillas, which when cold are leathery and tasteless, and hard to revive with any sort of soaking or heating, once dry manioc bread was dipped into chile sauce, broth, or water, it again became soft and palatable. It was berated as being as tasteless as sawdust by the Europeans, but it played a major role in the conquest of the New World by the military and the religious. Juan de Santa Gertrudis Serra, an eighteenth-century Franciscan missionary, gives us a description of his first encounter with manioc bread in Cartagena, Colombia, where it was called *cazabe,* a word related to *cassava,* the British colonial term for manioc:

> We also remember seeing some negresses coming bearing great platters on their heads. As they were so numerous our curiosity was roused to know what they could be doing with all those platters. We went up to a man selling *tasajo,* which is what they call meat salted and dried in the sun, and I must tell you that in Cartagena there is no fresh meat except that of fowl. I asked him, "Mister, what are all those platters for, that the negresses are carrying?" He answered me, "Father, those are not platters. That is the bread that is commonly eaten in this country. It is called *cazabe.*" He had a bit and gave it to us to try, and we thought it was terrible. (Serra 1970, 1: 49)

Father Serra may have had a low opinion of it, but manioc continues to be a major source of calories all over the tropics. It was taken to Africa by the Portuguese along with maize and westward across the Pacific by the Spaniards, who introduced it into the Philippines, whence it spread into Southeast Asia. Today Thailand produces a large crop of manioc, most of which goes into the only manioc product with which those of us who live in northern climes are familiar—tapioca.

POTATOES, SWEET POTATOES, AND YAMS

The role manioc takes in temperate climates as tapioca, thickener of
pies and ingredient of puddings, may seem trivial to us and a minor
contribution from the New World. Manioc is a plant of the humid
tropics, and it has stayed there. Maize, coming from higher altitudes
and having no specific requirements as to day length, spread rapidly
through the Mediterranean climates similar to its own. The last plant,
or more precisely one of the last set of staple plants that we shall discuss, was a gift of the New World to colder regions.

The history of the potato is inextricably mixed with the history of
the sweet potato and that of several other plants as well. If anyone has
doubts as to the utility and necessity of Latin names, let this be a lesson
for them, because the common names, *papas, batatas, patatas,* give us
only the vaguest idea of what is being talked about. When the Italian
traveler Francesco Carletti had a dish of roots called *papatas* in port at
the city of Santa, Peru, around 1600, roots that were white, eaten
roasted or boiled, and tasted like chestnuts, we have no idea what he
was putting in his mouth (Carletti 1701).

This being the case we must define our terms. By potato I mean the
tubers of *Solanum tuberosum* and other species of *Solanum.* By sweet
potato, or *batata,* I mean the thickened roots of *Ipomoea batatas.*
There are three kinds of sweet potatoes eaten in the United States today, an old-fashioned white kind, a hardy dry yellow kind, and a
moist, sweet, dark orange kind, miscalled a yam. True yams are members of the Dioscoridae family, among them one unfortunately named
Dioscorea batatas but domesticated in the Old World, and another
named *Dioscorea trifida,* a New World domesticate. With the New
World yams we will have nothing further to do, except to say that if
they were the *ages* or *ñames* Columbus and his successors found in the
West Indies, they were considered inferior to sweet potatoes, a quick-
growing food fit only for servants and slaves.

Sweet potatoes sparked immediate enthusiasm. Fernández de
Oviedo said, "a *batata* well cured and well prepared is just like fine
marzipan" (Fernández de Oviedo 1959, 1: 234). Las Casas' recipe for
sweet potatoes starts with washing them after the harvest and then
curing them under light shade for eight to ten days. After this curing
the sweet potatoes are to be roasted and then they will taste as if they
had been dipped in a jar of jam, they will be so honey-sweet (Las Casas
1958, 1: 39).

Fernández de Oviedo said that he had transported cured sweet potatoes to Spain, and though they were not quite what they had been before the journey, they remained a singular and precious fruit (Fernández de Oviedo 1959, 1: 235). As late as 1577 they were an important present, because we have a letter from the future saint Teresa de Jesús of Avila, written from Toledo on January 26, 1577, to Mother María de San José in Seville, thanking her for a gift of *patatas,* even though she admitted that she had had no appetite for them when they arrived (Teresa de Jesús 1959, 3: 318). Teresa was most punctilious about thanking people for the gifts they sent her, oranges, sweetmeats, and another curiosity, a coconut. She said it was the idea she liked, not the gifts themselves, so we have no way of knowing if she was temporarily indisposed or had other reasons for not tasting the sweet potato, if that is what it was.

The New World history of the sweet potato is complex. The Uto-Aztecan word *camotli* seems to be the root of all the words found for it in the Pacific area, for the sweet potato is found not only in the New World but also in Polynesia, from Hawaii to Easter Island to New Zealand. There is practically no use made of sweet potatoes in Mexico today, with the exception of *camotes de Santa Clara,* a soft candy made in the city of Puebla. Despite the linguistic evidence there is nothing in the way of archaeological material in Mexico, whereas on the coast of Peru sweet potato use goes back to at least 2800 to 2400 B.C. and possibly much earlier. A center of domestication in western South America seems more probable than one in southern Mexico and Central America. From either place the sweet potato could have been taken to Polynesia, either deliberately or on the drifting boat so beloved by the diffusionists. Polynesians could also have fetched it, although such visitors were probably much more in danger of being turned into foodstuffs themselves than returning with novel foodstuffs. The third possible scenario is that the sweet potato did not stop in Spain when it arrived there after Columbus but continued its eastward journey, so that when explorers got to Polynesia in the eighteenth century the sweet potato had had time to become thoroughly embedded in the culture. However, when there was a famine in Fukien province in 1593, the Chinese authorities sent a mission to the island of Luzon to find new food plants. The commission returned the following year with a new food plant, the sweet potato, which remains to this day the food of the indigent in China. The Philippines were of course in contact with Mexico via the Manila galleons which sailed from Acapulco to Manila and may have brought sweet potatoes as they brought many other New World plants.

The potato, *Solanum tuberosum* and allies, did not travel as swiftly as the sweet potato, even if we reject the possibility that the sweet potato could make it from Spain to the Philippine island of Luzon in less than a century. The potato was not even seen by the Europeans until the 1530s, when they conquered the cold highlands of Colombia and Peru. That is to say, cultivated potatoes were not seen by the Europeans until that time. More than two hundred species of wild tuber-bearing potatoes exist in the New World, growing from the state of Colorado in the United States south to Chile and Argentina, but if the Europeans ever noticed anybody eating them, they did not record it.

The many uses for cultivated potatoes in their native Andean highlands will be dealt with in the section on Inca food. Here I will sketch their early history and their impact on Europe. The earliest domesticated potato, *Solanum tuberosum,* has been found in a cave in central Peru which seems to date back to 8000 B.C. By 3800 B.C. potatoes were certainly well established in the highlands, although they did not appear on the coast until 2000 to 1750 B.C. This was not just one single kind of potato but a whole constellation of potatoes, varying among themselves in taste, color, hardiness, use, and everything else that potatoes can vary in.

There is a "just so story" that potatoes were sent to Philip II of Spain from Cuzco in 1565, and Philip II had them sent on to the then pope, Alexander VII Chigi, as a tonic. From the pope they were supposed to have passed through several hands until they reached the botanist Jules Charles de l'Ecluse, usually known as Clusius, who first described them. The purport of the story is that potatoes got their name *papas* because of the pope's role in transmitting them to Clusius. Any dictionary of Quechua, the language of the Inca, will give you the word *papa* for potato. The Quechua were perfectly capable of naming their staple food without papal intervention.

There was a flurry of descriptions of the potato in the herbals of the late sixteenth century. It was at this time that the British botanist Gerard planted the seeds, or perhaps one should say the potato eyes, of trouble when he confused *Solanum tuberosum* from South America with *Apios tuberosa,* the ground nut, which was eaten by Indians and early colonists in Virginia. For years the English-speaking world called

The Inca harvesting potatoes.
From Guaman Poma de Ayala 1936: 1047.

Solanum tuberosum the Virginia potato and thought it came from Virginia and had been domesticated there, even though there were no wild potatoes to be found there, nor any domesticated ones either.

After this almost everybody in Europe lost interest in the potato for several hundred years. The one place it did take root was Ireland, where the seventeenth-century diarist John Evelyn knew it as the Irish potato and thought it an acquired taste, only suitable for the poor, or for the servants when it was necessary to reduce expenses (Evelyn 1818, 2: 292).

What caused this early lack of success? If we look at the early herbals, the plants illustrated look like what used to be considered a separate species, *Solanum andigenum,* now considered just a variety of *Solanum tuberosum* and called *Solanum tuberosum* var. *andigenum.* It has more and thinner stems, more pigment, and longer and narrower leaves than *Solanum tuberosum* var. *tuberosum.* The *andigenum* variety was probably the one brought to Europe from highland Colombia, where it was first seen in 1537 by Jiménez de Quesada, who was leading an expedition into the interior. As *batatas* were compared to chestnuts, so potatoes were compared to truffles, "a delicacy for the Indians, and a dainty dish even for the Spaniards" (Juan de Castellanos, quoted in Hawkes 1967: 220). The defect of this early imported potato was that it was adapted to the short days of the tropics and could not produce a worthwhile crop during the long days of a northern summer. That is why it took hold in Ireland, where the climate was mild enough so that the potato could grow until November, when the shortening days would finally induce it to set a few tubers.

We do not know what happened next. It is suggested that because the *andigena* potatoes produce many flowers and berries they were perhaps propagated by planting seed, rather than pieces of tuber, which led to a more variable crop, and earlier ripening strains were selected from those. The alternative explanation is that stocks of *Solanum tuberosum* var. *tuberosum* were imported from southern Chile, which was far enough south so that they could produce tubers during long summer days. Being the same species, they would cross with the *andigena* potatoes, and even though cultivators might know nothing about genetics and plant breeding, they could still spot a superior early-cropping variety if it appeared.

The rival theory, that the European potato came exclusively from stock that originated in the Chiloe islands of Chile, where day lengths were like those of Northern Europe, was upheld by Vavilov, the Soviet investigator of plant origins. Working from his hypothesis that the likely place for the domestication of a plant is the place where the most cultivated varieties of that plant are to be found, he pinpointed Chile as the homeland of our present-day potato.

Vavilov, who died a martyr for science during the Stalin antigenetics campaign, has become a secular saint in Russia, but his view of the early history of the potato does not seem to be correct. Not only do the early illustrations resemble variety *andigenum* rather than variety *tuberosum,* but the Araucanian Indians of Chile put up an especially heated resistance to the Europeans, and that would have made it difficult to collect potatoes in Chile in the 1560s and 1570s. Any potato shipped from Chile up the west coast of South America, across the Isthmus of Panama into the Atlantic, and then across the Atlantic to Spain would have been rotten long before it got to its destination. No Europeans would have put potato seeds in their pockets, could they have found any of the rare *tuberosum* seed, because the primary reason for shipping the tubers was to eat them along the way, not to take them home to plant. The trip eastward to Spain, through the Strait of Magellan, was apparently not made until 1579 and would not have shortened the time by any significant amount.

In short, we do not know how or when the original, and rather unsatisfactory, Irish potato changed its ways. It could have been by means of selection, or by the addition of new genetic material, or both. We do know that by the late eighteenth century there was an improved version which led to an explosion of interest. This was the period when Marie Antoinette of France wore potato flowers in her hair, Frederick the Great of Prussia commanded the peasantry to grow potatoes, and even A. T. Bolotov, a superintendent on the far-off Russian estates of Catherine the Great, was experimenting with the new plant.

The Italy that accepted maize a few decades after the discovery of the New World took its time with the potato. It was not until 1766 that Antonio Zanon, an economist, got it straight that potatoes were not the same thing as cyclamen tubers. Even though a friend told him that in Holland the things were served daily, boiled, with poached fish and melted butter, he could not envisage them being much liked and consigned them to the peasants and the poor (Zanon 1982). It was in the third decade of the nineteenth century, some twenty years before the social and economic structure of Ireland, totally dependent on the potato, came crashing down, that the archbishop of Genoa first advised his priests in mountain parishes to persuade the peasants to cultivate potatoes, rather than depending on their chestnut trees.

The potato continued to expand its range throughout the nineteenth century. By this time Ireland had become essentially a one-crop country and gave the world a horrific lesson in the dangers of monoculture when the fungus *Phytophthora infestans* overnight destroyed half the 1845 potato crop and followed this with the total destruction of the 1846 harvest. The blight occurred in other portions of Europe as well, but nowhere else was the population so helplessly dependent on that single crop. A million people died in Ireland, and huge numbers of survivors emigrated to North America. Ironically, the fungus was probably imported from North America, perhaps on some potatoes brought to Ireland for breeding purposes.

The blight further spurred the efforts of the plant breeders. One way to avoid it was to plant potatoes that ripened early. In Utica, New York, the Reverend Chauncey Goodrich, one of the many nineteenth-century clergymen plant breeders, assembled a collection of potato breeding stock from Latin America. In 1851 a contact, the American consul in Panama City, then part of Colombia, sent him a collection of potatoes that he had picked up in the marketplace. One kind either came with the name "Rough Purple Chile" or was given that name by Goodrich. Why a Chilean variety, if such it was, should be found in a market in Panama City we do not know, but it did transmit one Chilean, or *tuberiferum*, trait to its offspring, namely, the ability to produce a crop of tubers during the long days of summer. If it had not happened before, and if the two strains involved were indeed *tuberiferum* and *andigenum*, they certainly became well mixed at this point.

Potato breeding is now the province of professionals more concerned with shipability, storability, and disease resistance than with taste. The varieties they produce are considered by Peruvians and Bolivians, all great potato connoisseurs, to be watery and insipid. They have hundreds of varieties of potatoes in their markets, compared with the miserable handful available in our own. To deal with their massive inventory of potatoes the Quechua of Peru independently developed a system of nomenclature very similar to that which Linnaeus used to order all living things in the eighteenth century. The Quechua, like Linnaeus, gave binomial names. Every variety had a noun for a name, sometimes quite a poetic or metaphorical noun, and for purposes of further discrimination an adjective was added.

The potato has carved itself a unique niche in the history of Europe, as well as in the lives of the Quechua. Other American plants became staples outside their hearths of domestication, but no other plant was so beguiling that it could lure a million people to their deaths and cause major political convulsions. There are those who laugh and think the study of the history of domesticated plants is a ridiculous and trivial occupation. The potato proves them wrong.

THREE

New World Produce

The New World offers a veritable cornucopia of fruits and vegetables to the hungry. From this abundance of "produce" (a handy term which avoids the question of what is a fruit and what is a vegetable, a distinction founded on culinary culture and not on botany), the modern world has selected a few and left the rest to languish in their native hills and valleys.

What led certain plant foods to be accepted by the Europeans and the modern world, while others were rejected? Four factors seem to have led to certain plants finding favor, given that they were basically amenable and willing to grow and produce with reasonable ease and speed and could adapt to more than a single specialized environment.

The first class of acceptable plants were those which fit nicely into already established European categories. Maize should be included here, although attaining due respect as the culinary equal of wheat took centuries. Father Serra, the eighteenth-century Franciscan missionary whose encounter with the manioc bread platters of Cartagena we have already quoted, illustrates the difficulties individuals newly arrived in the New World had with nonwheat bread almost three hundred years after Columbus.

At midday they brought us a meal of stewed and roast fowl. They brought *arepas* [thick maize tortillas], roast plantains, sweet manioc, sweet potatoes, etc. But we did not know how to eat without bread. Then I realized that bread was sustenance to someone who was brought up like me, and I remembered that when I was in Cádiz about to leave, a brother said to me, "Brother John, you are going to the Indies: God keep you from losing sight of bread." (Serra 1970, 1: 107–108)

Other foods which meshed with preexisting European food categories were the New World beans. They looked, cooked, and tasted like the pulses which were on every Spanish ship's manifest. The Old World *habas, garbanzos,* and *lentejas* translate into English as broad beans, chick-peas, and lentils and into botanical Latin as *Vicia faba, Cicer arietinum,* and *Lens esculenta.* The New World *Phaseolus* beans not only could be used like the Old World ones but also were related to them, all being members of the family Leguminosae, subfamily Papilionoideae.

Two other plants won acceptance because they could replace almonds in marzipan, which was then an elegant and expensive dish and loaded with prestige. Both the peanut (*Arachis hypogaea*) and the hulled seeds of the genus *Cucurbita* squashes could be toasted, ground, mixed with sugar or honey and some eggwhite, and then dried in the oven. This dough could be molded into different shapes and then gilded, silvered, or tinted according to the whim of the creator. In the next to last chapter we shall see it appearing on the tables of the great in early colonial Mexico City. The parts of the squash that we eat now, the flowers, the shoots, and the immature or ripe fruit, were scorned as belonging to the category of greens, that is to say poor people's food.

Even if food plants did not fit into a convenient European niche, some of them possessed unique qualities which led to their enthusiastic embrace by the Europeans. The pineapple (*Ananas comosus*) was taken back to the Old World very soon after the discovery. The fruit was sufficiently resistant to shipping so that some survived the trip unrotted and astounded the savants with their fragrance. Although avocados were not such good travelers and only spread through the culinary world in the twentieth century, their unctuous oily flesh, a trait shared only with the olive and the coconut in the edible plant world, intrigued the natural history writers enough to be given long chapters in their books on the vegetable wonders of the New World. As a peculiar form of endorsement the avocado was stripped of its perfectly good etymology in Nahuatl, the language of the Aztecs, where the word derives from *ahuacatl,* or testicle. The OED ignores this completely and claims that the word comes from "advocate," or lawyer. How lawyers could have become involved with the fruit of *Persea americana* is nowhere explained (one can only suggest that it is from the tendency of the legal profession to insinuate itself everywhere).

The third category of welcomed foods has already been encountered. These are the plant foods that may not have had instant appeal for reasons of taste but were cheap, efficient, and hugely productive sources of calories. Manioc and potatoes belong to this category. After the discovery of the silver mines of Potosí in Peru in 1545, fortunes were made by Europeans who provided *chuño,* a pre-Columbian invention of storable freeze-dried potatoes, to feed the Indian miners imprisoned in the dark galleries. The use of manioc to make military stores has already been mentioned.

Finally there is the fourth class of New World foods, which could be referred to as sleepers. The tomato barely received a word in the early writings. If mentioned at all, it was as an ingredient that gave a pleasing sourness to stews. There were fears that it might be poisonous, because of poisonous relatives in the family and the rank odor of the plants. It was also difficult to get it to fruit in places with a short growing season. But with time the tomato surmounted all these impediments and conquered the culinary universe. Today the food of the world is overwhelmed by this red tide.

There are hundreds of New World plants which are basically unknown. It is instructive to look at the attempts now being made to introduce them. Do they follow any of the four tracks outlined earlier in this chapter? Not a bit of it.

We cannot see proteins, vitamins, or minerals. We cannot smell them or taste them, but they are what we are expected to be looking for in new foods. Every little-known grain is guaranteed superior to wheat, rice, and maize, as far as protein content goes, or any vitamin or mineral that you might choose to mention. This is always the first thing that we are told. Yet even if the new foods have the added inducements of high fiber and low cholesterol, we persist in eating the same old ones. Could it be that the advocates of the new edibles are mistaken, and we do not eat wholly in the pursuit of complex nutritional goals but at least partially in search of a little pleasure?

What scanty enjoyment there is to be gotten from these would-be new foods seems to lie in the realm of texture. "Crisp" and "crunchy" are assumed to be the magic words, words that will induce us to take an *arracacha* between our teeth, or taste a *llacón.* As far as flavor goes, we are meekly reassured that these things taste "mild" or, at their most thrilling, "nutty."

The final and most odious inducement to try the novelties is the old "everybody is doing it" routine. See, this fruit is very popular in Japan. Look, this one is profitably cultivated and sold in New Zealand. The only effect this approach can have is to make one dislike the eaters as much as one already dislikes the thought of the substance to be eaten.

Instead of following the carefully researched and considered advice of the modern marketing experts, perhaps the would-be plant introducers should read some of the plant descriptions, many of them essay length, written by the early missionaries and explorers. These record the experiences of hungry men, encountering fruits and vegetables in their native climates, many prepared in the native manner. Some of them welcomed their experiences with the all-devouring curiosity which we now think of as an attribute of Renaissance men, which to a greater or lesser extent most of them were. Fernández de Oviedo, Las Casas, Acosta, Cobo, and Serra all wrote about the new foods they encountered with the exhilaration of discovery, not as some grim nutritional duty to be performed. They probably did not know the Japanese proverb that claims that every new foodstuff sampled adds seventy-five days to one's lifespan, but that is the spirit in which they wrote, and they make their reader want to rush out and try new foodstuffs too.

BEANS

There were beans in the Old World besides the *habas, garbanzos,* and *lentejas* mentioned earlier. Most of them were used in the Orient, including the adzuki bean (*Vigna angularis*), the mung bean (*Vigna radiata*), which produces some but not all bean sprouts, and *Vigna unguiculata sesquipedalis,* the yard-long bean. The soybean, recorded in China since the eleventh century B.C., is unquestionably a different genus, *Glycine.*

The New World domesticated its own beans, belonging to the American genus *Phaseolus.* These beans made an early and important contribution to the food of humans in the New World. Their protein profile dovetails nicely with that of maize, so that a diet of properly processed maize and beans provides all the protein requirements of the working males, although it is insufficient for the most protein-sensitive members of the population: lactating mothers and newly weaned infants.

There were four species of *Phaseolus* domesticated in the New

World. The northernmost in origin was the tepary bean (*Phaseolus acutifolius*), a fine drought-tolerant crop for the arid southwest of the United States and adjacent Mexico. There were many cultivars that differed in color and taste, but the advent of cash-crop farming in the beginning of this century meant their near extinction. The beans they produced could be soaked and then baked or boiled or made into powdered form. It would seem that there could be nothing more difficult than grinding hard ripe beans to a powder, even with the best of stone grinding tools, but the simple expedient of parching or toasting the beans first made it quite easy to reduce them to a fine flour. The flour could then be used to provide quick bean dishes. The tepary bean has been known since 3000 B.C., and there are attempts being made to revive its cultivation on otherwise unproductive dry land.

The scarlet runner bean produces gorgeous red flowers and is sometimes grown as a decorative. *Phaseolus coccineus* is unusual in that it is a short-lived perennial, not an annual like the other domesticated beans. If it gets less than thirteen hours of daylight a day, it puts off flowering and fruiting and instead produces a tuberized and edible root. The wild beans were gathered in Oaxaca and Tehuacan at 8750–6750 B.C. and 7050 B.C., respectively, but not cultivated, at any rate in Tehuacan, until shortly before the time of Christ. Clavigero says that they were the biggest beans in Mexico and were called *ayacotli*, and we are sure that they were this species because he mentions the fine red flowers (Clavigero 1780). But he said these were not the best beans, which were small and black and heavy and so fine that they were eaten as a delicacy by the Spanish nobility. These must have been one of the myriad varieties of *Phaseolus vulgaris*.

The origins of *Phaseolus vulgaris* are obscure. It is always difficult to differentiate between wild plants and cultivated plants that have gone back to the wild, but at least some authors have claimed that there is wild *Phaseolus vulgaris* growing for thousands of miles along the eastern slope of the Andes, as well as in Mexico and Central America (Berglund-Brücher and Brücher 1976). As older notions of single centers of domestication give way to newer views that have domestication as a more decentralized process, going on simultaneously over wide areas, we can imagine various strains of *Phaseolus vulgaris* being tamed by humans from Mexico to South America. Early dates range from 5000 B.C. in Tehuacan in Mexico, 5680 ± 280 B.C. in the highlands of Peru, and 2550 B.C. on the Peruvian coast.

If the domestication process took place over such a wide area it should not be surprising that different parts and stages of the bean plant were targeted by the domesticators. One possibility was to consume the whole young seed container, in other words, string beans. This was probably originally difficult and unpleasant because the young pod of the wild bean is protected by tough strings and parchment-like membranes. When the bean pod is dry these strings and membranes twist and expel the seeds, which is advantageous for the plant but not for the forager who wants to eat the young bean pods or the beans. The consumption of green beans as such is probably a late development, and indeed the last tiresome strings were removed by the breeders within this author's lifetime.

Most beans were and are used mature and dry. Scorned in the sixteenth century and the twentieth, and the centuries in between, as food for the lower classes, as well as for what has bluntly been called the fart factor, one variety nevertheless seemingly began its Old World career under the highest auspices.

Lamon beans are plump middle-sized beans with a background color of light tan, covered with an irregular pattern of reddish-brown speckles. They are sold by weight from sacks in food stores in Italy, the same way that lentils, maize meal for making polenta, and other varieties of beans are sold. Perhaps they only seem tastier because of their supposed history.

Hernán Cortés, the conqueror of Mexico, sent his emperor Charles V samples of gold, featherwork, jewelry, and textiles from the country he had added to the dominions of Spain. Little or nothing of this survives, although the inventories are enough to make students of New World material culture weep with frustration. Cortés also sent samples of the produce of the country, supposedly including a sack of beans. In his turn, Charles sent some of this tribute to the then pope, Clement VII, who became pope in 1523 and died in 1534. We do not know exactly when this gift was made, but the relationship between the two was hardly consistently cordial. In fact, halfway between the time that troops loyal to Charles destroyed the capital of the Aztec empire, Tenochtitlan, in 1521, and the time they destroyed the capital of the Inca empire, Cuzco, in 1534, they had looted and devastated another capital, which as it happens was Rome, the seat of their own religion. Contemporary humanists considered the sack of Rome in 1527 to be one of the cultural disasters of all time, to be mourned much as present-day scholars mourn the destructions of Tenochtitlan and Cuzco. But the complex demands of European politics being what they were, shortly thereafter Charles may have sent Clement curiosities from the New World and included the sack of beans.

The pope gave the sack of beans to a distinguished scholar who had been a teacher in the Medici household in Florence, one Giovanni Pietro delle Fosse di Bolzano, better known under his literary name of Pierio Valeriano. In 1532 Pierio Valeriano took his beans to his dwelling in Belluno, in northeastern Italy. There he planted them in pots and put some of the pots in his windows and the others up on the roof. The beans did so well that he had a large crop, which he distributed widely, first in the immediate area and then in the whole mainland territory of Venice, including the town of Lamon, which attached its name to the beans and where it is claimed that today the restaurants daily serve the beans. Pierio Valeriano wrote a poem in 1534 celebrating his horticultural triumph in Latin hexameters and mournfully asking himself if this was going to be his only claim to fame. Clement VII, on the other hand, commissioned Michelangelo to paint the Last Judgment on the wall of the Sistine Chapel.

This story of the introduction of what were to become Lamon beans into Italy was repeated by me once too many times. I told it to a bean expert, and perhaps I should have been alerted by the fact that neither he nor his wife had ever heard of Lamon and its beans. He asked me to describe the beans, which I did, in pretty much the same terms as you see on the preceding page. Lawrence Kaplan shook his head. Most large beans like the ones that I was telling him about came from the Andean area, he said; it was the little ones that came from Mexico. And with this simple statement the entire construction of conquerors, emperors, popes, and scholars came tumbling down. If the original Lamon beans had had the history that has been told, then at some point they were totally replaced by the variety that we see today. Or perhaps there lies waiting to be discovered in some archive an equally picturesque story of the arrival and adoption of the present-day Lamon bean from the Andean area. It is probably too much to ask that the introduction of any food plant be known with such precision.

While some variety of *Phaseolus vulgaris* was being hymned in Latin hexameters in Italy, the fourth and last species of domesticated American *Phaseolus* had just been discovered. If *Phaseolus vulgaris* was domesticated in a strip of mountainside from northwestern Mexico to northwestern Argentina, *Phaseolus lunatus,* the Lima bean, did it differently, having two or possibly three widely separated centers of domestication. Sporting the rare correctly informative common name,

the Lima bean is a plant which likes hot climates and will not germi-
nate if the soil temperature is too low. The large kind, *Phaseolus lunatus* var. *microcarpus,* grew only in Peru, where it got its name. It is
found in Preceramic sites on the coast of Peru dating from 3000 B.C.
and in the highlands from 6000 B.C. These were the beans which
Cobo, a Jesuit missionary in Peru between 1609 and 1629, said were
the best of all beans, whether eaten in their green pods with oil and
vinegar, or mature and stewed, again with oil and vinegar (Cobo
1890–1893). Juan de Velasco, who was among the Jesuits exiled from
Spanish possessions in 1767, agreed as to their exquisite taste, saying
that with one boiling they dissolved like butter (Velasco 1977).

The smaller sort of Lima beans, sometimes called sieva beans, were
independently domesticated in Mexico shortly before the time of
Christ and do not seem to have had any particular distinction to make
them noticed beyond any other beans by the chroniclers. If there is a
third variety it is to be found in a band running from Yucatan, through
Venezuela, and into Brazil. All the Lima beans could have pods and
leaves used as greens, but some dark-seeded varieties were bitter and
required boiling in several waters before they were edible.

PEANUTS

Like the beans, peanuts (*Arachis hypogaea*) are members of the family
Leguminosae, but they have some peculiarities of their own. They
produce a white flower at the end of a stalk, and after the flower is
fertilized the stalk bends down and pushes into the soil, so that the
fruit is produced underground. It is a small plant, rarely more than
knee high, so that this maneuver is easy to miss. The Europeans won-
dered for years how the flower could be in one place and the fruit in
another before they discovered the secret.

The peanut suffers from misapprehensions as to its place of origin.
It did not originate in West Africa. It was first imported into the United
States from West Africa, on the ships that brought the slaves. But the
peanut had been brought to West Africa from Brazil by the Portuguese, along with maize and sweet potatoes. While the Portuguese
were moving peanuts east, the Spaniards were taking them west across
the Pacific from Peru and introducing them to the Far East.

The first Chinese reference to peanuts dates from the 1530s, but
there was a flurry among plant historians and archaeologists a few
years ago when a few peanut shells were found in excavations at an

Early Lungshanoid site dating from 3200 to 2500 B.C. It was the site that was that old, but the peanut shells were contemporary with the excavators, not the site they were excavating.

The true proof of the place of origin of the peanut is the fact that there are no wild peanut species found anywhere outside of South America, and within South America there are fifteen species of wild peanut, mostly in or around lowland Bolivia. From here the domesticated plant ranged east and north into Brazil and the Caribbean, arriving in Tehuacan, Mexico, at about A.D. 500. It was never important in Mexico and had no native name, being called *tlal-cacahuatl,* a compound word meaning earth-cacao, or cacao which grew underground.

Peanuts spread west to Peru from their country of origin. Those that appear in Peruvian highland sites are imported, as the plant does not grow well above 6,000 feet altitude, but by 3100 to 2500 B.C. they were common on the coast of Peru, giving rise to comments by archaeologists about the sites looking like poorly swept baseball stadiums. We do not know how they were eaten in Peru, but the fact that shells were found sounds as if they were being eaten in exactly the way they are eaten today, toasted in the shell.

Contemporary Bolivians have other ways of consuming this native of their country. Toasted, shelled, and ground and mixed with water they become a drink called *chicha de maní,* which we are told is not alcoholic, although *chicha* usually refers to fermented drinks. *Maní,* like maize, is an Antillean word taken up by the Europeans on their arrival and spread by them back to the country where peanuts originated. Green *maní* fruit can be eaten whole, in which case the inhabitants of the southern United States call them goober peas.

This novel plant got mixed reviews. Fernández de Oviedo (1959, 1: 235) found it mediocre, and several sources said that eaten raw, or in immoderate amounts, it caused headaches. Cobo was among those who accused peanuts of causing headaches, giddiness, and migraine, but he succumbed when his sweet tooth was tempted (Cobo 1890–1893, 1: 359). He recommended peanuts as substitutes for almonds in almond milk; in *almendrados,* a sweet made of almonds, honey, and flour; and in *turrones,* which were either hard candies made of the nuts and honey or a softer version which included beaten eggwhite. Clavigero (1780, 1: 53) had simpler tastes and preferred the nuts lightly toasted. If given a darker roast, he found that the taste and odor were so similar to those of coffee that anybody could be fooled by it. He also mentioned an oil that could be made from peanuts which was acceptable in taste but thought to be harmful in some other way. The oil was useful for lighting but was too easy to extinguish.

This question of edible oils comes up over and over again when reading writers on pre-Columbian food. They just cannot believe that these people managed to survive without cooking oil and take every opportunity and every plant that could conceivably be an oil source to persuade themselves and their readers that the natives, despite all the evidence to the contrary, made cooking oil from plants. Not even the lack of any pre-Columbian pottery shapes suitable for frying has any effect on their arguments.

In the Old World things were ground with a rotary motion, whether in a hand-powered quern or in a larger mill powered by slaves, animals, or water. In the Americas things were ground with a to-and-fro motion, be it cassava being ground on sharkskin for the transparently thin cakes of the nobility or lime-treated maize being ground on a three-legged stone *metate* with a handstone, a *mano*. There was no technology available in the New World for grinding great heaps of peanuts or any other oily seeds, or for pressing them to extract oil. The only way vegetable oil was obtained on the American continent was by crushing or grinding some oil-bearing seeds and putting them into a vessel with boiling water. Any available oil would then rise to the surface, ready to be skimmed off, but oil so laboriously obtained was more likely to be used as a medicine, a skin salve, or a hair dressing than as a culinary ingredient.

The Europeans sorely missed their olive oil and their lard and assumed that the Indians felt deprived as well. Not at all. They had never used them and therefore did not feel their lack. The only use the inhabitants of the New World could see for the grease that the Europeans so longed for was for illumination. That European invention they all agreed was most excellent, as before the conquest they had only had torches with which to light the night.

It was the French who first began large-scale extraction of oil from peanuts in the 1840s, and it was a Frenchman in the previous century who was the most enthusiastic champion of the little seed. Juan de Velasco, who recorded life in Quito, Ecuador, in the 1780s, remembered, "M. Condamine always went with his pockets filled with them, even eating them in the streets, asserting that they were the best treasure that he had seen in America" (Velasco 1977, 1: 143).

SQUASH

Winter squash and summer squash, cushaw and calabash, pumpkins and gourds: what are they all? They are fine examples of how far folk taxonomy can go in confusing one. The only way to get out of this maze is to use Latin names, invented expressly to impose order on such situations. There are some 760 species in the family Cucurbit-aceae, which is divided into two subfamilies. The one that concerns us, the subfamily Cucurbitoideae, is in turn divided into eight tribes, three of which included Old World food plants. The tribe Joliffieae provides the Old World with the bitter gourd (*Momordica charantia*), the fruit and shoots of which are appreciated in the Far East. The tribe Melothrieae includes many common Old World edibles: the gherkins, the cucumbers, and all the melons and cantaloupes, these two last being varieties of *Cucumis melo melo*. The tribe Benincaseae gave the Orient its winter melon and fuzzy gourd and the rest of the Old World the watermelon, the luffas, which produce not only bathroom sponges but edible young fruit and seeds, and *Lagenaria*, one of the species of which, *siceraria*, is among the few domesticated plants common to both the Old World and the New before 1492. This is the white-flowered bottle gourd, one of the earliest cultivated plants in the New World and of respectable antiquity in Egypt as well. *Lagenaria* was widely eaten in the Old World, being what the Romans consumed as *cucurbitas* and considered pretty dull stuff. Virtuoso Roman chefs pre-pared multicourse meals which included *cucurbitas* in every dish, showing off their technical ability by disguising the neutral, or more honestly tasteless, base with complex and extravagant sauces and garnishes.

The *Lagenarias* were domesticated in the New World long before the invention of pottery and were probably mostly used for containers. This led to them being called *calabash*, an English generic term for any hard vegetable shell. There are other calabashes, especially the tree-calabash (*Crescentia cujete*), no relation to the Cucurbitaceae, al-though like some of the *Lagenarias* the young fruit and the seeds of some trees could be eaten. The fruit of the calabash tree was worked into elegant drinking vessels for the Aztec nobility, who took their chocolate from these *xicallis* and gave the word *jícara*, small cup or bowl, to contemporary Spanish, and *chicchera*, meaning cup, to Italian.

Three New World tribes of Cucurbitaceae are of culinary significance. Peru and surrounding countries ate *cayua* (*Cyclanthera pedata* of the Cyclanthereae), a small fruit which to European taste could replace cucumbers when young. When ripe the black seeds were removed and the body stuffed. Dried, these stuffed *caiguas* were among the edible supplies stored by the Inca in their state warehouse system.

The Sicyoeae are another New World tribe of Cucurbitaceae, producing in Mexico, Central America, and the Caribbean what is called by a swarm of names, including *christophine, mirliton, chayote, chocho,* vegetable pear, and scientifically and definitively *Sechium edule.* This plant was domesticated in Mexico and did not appear in South America until after the conquest. A large and aggressive vine, it provides shade as well as myriads of spiny green fruit of a flattened pear shape, each with a large flat soft seed in the center. The massive starchy root is also edible, in fact to some tastes it is superior to the rather insipid and watery fruit, but it must be harvested with caution, lest the vine be killed.

Finally, in the family Cucurbitaceae, subfamily Cucurbitoideae, tribe Cucurbitae, we reach the genus *Cucurbita.* Not to be confused with the *cucurbitas* of the Romans, the five domesticated species of the genus *Cucurbita* were important food plants in the New World. Like many edible New World plants they could be eaten in different stages of development, from the yellow flowers and the shoot-tips to the immature fruit, the ripe fruit fresh or dried in strips, and finally the ripe seeds. The first use was probably either for the hard shells for containers, the domestication taking place before the knowledge of pottery, or else for the protein- and oil-rich seeds. The flesh of wild *Cucurbita* is scanty, bitter, and stringy and does not sound as if it would attract even the hungriest forager.

Recent authors dealing with Mexico and the Maya area have proposed a Mesoamerican triad of food plants—maize, beans, and squash—and a cult to worship them. Maize was an important feature of Mesoamerican religion, and although we know that maize and beans are a happy nutritional fit, there is no evidence that this connection carried over into religious beliefs. Nor did these two have any sacred tie with the *Cucurbita,* which we shall call squash from now on. This triad was invented by foreigners and imposed on the high cultures of the New World, and the proof of this is to be found in the omission of chile peppers, which the outsiders viewed as a mere condiment, while the original inhabitants considered them a dietary cornerstone, without which food was a penance.

The squashes are curious plants. Their original distribution in the wild can be traced by the ranges of various species of bees of the genus *Peponapis,* whose sole sources of nectar and pollen are the squashes, and specific species of squashes for specific species of bees at that. Before the importation of European bees these native bees were the only available pollinators for the squashes. The largest concentration of *Peponapis* bees is in Mexico and Guatemala, from which we can deduce that the largest concentration of squash species should be found there, as is indeed the case. South America has its own indigenous species of *Peponapis* bees, dependent on the South American squash species but isolated from North American ones. Insect distributions, unlikely as it may seem, have a contribution to make to culinary history.

Cucurbita pepo is the northernmost species of squash and may have been domesticated twice, once in the eastern United States, where it is found by 2700 B.C., for the long-day-tolerant form, and once in Mexico for the short-day-adapted varieties. It is found in Oaxaca by 8750 to 7840 B.C. and has been in New World gardens ever since. Acorn squash, zucchini, summer squash, and the yellow-flowered decorative gourds are all *Cucurbita pepo,* as are some but not all pumpkins. It is characteristic of the species *Cucurbita pepo* that while certain cultivars have thick skins and will keep on the shelf for months, the flesh will lose flavor during this time and become bland and stringy. Therefore they should be eaten shortly after harvest or stored in the form of dried flesh, if that is what is being eaten.

The other exclusively northern hemisphere squash is *Cucurbita mixta,* the cushaw, found from the southwestern United States down to Costa Rica. A pear-shaped fruit, it can be distinguished by its corky peduncle, the peduncle being that convenient handle which connects the fruit to the vine.

Cucurbita moschata is considered the hinge species between North America and South America. It is adaptable to both hot humid regions and cold dry ones and has been suggested as a traveling companion for maize on the way south from its Mexican domestication, if a separate Peruvian maize domestication is not acceptable. It is earlier on the coast of Peru than maize, which might support the idea of two separate domestications, both for this squash and for maize, the squash being domesticated once in Mexico for the hard-shelled and white-seeded kind, and again in Colombia for those with soft shells and brown seeds. Today this species provides the butternut squash, a good keeper with a rather sweet flesh.

The Peruvian domesticate is *Cucurbita maxima,* which was known on the cool coast of Peru by 1880 B.C. The peduncle is the only one which is round in cross-section, without any ridges or striations, as among the other squashes. Today it is considered a good keeper, with the sweetest and most fiber-free flesh, but who knows what the original Hubbard squash was like in its homeland amidst the fogs of coastal Peru.

The only perennial of the lot, *Cucurbita ficifolia,* was domesticated in Mexico but spread to South America before the European conquest. Its main attraction to the cultivator, aside from being perennial, is that it is adapted to high altitudes, growing best above 3,000 feet.

The Europeans writing about the squashes did not fiddle around inspecting peduncles and seeds to tell us which species they were writing about. They used the ground seeds as another substitute for almonds in preparing marzipan or mixed with water to make a cool drink, in the same way that ground melon seeds were used to make *horchata* in the Old World. They ate squash flesh roasted or boiled, sometimes with oil and vinegar, or they made *conservas* with it. *Conservas* were fruits cooked and preserved in sugar syrup or allowed to dry after cooking in syrup. Supposedly this is an Arab invention which was taken up by seafaring nations like the Spaniards and the Genoese to use as shipboard supplies. In those times sugar and sweet things were thought to have medicinal properties. Perhaps the citrus and other fruit in the syrup retained some of their vitamin C, or they tasted good to the hungry sailors. The method was applied to New World fruit and is still in use in the Americas with hard-shelled and firm-fleshed *Cucurbita.* The mature fruit with its shell is cut up, if necessary with an axe, and the resulting chunks are cooked slowly in a syrup of brown sugar, water, and whole spices.

This method of cooking squash is mentioned by several sources, but it is not clear if it was brought from the Old World or independently invented in the New World. The New World had plenty of sweetening available, including honey and various syrups made by boiling down plant saps and juices. Cobo says flatly that New World Indians did not make *conservas* because they lacked sugar, equipment, and knowledge, but Cobo wrote about Peru and tended toward broad generalizations (Cobo 1890–1893, 1: 335). If we accept *alegría*, the candy made in Mexico of popped amaranth seeds held together by boiled-down syrup, as a pre-Columbian dish, then knowledge of the properties of boiled syrups was available in the New World before Columbus. The question as to whether or not squash *conservas* were among the methods of utilizing squash in America before the conquest must remain an open one.

PINEAPPLES

The pineapple grows best in hot humid climates, as it was originally from Brazil and Paraguay and was later distributed over the South American continent by the Tupi-Guarani tribes as they expanded their territory. By the time of the European conquest it was known in the West Indies, Mexico, and the Maya area, as well as South America. It is hard to think of a less plausible plant to cajole into fruiting under English conditions, but that is what the competitive gardeners of the British nobility succeeded in doing in the late seventeenth and early eighteenth centuries. It was an abstruse and expensive business, calling for specialized buildings named pineries, which were built alongside the vineries, where grew the grapes which also would not mature under sullen Northern European skies. Heat was provided by beds of manure and specialized furnaces, and every gardener had a secret formula for soil which would best bring his or her plants of *Ananas comosus* into fruit. The result of all this was that the pineapple became not just a fruit but the embodiment of everything the nobility liked to think that it stood for—wealth, hospitality, and friendship. Its likeness carved in wood became an architectural motif considered particularly suitable for entrance halls and dining rooms, and it spread to the American colonies in this form. Care needs to be taken, however, that all mentions of pineapples are not automatically considered derived from the New World fruit. The Old World pinecone, which because of a vague similarity in look and shape gave its name to the New World pineapple, was also used as an architectural motif from Roman times on and was often referred to as a pineapple.

By the 1820s pineapples could be imported from the West Indies on their plants, so that they became common, and therefore uninteresting to fashion pacesetters. In England it stopped being profitable to rent out pineapples as centerpieces for dinner tables, but in Russia, not reached by West Indian shipments, pineapples in champagne were the last word in luxurious extravagance until the beginning of the twentieth century.

The pineapple moved in the best social circles from the beginning of its European career. Difficult but not impossible to bring fresh from the West Indies in an early sailing ship, it was picked slightly green, and if the ship was favored by the winds and the seas, a few pineapples might arrive unrotted. Peter Martyr records King Ferdinand of Spain, who died in 1516, tasting a pineapple. Only one fruit, the one the king ate, had arrived in edible condition. He said it was the best thing that he had ever tasted. There was not enough left for Peter Martyr to try, but he consoled himself by telling us that in shape and color it was like a pinecone, and that people who had eaten them on their native soil had been amazed at the flavor (Anghera 1912: 262).

By the time Andrea Navagero was in Spain in 1525 as the envoy of the Venetian Republic to the court of Charles V, the grandson of Ferdinand, there were enough imported fresh pineapples to go around, and he could have a taste. He thought it a most beautiful fruit, tasting like a highly scented combination of melons and peaches, and very agreeable indeed (Navajero 1879: 274).

Navagero is worth a brief excursion away from the pineapple. It is sometimes said that the idea of the botanical garden came to Europe in the letters of Cortés to Charles V, in one of which he described the botanical gardens of the Aztec emperor Motecuhzoma (Cortés 1986: 196). These letters were published in Latin in 1522 and in Italian in Venice in 1524. Navagero left Venice in October 1524 and when he arrived in Spain wrote to his friend Giovanni Battista Ramusio, promising to send him all the written material he could find on the New World if Ramusio would see to tending his two gardens, one on the mainland at La Selva and the other on the island of Murano. This last, supposedly the first private botanical garden in Europe, had been planted in 1522. The earliest public botanical gardens in Europe were in Pisa and Padua, founded respectively in 1544 and 1545. If Ermolao Barbaro really founded, or even thought of founding, a private botanical garden in Padua in 1484 this of course predates any possible New World influence. The last decade of the fifteenth century saw the republication in Venice of many of the botanical works of antiquity—interest in the world of plants was part of the Renaissance ferment. The best conclusion about the origin of the botanical garden is to consider it a joint effort, with the Old World and the New cooperating to add this weapon to the armament of science.

If Navagero, the Venetian envoy to the emperor, had tasted a pineapple, we can be sure that it had been offered to the emperor himself. Acosta, who was not a contemporary, tells us that it had cost a pretty penny to bring a potted pineapple plant bearing a pineapple to Charles V from the West Indies, but that when it arrived the emperor praised the odor of the fruit but did not wish to taste it (Acosta 1954: 113). Charles was considered to have an incomparably handsome leg, which he was suitably proud of, but he also had a Hapsburg jaw, a hereditary malformation which resulted in his lower jaw jutting far beyond his upper jaw, making chewing difficult. Perhaps because of this he suffered from digestive difficulties, and while the pineapple soon got a reputation for stimulating the appetite and aiding digestion, it was considered bad for the teeth. Whatever caused Charles to refuse to taste that particular pineapple, we are left to wonder if he did ever try the fruit which aroused such enthusiasm among his subjects.

Columbus was the first European to eat a pineapple, which he did on November 4, 1493, when he landed on the island of Guadeloupe on his second voyage (Colón 1749, 1: 43). He gave a straightforward description of it, saying that cultivated pineapples were better than wild ones, which is not true, because there are no wild pineapples. All pineapples are seedless and propagated either from their crowns or from sprouts which appear around the base of the pineapple. A sprout tossed aside might have rooted in poor conditions and produced a scrawny sour fruit, or Columbus may have sampled one of the pineapple's poor wild relations.

Fernández de Oviedo was the great publicist of the pineapple (Fernández de Oviedo 1959, 1: 239–243). He wrote pages in its praise, giving a rather contrived description of how it appealed to every sense but that of hearing, and how it was the most beautiful fruit he had ever seen, not excepting the fruits which King Fernando of Naples had planted in his three gardens, or those grown for the duke of Ferrara on an island in the Po, or even those from the portable garden of Lodovico Il Moro, the duke of Milan, who had the fruit-laden trees brought to his table. No wonder his rivals accused him of being a great self-advertiser, as well as a great liar. The only drawback that he could see was that neither wine nor any other liquid tasted good after eating pineapples, and he managed to turn even that fault into a virtue by suggesting them as a cure for drunkenness.

This fruit, so successfully competing with the Old World peaches, quinces, melons, and muscat grapes, to which it was constantly being compared, reached its culinary apotheosis at the hands of the nuns of Huánuco, Peru, in the eighteenth century.

> The nuns of Huánuco have a singular method of preparing pineapple sweets, which they do in the following manner: first they clean them, then they cook them in water to rid them of their sourness and stickiness; in this condition they remove the core, which is about half of the flesh, which they grind with almonds, raisins, sugar, and cinnamon, forming a smooth filling, with which they fill the hollow of the fruit which has been previously cooked in sugar, and afterwards they give this two or three baths of sugar; which results in the most delicate pineapple sweets, weighing three to six pounds each. (Ruiz López 1952: 297)

AVOCADOS

If the pineapple had to go abroad to attain status, the avocado rested on its laurels at home. A happy chance turn of phrase, because the avocado is a member of the laurel family and therefore related to such fragrant plants as cinnamon, the Old World bay tree, and the sassafras of the New World. Certain avocado varieties have strongly anise-scented leaves and fruit and are used as a condiment in Mexico, as well as being flavor-adding wrappers for foods to be steamed or baked in pit ovens.

The small, nearly spherical seeds of wild avocados are found in archaeological sites in Oaxaca and the Tehuacan valley of Mexico at dates of 8000 to 7000 B.C. They are seeds of the cold and drought-tolerant upland avocado (*Persea americana* var. *drymifolia*) trees, which have anise-scented foliage and produce small, thin-skinned, loose-seeded fruit. By 6000 to 5000 B.C. they were being cultivated in Tehuacan, as shown by the increasing size of the fruit and the change in seed shape from the round wild type to egg-shaped.

The other two races are the Guatemalan, distinguished by its thick woody skin and a relatively small clingstone seed, and the misnamed West Indian race, which was not found in the West Indies until after the arrival of the Europeans. This race was adapted to low country, growing from sea level to 3,000 feet in Mexico and Central America and Peru, where the seeds have been found in coastal sites dating to 2400–2000 B.C.

There was a good reason for the popularity of the avocado. The diet of pre-Columbian America was what we would consider low fat. The avocado is one of three fruits that contain large amounts of oil in their flesh, up to 30 percent in the case of the avocado. (The other two fruits, by the way, are the coconut and the olive, both mightily important where they are grown.) In addition to fat, avocados also contain two or three times as much protein as other fruits, and many vitamins as well.

We know little about how avocados, or *paltas*, as they are called in Peru, were eaten in pre-Columbian America. The one recipe that we may be sure of is the Aztec *ahuaca-mulli*, or avocado sauce, familiar to all of us today as guacamole. This combination of mashed avocados, with or without a few chopped tomatoes and onions, because the Aztecs used New World onions, and with perhaps some coriander leaves to replace New World coriander, *Eryngium foetidum*, is the pre-Columbian dish most easily accessible to us. Wrapped in a maize tortilla, preferably freshly made, or even on a tortilla chip, it might ever so distantly evoke the taste of Tenochtitlan.

If few pre-Columbian recipes for the avocado survive, the European writers more than made up for the lack. The Europeans fell into three camps. There were those who ate their avocados with salt, those who ate them with sugar, and those who liked them both ways. Fernández de Oviedo allowed himself to be led astray by the avocado's superficial resemblance to a pear and ate it with cheese, like a European dessert pear, but this did not find favor with later authors. Acosta liked sugar with his avocado. To eat it thus, he said, was to eat a very delicate sweetmeat. He said it was delicate and buttery plain and complained of lacking the vocabulary to describe all the subtle new tastes that he encountered (Acosta 1954: 119). Two eighteenth-century commentators, Serra and Velasco, liked it with salt, and Serra also added pepper. He said he hadn't cared for the fruit at first but had been told that it would grow on him. He ended up eating avocados twice a day when he could get them (Serra 1970, 2: 118–119). Juan de Velasco described the many varieties which were distinguished by the color of their skins (green, black, or purple) and their flesh (green, white, or egg-yolk yellow). All of them, he said, could be eaten with salt or without, but always with a spoon (Velasco 1977: 146–147).

Cobo reported that oil good for cooking and lighting had been extracted from avocado pits. He ate the flesh with sugar, or with salt, or plain. The resemblance of the oily flesh to that Spanish staple the olive did not escape him, and he suggested making mock olives by brining pieces of avocado (Cobo 1890–1893, 2: 19–20).

All the sources quoted so far give the impression that the Spaniards had a monopoly on the news from the New World. Not so. The discovery of the New World attracted fortune hunters from most of the world. The Spaniards tried to keep them off the mainland but could not prevent them from attempting to get a share of the booty on the high seas. These privateers, pirates, or just plain thieves, depending on your nationality and point of view, could fill their pockets by publishing accounts of their adventures if they had not come across enough Spanish galleons. William Dampier, an Englishman, was one such adventurer who realized that not all wealth came in the shape of gold bars and pieces of eight and that books could bring in the cash as well.

> This Fruit [the avocado] hath no taste of itself, and therefore it is usually mixt with sugar & lime-juice, and beaten together in a Plate, and this is an excellent dish. The ordinary way is to eat it with a little salt and a roasted Plantain; and thus a Man that's hungry, may make a good meal of it. It is very wholesome eaten any way. It is reported that this Fruit provokes to Lust, and therefore is said to be much esteemed by the Spaniards. (Dampier 1906, 1: 223)

TOMATOES

The Aztecs, we are told, ate tomatoes. Well and good, but what were they eating when they ate tomatoes? Were they eating what we eat when we eat tomatoes? Not necessarily.

The word *tomatl*, in Nahuatl, the language of the Aztecs, means something round and plump, and they used it for many fruits, mostly members of the Solanaceae family. The Solanaceae provide many edibles in both the Old World and the New. The eggplant (*Solanum melongena*) is an Old World member of the family. We have already met some of the New World members like the potato (*Solanum tuberosum*) and will shortly meet others like the chile peppers, genus *Capsicum*. Unfortunately the Aztecs called several genera of the Solanaceae family *tomatl*, or plump fruit. Nahuatl is an agglutinating language, which means that the root words were modified by adding prefixes and suffixes. To find out exactly which plump fruit was being eaten one must distinguish between a *miltomatl,* a *xitomatl,* a *coyo-tomatl,* and many another kind of *tomatl.* Some Europeans, who did not understand the structure of the language they were dealing with, thought they were simplifying things by shortening the name of the larger fruit which we know as the tomato from *xitomatl,* meaning plump thing with a navel, to plain *tomate.* European settlers in central Mexico also shortened a word, in this case *miltomatl,* to *tomate,* but the fruit that word referred to was the most common *tomatl* in the valley of Mexico, which was not the same as the red tomato, or *xitomatl.* It was not *Solanum lycopersicon* at all. This fruit, the husk tomato, genus *Physalis,* was a small, green, plump fruit that nestles in, or bulges out of, a papery husk. When we hear of the inhabitants of Mexico eating tomatoes we need to ask who is eating, where, and when.

Of these two *tomates*—there are more, but the situation is complicated enough—the *Physalis, miltomatl,* or husk tomato, was domesticated in Mexico. They were found in late levels of the Tehuacan caves, dating to A.D. 825–1225, and something vaguely described as tomato tissue was found in dried human feces from the same caves, which dated to 800 B.C. One cannot expect an extensive archaeological record from something so lacking in hard parts and producing such small and inconspicuous seeds.

Today, in the highlands of Mexico, *Physalis* grows better than *Solanum lycopersicon* and is preferred for cooking. The cultivated *Physalis* is called *tomate* in contemporary Mexican markets, and the wild *Physalis,* which is sought after for its superior flavor, is called *miltomate.* Our common tomato is a *jitomate.*

The common tomato (*Solanum lycopersicon*) originated in South America. There are seven species of tomatoes growing wild from Ecuador south into Chile and one on the Galápagos Islands. The ancestral form of our edible tomato is the currant tomato (*Solanum pimpinellifolium*), which bears a long spray of tiny red fruit which when ripe split on the plant. With or without human intervention, a tomato diverged from its miniature relative and spread north, probably carried by birds. Desiccated tomato flesh has been found in the stomach of a Peruvian mummy, but it was not commonly used in Peru. When it arrived in Mexico, the already existing tradition of *Physalis* cultivation made it a logical candidate for horticultural attention. The two plants fill different ecological niches, meaning that the tomatoes could grow successfully where *Physalis* did not do well.

Tomatoes, who knows whether *Solanum* or *Physalis,* make a fleeting appearance on the pre-Conquest Aztec tribute lists. They do not appear among the tribute given to the Cortés establishment in Cuernavaca in 1532 unless they are hidden in some general category like "fruit." Around 1550 Don Juan de Guzmán, the governor of Coyoacán in the Valley of Mexico, received daily 3 fowl, 2 baskets of shelled maize, 400 cacao beans, 200 chiles, 1 piece of salt, tomatoes, squash seeds, and the services of 8 women to grind the maize. Another list has this same Don Juan getting 700 chiles and 700 *tomates* a week. Presumably these tribute tomatoes were highland *Physalis,* green husk tomatoes, and not lowland *Solanum lycopersicon,* our modern red tomato.

Don Juan's tribute list illustrates the consistent linkage between chiles and tomatoes. Sometimes the lists give a combined total, and it seems probable that they went together for culinary as well as accounting purposes. Cervantes de Salazar said that tomatoes were added to sauces and stews to temper the heat of the chiles but also agrees with other sources that they added a pleasing tartness to the food (Cervantes de Salazar 1914: 18).

The further history of the tomato (*Solanum lycopersicon,* because *Physalis* barely got beyond its native shores until recently) is well known. As one would expect from its climatic requirements, it successfully adapted to Mediterranean conditions although its welcome was not immediate or unanimous. The first printed recipe for spaghetti with tomato sauce was published in a Neapolitan cookbook in 1837, although we do not know how long the dish had been eaten before that. It must have been late in the nineteenth century before "as easy as spaghetti with tomato sauce" became the Italian equivalent for our "as easy as pie." And then it was hardly welcomed all over Italy. Even today the Genoese have reservations about the compatibility of tomatoes with fish, thinking them too sour and aggressive to go with the delicate flavors of the sea. In fact the myth of tomato-soaked Italian cuisine is a product of American perception of Italo-American food, which is not at all a realistic assessment of Italian food as it is or ever was.

Queasiness about the tomato increases as you go farther north, in both Europe and North America. Modern authors snicker at the herbalists speaking of the rank smell of tomato plants, but they should go out into the garden and stake and tie a hundred plants, and they will find that tomato plants do indeed have a powerful and distinctive odor which is totally absent from the fruit. A. T. Bolotov, whom we met experimenting with potatoes in eighteenth-century Russia, also tried growing tomatoes and developed a routine for cultivating them in his cold climate: starting them indoors, transplanting them outside, and then bringing them back inside, just before the first frosts, to ripen. The Decembrists introduced the plant to Siberia during their exile there during the late 1820s and the 1830s, but much of Northern Europe and North America still looked askance on this relative of the deadly nightshade. As always, there were the innovators, people like Thomas Jefferson, who grew tomatoes in the 1780s, and conservatives who had their doubts about them a hundred years later. Dio Lewis, who published a guide to good health called *Our Digestion; or My Jolly Friend's Secret* in 1872, considered tomatoes medicinal and recommended their use in small doses, a teaspoonful or two at a time, as a sauce. According to him, excessive indulgence in tomatoes led to the loosening, and eventual loss, of the teeth (Lewis 1872: 183). A few decades later Montagu Allwood, who grew up to be a distinguished British horticulturalist specializing in carnations, was introduced to the tomato, which obviously had not been encountered in even single-teaspoon quantities in his circles.

> The great event during tea was to be the introduction to this wonderful new fruit—or was it a vegetable? About halfway through the meal, a parlour-maid, of course, a tall elegant girl, dressed in black, and with a white apron and cap with streamers, came in carrying a small dish of cooked tomatoes, which looked and smelled—oh so good! . . . Those wonderful tomatoes were not handed round, but the few grownups tasted them, adding salt and pepper to taste . . . After tea, we all went to see the plants growing in the conservatory, and the head gardener gave a brief discourse upon the tomato. (Allwood n.d., 2: 392–393)

One can laugh at the hesitation with which Northern Europe and the United States accepted the tomato, but there may have been a reason for it. The tomato is a plant adapted to warm climates, and it is quite possible that older varieties, grown in unfavorable conditions, were not in fact very palatable. The taste of a tomato depends on many things, first of all the cultivar planted, but also the growing conditions: the amounts of sunlight, warmth, and moisture. It takes precisely the right conditions to produce the perfect balance between the sugars, the acids, and the more than three hundred volatile compounds that combine to make a flavorful tomato, and poor conditions will make a poor tomato.

Today the pursuit of richly savory tomatoes is made even more difficult by the fact that the tomato is the most studied and genetically manipulated New World plant after maize. Most tomatoes available today grow on plants bred to give fruits that are impervious to machine harvesting and shipping and that also possess a startlingly long shelf life. The savor and acidity which made the Europeans add the fruit to their stews has been replaced by a monotonous and uninteresting sweetness, more suitable to the palate of a three-year-old than that of an adult capable of appreciating complexity. What do you suppose the deeply lobed tomatoes pictured by sixteenth-century herbalists and seventeenth-century still life painters tasted like?

FLAVORS

Chocolate

Trying to boil the history of chocolate down to a few pages is like trying to put the ocean into a walnut shell. This New World foodstuff, the prerogative of the Mesoamerican aristocracy, established itself firmly among the royalty, courtiers, and prelates of Europe; no other substance from the New World appears so often in the letters and diaries of the nobility and men of letters of the seventeenth and eighteenth centuries. With the fall of the absolute monarchies, drinking chocolate went into an eclipse, but cacao returned in the later nineteenth and the twentieth centuries in a role more suited to the egalitarian nature of the times.

The words "chocolate," "cacao," and "cocoa" need definition. This product must not be confused with sound-alikes like coconuts, produced by the now circumtropical palm *Cocos nucifera*, the universal symbol of tropical island paradises; *coca*, the leaf of *Erythroxylum coca* and the source of cocaine, of great importance to the Inca of Peru, who neither consumed cacao nor knew of the plant *Theobroma cacao;* and coco, cocoyam or cocoa-fingers (*Colocasia esculenta*), an Old World starchy root much used in the West Indies. "Cacao" is used to refer to the tree and its products before processing, and "cocoa" used to be the product after processing had begun. "Chocolate," before the end of the eighteenth century, referred to the drink, usually made of water and "cocoa" with the addition of flavorings. Nowadays chocolate means any manufactured cacao product, and cocoa is the defatted powder invented by Van Houten in 1828.

The word "cacao" has provisionally been traced back to the Olmec, the mother culture of Mesoamerica during the first and part of the second millennia before Christ. Mesoamerica is the high culture area of Mexico, Belize, Guatemala, Honduras, and El Salvador, much of it hot and humid lowland country eminently suited for cacao cultivation. The Olmec may have given the word and the substance to the Maya, who succeeded them in a large part of the territory. The Maya in their turn introduced the word and the substance to the Aztecs or their predecessors in the valley of Mexico, all of whom had to import every cacao bean they used, because the valley of Mexico is much too high, dry, and chilly to suit *Theobroma cacao*. One explanation of how we got the word "chocolate" is that the Aztecs called one of the many drinks they made out of the prized imported cacao *cacaoatl*, or cacao water, *atl* meaning water in Nahuatl. How did this become our word chocolate? The simplest explanation is that the Spaniards did not care enough to transcribe the language of the conquered with any precision, or perhaps first met with the word in some aberrant dialect.

If that explanation seems feeble one can always accept the folk etymology that the "choco" was really onomatopoeic, imitating the noise made when the chocolate was being beaten, "choco, choco, choco." This story goes back to Thomas Gage, an Englishman who traveled in Mexico and Guatemala in the 1620s and had a great deal to say about chocolate (Gage 1958: 151). The chocolate was beaten to raise the foam, which was considered the best part of the drink and the sign of quality. After the conquest chocolate was beaten in a deep cylindrical pot, twirling a more or less elaborately carved stick between the hands as a beater. Chocolate pots of materials from copper, through porcelain, to silver by the greatest masters may be seen in museums, with holes in their lids for the introduction of the beater. There are no pre-Columbian depictions of chocolate being beaten with a beater, or *molinillo* as it is called in Spanish, although spoons for chocolate appear in conquest period inventories. In the first Maya dictionaries the word for beater is the same as that for any stirring stick, as if the beater was not an indigenous object. All pre-Columbian illustrations of chocolate preparation show the foam being raised by pouring the liquid from one cylindrical vessel into another. Sahagún mentions a beater in one of his passages on chocolate, but his description of the seller of fine chocolate in book 10 has the chocolate being aerated, filtered, strained, poured back and forth, made to form a head, and made to foam, in other words every possible manipulation except beating (Sahagún 1950–1982, 10: 93). If beating the chocolate with a beater was a postconquest introduction it seems unlikely that the drink would be named for the noise made by beating.

The third explanation, which also has unsatisfactory aspects, is that the word chocolate came from the Nahuatl *xoco,* meaning "sour," added to *atl,* water. Our immediate reaction, to say that chocolate is not sour, only shows our cultural limitations. The Aztecs had myriads of chocolate drinks, some sweetened with honey, some stepped up with chile peppers, and many with spices and ingredients unfamiliar to us. It is we who have relegated chocolate dishes to the department of sweets. The objection to this derivation of the word chocolate lies in the fact that *xoco-atl* was used to refer to another, very common drink. This was made of maize dough soured by a continuing yeast, bacterial, and fungal culture, a sort of maize dough tempeh or yogurt if you will, with the dough then being mixed with water for consumption. There is, of course, no reason why the same name might not have been applied to different drinks in different places. All we can conclude is that the origin of the word chocolate has yet to be pinned down.

The origin of the word is a mystery, and so is the origin of the tree. The cacao tree (*Theobroma cacao*), of the same family (Sterculiaceae) as the cola nut (*Cola acuminata*), also caffeine containing, of tropical Africa, is rather small and impressed all the early writers with its fragility. It requires shade, shelter from the wind, a hot humid climate, and a well-drained soil. It is easy to tell which of the early illustrators of cacao had not seen the actual tree, because they persist in showing the cacao fruit hanging from the branches, in the way that normal temperate fruit—apples, or pears, or peaches—grow. In reality the cacao bears its flowers and its fruit on the trunk, or on the larger limbs, in a manner common to tropical trees, but not, for some reason, to trees growing in temperate climates.

Most of the wild species of cacao grow in South America, in the drainages of the Amazon and the Orinoco, and if we accept the classic theory of plant domestication, cacao should have been domesticated there. However, the aborigines of this area never used the seeds in the cacao pods, only sucking off the sweet white pulp that covers the seeds and discarding the source of chocolate, the seeds. The seeds retain their ability to sprout for but a few weeks, so that it is hard to imagine these objects of no known use being traded northward until they finally found appreciative cultivators and consumers in Mesoamerica. For the same reason it is improbable that cacao seedlings made the trip.

The alternative theory, recently bolstered by the apparent discovery of populations of wild *Theobroma cacao* trees in Mesoamerica, is that the plant was domesticated there, despite the scanty inventory of wild trees and wild species. The difficulty of distinguishing genuine wild populations from cultivated trees that have gone back to the wild and the offspring of such trees makes it hard to expect certainty in such discussions.

Whether domesticated in South America or in Mesoamerica, it was probably in Mesoamerica that someone hit upon the proper processing of cacao beans. It is no easy thing to transform the beans, wrapped in their white flesh inside the pod, into something that tastes and smells like chocolate. The first step is to gather the ripe pods and allow them to ferment for a few days, which causes many chemical changes in the seeds. After this the seeds are removed from their pods and from their flesh and allowed to dry; then they are carefully toasted and peeled. The peeled nut is ground, and reground, and reground again on the *metate,* preferably heated by a small fire or a pan of hot coals under it. The *metate* is the same three-legged stone used to grind the maize. Indeed, the heavy, humble, bulky, stone *metate* was imported into Europe at the height of the chocolate craze so that the precious substance could be prepared in the manner to which it was accustomed. After grinding the chocolate would be formed into small storable cakes or immediately made into a drink.

Drinks made of processed cacao beans were the first stimulating drinks, meaning beverages containing caffeine and theobromine, alkaloids which affect the human body, to be encountered by Europeans. At that time tea and coffee were Oriental exotics, and their dissemination and widespread popularity did not begin until the middle of the seventeenth century. Before the discovery of the New World the only things there were to drink were water, flavored waters, wines, milk products, cider, berry and other fruit-based drinks, meads, beers, and a wide range of gruels and starchy liquids that intergraded with soups and stews. Distilled liquors were the province of the alchemists and medical men. When we think of the huge meaning tea, coffee, and chocolate drinking have for our social lives as well as for our liquid balance, it is obvious that the impact of this first drink to contain psychoactive agents other than alcohol was enormous.

Columbus was the first European to lay eyes on cacao beans. On his last voyage, in 1502, he came across a great Maya trading canoe in the Gulf of Honduras, an encounter which pleased him very much, because it allowed him to sample the resources of the country without the possible risks of military action. He saw some almondlike objects dropped and everybody scrambling to pick them up "as if their eyes had fallen out of their heads" (Morison 1963: 327). The text adds that these were the almonds used as coins in New Spain, that is to say Mexico, but that is clearly a later addition, as Mexico had not yet been discovered.

Cacao beans were used as small change in Mexico, and it was suggested that they be introduced to Spain in this capacity, the idea of a coin that could rot and decay pleasing the moralizing friars. But the triumph of cacao was not to come about by means of earnest monks, and its adoption took place in the salons of the nobility, not the merchants' counting houses.

The idea of this new and different kind of drink was a difficult one to get across to the Spanish public. Peter Martyr, who was probably relaying information rather than speaking from personal experience, wrote of chocolate as being a kind of wine, drunk by the Aztec aristocracy and intoxicating if taken in large quantities (Anghera 1912: 355). Fernández de Oviedo, who had had personal experience in the New World, was told by the natives that if he drank chocolate in the morning he would be immune to attack by poisonous snakes during the day (Fernández de Oviedo 1959, 1: 270). He found that interesting, but less interesting than the fact that cacao beans could be a source of fat, which he obviously sorely missed.

> The ... cacao ground, and cooked with a bit of water, makes excellent fat for cooking, and other things; and I remember that in a place called Mambacho, there was an Italian, a good fellow, and a friend of mine, named Nicolá, ... and he gave me and my people a very fine dinner of much fish, and many eggs, cooked in this fat. When I asked him where he had gotten the lard, he said it was not lard but cacao fat, and that he had tried it a couple of times when he was wounded, or had pains and ills ... and it helped everything. (Fernández de Oviedo 1959, 1: 272)

An Italian, Girolamo Benzoni, expresses the final conversion of Europeans to the use of chocolate, not as a coin, or a snake-bite preventive, or a healing ointment, but as a drink. The first sentence is usually misleadingly quoted alone, to make him a denigrator of chocolate, but he is nothing of the sort.

It [chocolate] seemed more a drink for pigs, than a drink for humanity. I was in this country for more than a year, and never wanted to taste it, and whenever I passed a settlement, some Indian would offer me a drink of it, and would be much amazed when I would not accept, going away laughing. But then as there was a shortage of wine, and so as not to be always drinking water, I did like the others. The taste is somewhat bitter, it satisfies and refreshes the body, but does not inebriate, and it is their best and most expensive merchandise, according to the Indians of that country. (Benzoni 1962: 103–104)

It was necessary for all the new foodstuffs from the New World to be incorporated into European schemes of thought about food, especially those having to do with religiously required fasting and abstinence. Abstinence meant abstaining from meat, and fasting meant that but one solid meal a day could be consumed. The question of how to classify chocolate, as food or drink, had to be referred to Rome for decision. Gregory XIII, who was pope from 1572 to 1585, was twice consulted by the residents of Chiapas on this question and both times responded that chocolate did not break the fast because it was a drink. Other authorities were less decisive and wrote long tomes on the question, in which they made a distinction between chocolate mixed with substantial things like milk, eggs, and broth, which might break the fast, and simple chocolate made with water and honey, which would not.

While the ecclesiastical authorities were splitting hairs, chocolate was spreading over Europe. A Florentine, Francesco d'Antonio Carletti, went around the world between 1594 and 1606 and is supposed to have brought the art of chocolate making back to Florence. His account of the journey, not published until 1701, speaks of the Spaniards of Mexico as being so addicted to the drink that their strength failed them if they did not have their chocolate at their accustomed hour (Carletti 1701: 91). Spanish princesses who married into the French royal family took their morning chocolate habit with them and introduced it to the French court. Even the pirates off the Spanish Main were drinking chocolate for breakfast by the end of the seventeenth century. Esquemeling tells us of a successful raid after which the pirates had "each morning a dish of that pleasant liquor, containing almost a pint" (Esquemeling 1684, 4: 99).

The pirates' morning drink was probably nothing very elaborate, but some of the chocolate consumed at this time was distinctly complex. Cosimo III Medici, who was grand duke of Tuscany from 1670 to 1723, practiced international diplomacy by plying other European rulers with gifts of Tuscan wine and chocolate, especially chocolate scented with jasmine flowers, made from a special recipe. His physician, Francesco Redi, was asked for the list of ingredients by a friend and had to reply in his most courtly style that he was sorry, he had specific orders that the secret not be divulged (Redi 1811: 345). He would talk about chocolate flavored with citron peel, chocolate flavored with lemon peel, with ambergris and with musk, but the recipe for jasmine chocolate he could not part with, by order of the grand duke himself.

Most sixteenth-, seventeenth-, and eighteenth-century cacao was for drinking, but its consumption in solid form was not unheard of. To make a drink out of processed cacao beans they must be ground, and then, unless they are immediately made into a drink, the mass congeals. In 1591 Cárdenas credited some Guatemalan ladies with the invention of storable chocolate tablets that could later be dissolved in sweetened hot water (Cárdenas 1913: 105). From this it was easy to move on to adding sugar and spices to the cacao while it was being ground. A tablet of this nature could be dissolved in hot water to make the breakfast chocolate, but it could also be nibbled. There is no way of exactly dating the birth of the chocolate confection, but by 1685 Dufour was writing that "The Ladies also, and Gentlewomen of *Mexico,* make little delicate Cakes of *Chocolate* for daintiness, which are sold likewise in the Shops, to be eaten just as Sweet Meats" (Dufour 1685: 73). A century later Buc'hoz could give recipes for chocolate biscuits, chocolate pastilles, chocolate mousse, chocolate marzipan, chocolate ice cream, chocolate olives, which were like chocolate truffles but baked in a slow oven, chocolate dragées, and chocolate diablotins, which were a sort of small flat wafer (Buc'hoz 1787: 46–56).

In 1828 Conrad Van Houten developed his process for removing the excess fat from cacao beans. This left him with cocoa to make into drinks and a supply of cacao butter. This could be added to other

hocolate, giving it more than the allowance of cacao butter that it
as born with. With the addition of sugar this began the production
f what are called modern chocolates. Many people take it to mean
hat solid chocolate was not eaten before Van Houten's time, but as
he preceding paragraph has shown, this is not so.

This is running ahead of the story. The decline of European royalty,
egun by the French revolution, led to the decline of chocolate, an
ristocratic drink. Chocolate was tainted by its association with court-
rs and the clergy, especially the Jesuits, who had been accused of
ying to monopolize the trade in cacao, for the greater glory of God
nd their own profit. Coffee: middle-class, Protestant, businesslike,
hat was the coming drink of the common people. No longer did the
iceroys of New Spain send the Spanish court shipments of the finest
oconusco cacao from the south coast of Guatemala, a rarity by then
nd almost extinct now. No longer could the Spanish court present
his delicate, buttery, and flavorful cacao to the other royal houses of
urope. The fine Soconusco Criollo varieties, even more subject to
isease than the rest of the species, were replaced by more robust
orastero types from the Amazon, or by Trinitario trees, hybrids be-
ween Criollo and Forastero.

The story of chocolate in the last 150 years is one of industrializa-
ion and changing patterns of consumption. Chocolate drinks became
omething fit only for children, but eating chocolate blossomed into
housands of expensive and exotic forms. In 1874 the invention of
conching," which makes the chocolate mass infinitely smoother, gave
nother impetus to the consumption of solid chocolate, as did the
oming of milk chocolate. This last, dismissed as something Swiss
ows had found to do with their surplus milk, is now far more popular
han the more vivid-tasting dark chocolate. The invention of the choc-
late chip by Ruth Wakefield in 1939 added another dimension to
hocolate use. Today our supermarket shelves hold miniature choco-
ate chips, gigantic chocolate chips, and milk chocolate chips, as well
s the old original chocolate chips. There are even chocolateless choc-
late chips containing no cacao but a cheaper artificial flavor.

The view expressed by Jean-Paul Aron, that the Aztec chocolate of
he Emperor Motecuhzoma, bitter, spiced, and "rendered more savage
et by chile" (Bernachon 1985: 7), was tamed and made drinkable by
he Europeans is a typical piece of Europe-centered thinking. Cacao
n the Old World has undergone a complex evolution, moving from
eing the nectar of the elite to becoming a gamut of sweets ranging

from the plebeian chocolate bar to the most luxurious and expensive of confections. All foodstuffs change their uses through time, and there is no need to single out the American ones as being in special need of defanging. In fact we would do well to return to the kitchens of the Emperor Motecuhzoma and see what we could learn there. Hot chocolate with chile is quite delicious!

Vanilla

Vanilla logically follows chocolate. Vanilla went to the Old World as an accompaniment to chocolate, and now that it has expanded its field beyond chocolate has become such a common and all-pervasive flavor in the United States as to be a synonym for the humdrum—plain vanilla.

Vanilla planifolia is one of the few members of the enormous orchid family that is valued for anything besides cut flowers. There are about a hundred species of the genus *Vanilla,* all tropical vining orchids which look rather like green garden hoses scrambling through the supporting trees, if garden hoses had occasional nodes with occasional leaves sprouting from them. The flower of *Vanilla planifolia* is recognizably an orchid flower, yellowish green and fertilized, not very efficiently, by *Meliponid* bees. The product of fertilization, the vanilla bean, looks like a string bean, but instead of containing a few beans it contains millions of tiny seeds. Orchid seeds are minuscule because they store little but genetic information, leaving the job of providing the nourishment for the new plant to a fungus which a few fortunate seeds are lucky enough to come across. These seeds are the black specks that enable us to identify a vanilla ice cream as the genuine article.

The bean when picked does not smell like vanilla. To do that, it must be cured, and there are many curing regimens, each providing different nuances of taste. Brief scalding, "sweating" in heat generated by their own enzymes, sun drying, drying over wood fires, and months of "conditioning" are all employed. The secrets of curing and the special requirements of orchid cultivation made vanilla a mystery plant to seventeenth- and eighteenth-century Europe. The 1779 edition of Diderot's Encyclopedia hints that blood-curdling oaths were sworn by the native inhabitants of Veracruz, Mexico, to prevent the dissemination of their knowledge of this subject. Raynal, a contemporary, blamed his ignorance on the indolence of the Spaniards, whom he accused of being content to enjoy their ill-gotten riches and equally unwilling to apply themselves to the study of natural history, or honor those who did (Raynal 1774: 79).

Vanilla was known to the Aztecs as *tlilxochitl,* which means black flower, although the flower is not black. This has been explained by assuming that the Aztecs did not know the difference between the flower and the black cured pod, which is absurd considering their great skill as horticulturalists. It is far more likely that the name is a complex metaphor, something the Aztecs were very fond of, for which we may never know the explanation. The word vanilla comes from the diminutive of the Spanish *vaina,* or pod.

Vanilla arrived in the Old World as one of a flock of spices that were used in the preparation of chocolate drinks. A basic Baroque recipe for chocolate contained cacao, *achiote* (a red coloring and flavoring derived from the greasy coating on the seeds of *Bixa orellana*), vanilla, cinnamon, and sugar. During the eighteenth century a great change of taste took place in Europe, with the complex and highly spiced flavors favored during the Baroque giving way to the simpler and lighter tastes of the Enlightenment. Chocolate shed some of its ingredients during the eighteenth century, but it was not until the nineteenth century that the link between cinnamon and vanilla in drinking chocolate was broken.

When chocolate scented with vanilla alone was first drunk is uncertain. A century before Diderot, Lorenzo Magalotti, a friend of Francesco Redi and like him a passionate amateur of things scented, described a strong and inexplicable odor of vanilla in his room. "Only last fall, in the two rooms where I live in the wintertime, I began to smell a smell of vanilla so vivid . . . especially in the heat of the day, that nobody who entered could think otherwise than that I had a box of vanilla with which to make chocolate" (Magalotti 1924: 142). Unfortunately he does not explain this sensory hallucination or tell us whether vanilla was the only thing that he was going to put in his chocolate.

The French were certainly involved in the expansion of vanilla cultivation. There were French colonists in the state of Veracruz in Mexico in the eighteenth century, growing vanilla. The first commercial plantations were there, on vanilla's native territory, but they suffered from the inadequacy of the natural pollinators until a series of experiments on greenhouse plants in the Old World showed how to do it better than the bees. The French colonists had to share the technique, developed by Charles Morren in Liège Belgium in 1836, with the neighboring Totonac Indians, who also raised vanilla, because the Totonacs, seeing the vastly increased crops of the French, accused them of thievery. In 1841 a former slave, Edmond Albius, on the island of Réunion, in the Indian Ocean, discovered an even quicker and easier method of pollinating the flowers. This raised the productivity of the vines by a factor of five and encouraged the French to expand vanilla cultivation on their tropical island possessions.

The invention of vanilla extract by Joseph Burnett in the United States in 1847 also aided the emancipation of vanilla from chocolate. It was produced by forcing a mixture of water and alcohol through chopped-up vanilla beans. Although there is nothing terribly difficult in splitting a vanilla bean and letting it stew in the milk for a custard, or kneading the split bean with the dough for sweet bread, the dominant opinion of the age that cooking was some sort of scientific endeavor led many to find it more acceptable to measure a precise teaspoonful of vanilla extract or throw in a standard packet of vanilla sugar.

In 1874 German chemists synthesized vanillin. It is the dominant contributor to the flavor of vanilla beans, but the real thing contains some two hundred other substances for added nuances. Today the world is overwhelmed with vanillas. There are pure natural vanillas, combinations of natural and artificial vanillas, vanilla extenders, and artificial vanillas, all available in liquid or powder form.

Recently an effort has been made to lessen the preeminence of *Vanilla planifolia* by promoting a rival, *Vanilla tahitensis*. As the species name suggests, it grows in French Polynesia, where it produces a very small percentage of the world vanilla crop. It has a different flavor, which is praised by admirers as being reminiscent of heliotrope and damned by detractors as smelling like prunes.

There is room for many different kinds of vanilla. The hundred species give visions of a host of flavors waiting to be discovered. But there is also a sinister prospect before us, the appearance of a virus which is attacking the vanilla plantations. The prospect of life without plain vanilla, or with only artificial vanilla, is a desolate one.

Chile

The fruits of *Capsicum* species seem to have a magnetic attraction for confusing colloquial names. It began with Columbus discovering them on his first voyage and calling them peppers of the Indies, initiating a mix-up which has lasted to this day. We will call all the fruit of *Capsicum* plants chiles. Cayenne is the ground pungent fruit, usually misleadingly called "hot" in English. The British call the nonpungent ones capsicums, but we will ignore that distinction, because pungency is a relative matter. Chilli is the Aztec and British term for the pungent varieties. Chili should be reserved for the dish known as "a bowl of red," or *chili con carne,* bitingly dismissed by Santamaría (1959: 385) in his *Diccionario de Mejicanismos* as "a detestable dish which under the false title of Mexican is sold in the United States of North America, from Texas to New York." Detestable it may be, but there are people who wish to make it the national dish of the United States. In its original form it was a stew of chiles and meat; nowadays just about anything else can be, and is, added.

This fruit with the many names grows on plants of the genus *Capsicum,* members of the Solanaceae family like the tomatoes and the potatoes and another New World domesticate, tobacco, which we shall not discuss. There were three species, or species groups, of cultivated chiles in ancient America. The most aberrant species is *Capsicum pubescens,* unique in having purple flowers, dark seeds, slightly fuzzy leaves and stems, and a great tolerance for cold. It was probably domesticated in the highlands of Bolivia, from which it spread to the highlands of Peru. The taste is quite different from that of our daily pungent chiles, mostly the fruit of *Capsicum annuum.* Possessed of a piquancy quite their own, Peruvians consider them much superior.

The white-flowered and white-seeded *Capsicum annuum, chinense,* and *frutescens* complex originated in tropical South America, but *Capsicum annuum* was in Mexico to be found, wild, in cultural deposits in the Tehuacan valley dating from 7200 to 5200 B.C. *Capsicum frutescens* produces the chile that makes Tabasco sauce, and *Capsicum chinense* gives us the so-called Scotch bonnet, or Habañero chile, which is found in lowland South America, the West Indies, and Central America. *Capsicum annuum* provides most of the chiles which we know today. They come in nearly all colors, shapes, sizes, and degrees of pungency. There is no point in worrying about their common names, as they change from one side of the street to the other.

The third species, practically indistinguishable as far as fruit appearance goes, is *Capsicum baccatum,* white seeded like the preceding group, but with brown or yellow spots at the base of its white flower petals. Probably domesticated in lowland Bolivia, it is used in tropical South America.

Why do people grow the things and eat them? Archaeologists tend to be rather dismissive of chiles, considering them mere seasonings because they do not provide proteins and calories. Presumably these same archaeologists would deny the spice trade any role in European history because spices, like chile, do not add calories to the human diet. Had they read the writings of the early soldiers, missionaries, and travelers in the New World they would have discovered that chiles were omnipresent, that the natives ate nothing without them, and that they would eat the bitterest and wildest herbs with them. Chiles were as significant when they were absent as when they were present. The concepts, familiar to the Europeans, of fasting and penance were widespread in Mesoamerica and South America, and without exception the basic penance was to deny oneself salt and chile. Perhaps it did not provide proteins and calories, but the chile still had a mighty significance in the culinary culture of the New World.

Chiles provide quantities of vitamins A and C, but so do plenty of other vegetables. What chiles have that is absolutely unique is capsaicin. Capsaicin is, unexpectedly, colorless, odorless, and tasteless. It is a powerful irritant, noticeable when diluted to one part in eleven million. It is produced by glands where the seed-bearing part, the placenta, meets the wall of the chile fruit. The capsaicin spreads to the placenta and sometimes to the seeds. Cooks, who for years have recommended removing the placenta and the seeds if mildness is desired, are correct. Water will not wash it off, as capsaicin is not soluble in water, but it does dissolve in fat or in alcohol, as chile oil and chile vodka prove.

There have been efforts made to measure pungency scientifically, mainly by manufacturers who want to produce a uniform product. The pungency of chiles can change even within varieties, so that without some sort of a test the manufacturers would not know if the same plants in the same chile field were producing chiles making mild chile sauce one week and three-alarm-fire chile sauce the next. The Scoville test was invented in 1912 and consisted of a tasting panel that came up with a consensus score, but depending on human tasters is risky, because they get accustomed to the capsaicin and tolerate higher concentrations. More recently high-pressure liquid chromatography has been used, not entirely to everyone's satisfaction, as pungency seems to consist of more than just the amount of capsaicin.

Antidotes to the effects of capsaicin depend on the individual addressed and the school of folk medicine he or she subscribes to. Milk products are prescribed by many, and there are believers in the efficacy of bread or rice. Capsaicin the irritant does not confine its action to the mouth and tongue but also attacks the hands that cut, pick, and chop the chiles and any body parts those hands touch. Washing with vinegar is advised by some but doesn't seem to do much good. This irritating property of capsaicin is the basis of many liniments, ointments, and devices to keep hunters' hands and feet warm in winter.

The uses of chiles in the New World were not confined to food. When the Indians attacked the fort that Columbus had built on the island of Santo Domingo they lobbed calabashes full of wood ashes and ground chiles into the enclosure. Chile smoke was used as a fumigant, as well as a means of chemical warfare, and the Aztecs disciplined their recalcitrant offspring with it.

Early European writers agreed that chiles could replace expensive black pepper imported from the East and suggested that they be chopped into pieces and added to the dishes being prepared in just the same way that black pepper was added. The decorative aspects of the plant and fruit appealed to them too, and it was universally agreed that in small quantities chiles aided digestion. In fact, the descriptions tend to be truncated because it was assumed that everybody in Spain knew all about these useful plants. There is, however, one use in the early texts that strikes the modern reader as a novelty, and that is the use of chile leaves as greens, cooked in stews or chopped and put in sauces like parsley. It works.

One important feature of the chile plant may have contributed to the disappearance of the powerfully spiced status dishes of the Renaissance and Baroque. The chile was cheap and easy to grow. It did not have to be imported from across the seas, passing from rapacious middleman to rapacious middleman and increasing in price every time it changed hands. Not being expensive, it could not be a status symbol. Peasants in a decent Mediterranean climate could grow it and feast on flavors their ancestors could not have afforded to dream of. The old saw about spices being imported to disguise the taste of tainted meat in medieval times was buried long ago, when people realized that what one person considers tainted another considers well hung. With chile available to every peasant strong spices and high flavors could no longer be the prerogative of the tables of the prominent. It was not only the availability of cheap chile which led to the decline

Girl of eleven being threatened with chile smoke as a punishment.
From Cooper-Clark 1938, 3: 60 recto.

of heavy spicing in the centuries following the conquest, but it may
have contributed to the change.

Northern Europe seems to have always had doubts about chile.
John Evelyn, writing to the Earl of Sandwich, ambassador extraordinary to the court of Spain in 1668, says that he has raised many
plants of chile and praises the beauty of the fruit, which he compares
to polished coral. But he goes on to warn that "a very little will set ye
throat in such a flame, as has ben [sic] sometimes deadly" (Evelyn
1818, 2: 184). Who it was that had expired after eating chiles is not
identified. Diderot had heard that the Indians ate the ripe fruit without
cooking but did not believe it. "No amount of habit would seem to
be capable of making an innocent food out of such an active material"
(Diderot 1779, 25: 917).

The division of the world into chile-users and chile-avoiders almost
became a moral issue in the nineteenth century. Chiles were said to
have no nutritive qualities whatsoever; they were a bad habit, like

using tobacco. Not only were they physically bad for you, they were bad for you morally. As proof of this one Professor La Fayette said all you had to do was to study the habits of the average Mexican who ate what La Fayette calls cayenne every meal of every day (La Fayette 1885: 15). He did not elaborate; presumably it was self-evident. If anybody was persuaded by statements like these, the feeling did not last, because one of the most notable recent changes in the cuisine of the United States has been the revival and spread of chile use.

These plant biographies have provided us with a convenient bridge from our world into the culinary world of the original domesticators and users of these substances, the Aztecs, the Maya, the Inca, and their predecessors. Using native and European sources, I will attempt to recount what is known about the food eaten by these peoples before the conquest, before European influence, at the time when indigenous American cuisine had probably reached its highest level.

FOUR

The Aztecs

We know far more about the day-to-day life of the Aztecs than we do about the life of the Maya and the Inca. That we know so much is entirely due to the intellectual curiosity of one man, the Franciscan friar Bernardino de Sahagún. A scant decade after the conquest of Tenochtitlan he was collecting material on the Aztec way of life from native informants, having it recorded in Spanish and Nahuatl, and commissioning illustrations from native artists. It is not enough to call him a great ethnographer born before his time, because from the point of view of a culinary historian he is far superior to a mere ethnographer, as he gives exhaustive lists of foodstuffs and dishes, and few if any ethnographers do that. In fact, one could call him one of the fathers of culinary history. His zeal resulted in his ending his life under a cloud, although his manuscripts were securely stored where they, to our great good fortune, escaped fire, flood, and military depredations to surface in the late nineteenth century. The following royal cedula, dated April 22, 1577, expresses the opinion of Philip II of Spain on ethnographic investigations.

By some letters that have been written to us from the provinces [Mexico] we understand that friar Bernardino de Sahagún of the Franciscan order has composed a Universal History of the most notable things of that New Spain, and it is a copious compendium of all the rites, ceremonies and idolatries which the Indians used when they were pagans, divided into twelve books, and in the Mexican language; and while it is understood that friar Bernardino did this with the best intentions, and hoped that his work would be useful, it is my opinion that this book should not be printed or circulated in any manner in this country, for weighty reasons; and thus we order that as soon as you receive this cedula, you use much care and diligence to get hold of these books, omitting no originals or copies, and send them immediately to our Council of the Indies, who will see to them; and be warned that you are not to allow any person to write anything concerning the superstitions and way of life these Indians had, in any language, because this is advantageous to the service of God our Lord, and our own. (*Códice franciscano* 1941: 249)

Fortunately Philip's orders were not faithfully observed, and besides Sahagún's magnificent compilation we have many other sources, although they may seem run-of-the-mill compared to his. The conqueror himself wrote letters to Philip's father, Charles V, and while Cortés was more interested in aggrandizing himself and denigrating his enemies, the letters contain items of interest. The most famous narrative is that of Bernal Díaz del Castillo, who was an eyewitness of the events he describes but wrote it all down long afterward, when he was an old man living in Guatemala and the oldest surviving conquistador.

With these, and with all the other sources, we must always remember that they are in no way objective accounts. Everyone wrote with a prejudice, or a political agenda, or a cause in mind. The conquest of Mexico was not an operation undertaken in a spirit of perfect consensus. The crown had its wishes, which mostly boiled down to more revenue. The religious had theirs, which involved more souls for Christ, but also more power, revenue, and territory for their religious order, or for the secular clergy, if that is what they happened to be. The conquerors turned colonists also wanted more revenue, but they wanted it for themselves; they wanted dowries for their daughters and an opportunity to set their sons up in life. Every source we read reflects these differing points of view, especially on matters concerning the Indians, and they must be read with such concerns in mind.

Who were the Aztecs, whose way of life Philip II found so distasteful, if not downright dangerous? The Aztecs were originally a barbarian tribe from the deserts of northern Mexico whose wanderings led them to the valley of Mexico some time in the fourteenth century. It was by no means uninhabited country: there were major settlements along the margins of the lakes in the valley, and not too far distant lay the ruins of two great ancient cities, Teotihuacan and Tula.

The valley of Mexico, today one of the most polluted places on earth, must have seemed a place of astonishing lushness to the desert tribe. The lakes were one of the end points of the North American flyway, with incredible numbers of migratory birds arriving every fall to spend the winter. When they departed in the spring the permanent avian residents made their nests in the reeds and among the marshes. The Aztecs, sent to live in the swamps by the Culhuacans, who had prior claim to more solid ground, adapted to their circumstances with a speed that amazed those of Culhuacan.

> And they went and found them content and multiplying, and saw that they were eating the snakes roast and stewed in a thousand manners and tastes, with another thousand dishes and soups made of fish and lake frogs and the eggs of *juhuiles* and even the flies that sprang from the foam on the water, and these were the first of these inventions and edibles, as before they did not use them, and necessity and hunger forced them to innovate, and thus they were fat and happy. (Dorantes de Carranza 1902: 6)

It is evident that their lake-centered diet was part of their mythology as a nation, because as the Aztecs began expanding their territory, at the expense of their neighbors, they used their foodstuffs as a weapon. The erstwhile desert dwellers had obviously become completely acclimated.

> You know how tasty are the viands which we obtain from our lake, let the guards take [to Coyohuacan] small ducks, large ducks, fish, and all sorts of things which breed on our lake, which they cannot obtain and greatly desire, and there, at their gates, roast, toast, and stew all this, so that the smoke will enter their city, and the smell will make the women miscarry, the children waste away, and the old men and old women weaken and die of longing and desire to eat that which is unobtainable. (Anon. 1987: 89)

By dint of such stratagems, as well as plain force of arms, the Aztecs expanded their territory, until at the time of the arrival of the Europeans they controlled land up to the Guatemalan border and sent their merchants far beyond, to what is now Nicaragua and Panama. It was not an empire, or even a state, as we know it. It was a looser sort of dominion and a patchwork one at that, with some of the other cities in central Mexico being independent. In part this was to provide an opportunity for a sort of ritualized enmity, the "Flowery War," which gave the warriors a chance to prove themselves, as well as supplying sacrificial victims for the gods, who preferred the blood of captives. Other areas were allowed to keep their indigenous rulers as long as the proper tribute was paid to the Aztecs. This haphazard structure greatly helped the Europeans, as many of the Aztecs' subjects were tired of their overlords and their heavy demands for tribute, and only too glad to jump from the frying pan into the fire.

It used to be thought that the Aztecs were softened up for the European conquest by a series of portents and omens that preceded the Europeans' arrival. Present-day wisdom considers most of these to have been invented by the occupying forces after the conquest, and if we compare the eight prodigies that foretold the collapse of the Aztec empire with the phenomena that are supposed to have occurred before the death of Lorenzo de' Medici in Florence in 1492, the similarities are certainly striking. There are the same strange lights in the sky, the same portentous lightning strikes, the same bizarre animal behavior. Perhaps the most widely disseminated explanation for the capitulation of the Aztecs has to do with their belief that the culture hero, Quetzalcoatl, who among other things had practiced the cultivation of cacao, had at some point in the past sailed off to the east, promising to return some day, and the arrival of the Europeans was interpreted as the god keeping his promise. But the Emperor Motecuhzoma II (Montezuma is a Spanish mangling of his name, which means "angry like a lord"), whatever may have been in his mind at first, devised an efficient and indeed rather scientific method for determining whether the new arrivals were gods or humans. He accomplished this by ordering his messengers to present Cortés and the Europeans with two kinds of food, one suitable for gods and the other for mortals, and asking the messengers to report the reactions of the strangers.

The landing of Cortés and his troops in 1519 was not the first time that Europeans had come to Motecuhzoma's attention. The earliest expeditions to the coast of Yucatan will be treated in the Maya section; here it is enough to know that the preceding summer Juan de Grijalva had touched the coast of Mexico and Motecuhzoma had been apprised of the fact. How he had learned of this landing is unclear, because while many secondary sources blithely assure us that runners brought Motecuhzoma fish fresh from the sea, the existence of a system of runners and the necessary posthouses is not substantiated by any early texts. Alvarado Tezozomoc (1944: 519) says it was a *macehual,* a commoner, who of his own volition made the journey from the coast to tell Motecuhzoma of the new visitors to his shores. He was no mortal *macehual,* however, because he was put into custody while his story was checked, and he vanished there. Other histories say that Motecuhzoma ordered a system of runners and posthouses set up especially to report news of the strangers, while still others have individuals going to Tenochtitlan to deliver reports, or in one case paintings of the Europeans and their equipment, done by Motecuhzoma's artists on white cloth, and taking anything from an impossible twenty-four hours to three or four days for the journey.

Perturbed by these reports, Motecuhzoma sent his magicians to consult an oracle. The oracle sent a gift to Motecuhzoma, a gift of *chilchotes,* a very hot variety of chiles; *xitomates,* probably what we know as tomatoes; *cempoalxochitl, Tagetes lucida,* or *Tagetes erecta,* also known as Mexican tarragon and related to our annual garden marigolds (British marigolds are our calendulas); and green maize ears. What the oracle intended should be done with this is not clear, because on a later visit it demanded that Motecuhzoma do penance by abandoning delicacies, flowers and perfumes, and sexual relations with women; eating only cakes of *michihuautli* and the seeds of *Amaranthus* or *Chenopodium;* and drinking only water boiled with parched bean powder, presumably as a penitential replacement for his usual chocolate drinks. Motecuhzoma observed this fast for eighty days. The theme of fasts and feasts is a recurrent one in accounts of Aztec food, and of course one that was also familiar to the Europeans from their own religious practices.

There is no record that the 1518 encounter between Grijalva's Europeans and the local inhabitants involved any sort of food tests to determine if the former were mortal or divine. We will have to assume therefore that the population offered them the foodstuffs that become almost a standard refrain in the later narratives, the birds, bread, and fruit. The Europeans reciprocated, giving their visitors standard shipboard stores. The visitors ate some and sent the rest up to the emperor in Tenochtitlan.

He categorically refused to sample the ship's biscuit, the fat salt pork, and the dried meat given by the strangers, on the pretext that they were the food of the gods, but had his hunchbacks taste them, and they said that the bread was sweet and soft. By orders of Mote-

cuhzoma it was put into a gilt *jícara* [calabash], and covered with
the richest mantles. The priests formed a procession, with incense
and the songs consecrated to Quetzalcoatl, and took it to Tollan
[Tula], burying it in the temple of that god. (Orozco y Berra 1880,
4: 47)

By the time Cortés had landed on his shores one year later, Motecuhzoma was ready to proceed in a more scientific and experimental
fashion. No matter who he thought the new arrivals were, and it was
possible that they were gods, after all, he was going to offer them a test
meal and find out.

Western readers often accuse the Aztecs, and all New World peoples, of submitting too soon, of not resisting sufficiently, of suffering
from cowardice and lack of guts. In part this goes back to the European myth of the inferiority of the New World, which was set in motion by Columbus on his return from his first voyage, when he is said
to have described the shallow-rooted trees to Queen Isabella, and she
is reputed to have answered that if the trees had shallow roots the people were probably shallow and worthless also. In part this accusation
of cowardice stems from the arrogance and thoughtlessness of the
modern world, which forgets that the New World had never seen anybody remotely approaching the strangers with their ships, horses, and
cannons. It is worthwhile contemplating the effect on us of the arrival
of a combination of the Second Coming and a landing of beings from
outer space before we condescend too much to Motecuhzoma and
mock his efforts to determine whether the threatening presences on his
coast were mortal or divine.

And he sent the commanders, the strong ones, the braves, to purvey
[to the Spaniards] all that would be needed of food, among them
turkeys, turkey eggs, white tortillas; and that which they might demand, as well as whatsoever might satisfy their hearts. They would
watch them well. He sent captives so that they might be prepared if
perchance they [the Spaniards] would drink their blood. And thus
the messengers did it.
    And when they [the Spaniards] saw this, they were nauseated,
they spat, they blinked, they shut their eyes, they shook their heads.
For the food, which they had sprinkled and spattered with blood,
greatly revolted them, for it strongly reeked of blood.
    And thus Motecuhzoma did it, for he thought them gods; he took

them for gods; he paid them reverence as gods. For they were called, they were named "gods come from the heavens." And the black ones were said to be black gods.

Later they ate white tortillas, grains of maize, turkey eggs, turkeys, and all kinds of fruits [there follows a list of twenty-five varieties of "fruit," including four varieties of sweet potato, sweet manioc, avocados, and five kinds of cactus fruit]. (Sahagún 1950–1982, 12: 21–22, retranslated)

Another account tells us that the Europeans were hesitant about eating the food for mortals and the Aztec ambassadors had to coax them. Even more fearsome was the chocolate, in what seems to have been the Europeans' first encounter with that beverage.

The two Aztecs tasted the different foods and when the Spaniards saw them eating they too began to eat turkey, stew, and maize cakes and enjoy the food, with much laughing and sporting. But when the time came to drink the chocolate that had been brought to them, that most highly prized drink of the Indian, they were filled with fear. When the Indians saw that they dared not drink they tasted from all the gourds and the Spaniards then quenched their thirst with chocolate and realized what a refreshing drink it was. (Durán 1964: 266)

Unaware of the examination to which they had been subjected, the Europeans landed and began marching toward the distant highland capital, Tenochtitlan. Bernal Díaz records the constant gifts of food they were offered by the inhabitants of the settlements along the way: fowls and honey; fowls, roasted fish, and maize; fowls, maize bread and "plums"; fowls, fruit, and roasted fish; "plums" and maize bread; fowls, maize bread, and fruit. Such gifts were considered signs of peace, although we know that the people the Europeans passed differed widely in their views of the Aztecs, and surely of the Europeans as well. The fowls they presented to the marchers were probably, but not certainly, turkeys, there being many other large fowl that the donors could have used for their gifts. The "plums" are *Spondias* fruit.

Motecuhzoma was not the only person who wished proof of the heavenly or earthly origin of the visitors. Somewhere en route, and the sources differ among themselves as to whether it was in Tlaxcala, one

The Europeans encounter the Tlaxcallans.
Adapted by Jean Blackburn, from Muñoz Camargo 1981: 266 recto.

of the enemy enclaves in Aztec territory, or outside of Tenochtitlan itself, an even more complex test was devised and administered.

They sent Cortés five slaves, incense, domestic fowl, and cakes, so
that if he was, as they had heard, a fearsome god, he could feed on
the slaves, if a benevolent one he would be content with the incense,

and if he was human and mortal he would use the fowl, fruit and
cakes that had been prepared for him. (Hernández 1945: 207)

At last Cortés and his men reached Tenochtitlan, the Aztec capital,
which Bernal Díaz in a famous passage of his narrative compares to an
enchantment from the legend of Amadis, as well as quoting the opinion of his fellow soldiers who had fought in the wars of the League of
Cambrai and thought that Tenochtitlan in the middle of its great lake
looked exactly like what they had seen of Venice in the middle of its la-
goon. Once within Tenochtitlan Bernal Díaz gives us an even more famous, from the culinary point of view, description of what is called
Motecuhzoma's banquet but was really just a routine daily meal when
he was not under the obligation to fast.

For his meals his cooks had more than thirty styles of dishes made
according to their fashion and usage; and they put them on small
low clay braziers so that they would not get cold. They cooked more
than three hundred dishes of the food which Motecuhzoma was going to eat, and more than a thousand more for the men of the guard;
and when it was time to eat, sometimes Motecuhzoma went out
with his nobles and mayordomos, who showed him which dish was
the best or of which birds and things they were composed, and as
they advised him, so he ate, but he went out to see the food on rare
occasions, and only as a pastime. I heard it said that they cooked the
meat of young boys for him; and as they had so many different
dishes of so many different things, we could not see if it was human
flesh or something else, because every day they cooked him fowl,
wattled fowl, pheasants, native partridges, quail, domestic and wild
ducks, deer, peccary, reed birds and doves and hares and rabbits,
and many other birds and things that are native to this country, that
are so numerous I could never finish naming them, and so will leave
them. I know that after our captain reprimanded him for sacrificing
and eating human flesh, from that time forward he gave orders that
that sort of food not be cooked for him. Enough of this, let us return
to the manner that they served him during his meal, and it was thus:
if it was cold they made him a fire of glowing coals made from the
bark of certain trees, which did not smoke; and the odor of the bark
of which they made those coals was most fragrant; and so that they
did not give him more heat than he wished they put in front of him a
screen worked in gold, depicting idols. He sat on a low, richly

worked soft seat, and the table was also low, and made in the same
manner as the seat, and there they put the tablecloths of white fabric, and some rather large handkerchiefs of the same, and four very
beautiful and clean women gave him water for his hands out of a
kind of deep acquamanile, which they call *jicales,* and to catch the
water they put down a kind of plate, and gave him the towels, and
two other women brought him the tortillas; and when he began to
eat they put in front of him a thing like a door of wood all painted
up with gold so that he could not be seen eating; and the four
women stood aside, and there came to his side four great lords and
elders, who stood, and from time to time Motecuhzoma chatted
with them and asked them questions, and as a great favor gave each
of those old men a dish of what he had been eating; and they said
that those old men were his near relations and councilors and
judges, and the plates of food that Motecuhzoma gave them they ate
standing, with much reverence, and without looking him in the face.
They served him on Cholula pottery, some red and some black.
While he was eating it was unthinkable that there be any distur-
bance or loud speech among his guard, who were in rooms near that
of Motecuhzoma. They brought him fruit of every sort available in
that country, but he ate very little of it, and from time to time they
brought him some cups of fine gold, with a certain drink made of cacao, which they said was for success with women; and then we
thought no more about it; but I saw that they brought more than 50
great jars of prepared good cacao with its foam, and he drank of
that; and the women served him drink very respectfully, and sometimes at meal times there were very ugly hunchbacked Indians, who
were very short of body and deformed, and some of them told ribald
stories; and there were others who must have been jesters, who
made witty remarks, and others who sang and danced, because Motecuhzoma was very fond of pleasures and songs, and he ordered the
leftovers and the jars of cacao given to them. The same four women
removed the tablecloths and returned with water for his hands,
which they did with much reverence. Motecuhzoma spoke to those
four old noblemen of worthwhile things, and they took their leave
with great respect, and he rested. When the great Motecuhzoma had
eaten then all of his guard and many of his house servants ate, and it
seems to me that they took out more than a thousand plates of
dishes that I have spoken of, as well as more than two thousand jars
of chocolate with its foam, as they make it among the Mexicans, and

no end of fruit. And then there were his women and his servants, breadmakers and cacao makers; it was a great establishment that he had. . . . And I will say what I had forgotten, and it is good to return to it, that when Motecuhzoma was at the table eating he was served by two other very graceful women who made tortillas kneaded with eggs and other nourishing ingredients, and the tortillas were very white, and they were brought to him in plates covered with clean cloths, and they also brought him another kind of bread which was like long rolls, made and kneaded in another manner with nourishing things, and what is called *pan pachol* in this country, which is a kind of wafer. They also put on the table three highly painted and gilt pipes, which contained liquidamber [*Liquidambar styraciflua?*] mixed with some plants which are called tobacco [*Nicotiana* sp.], and when he had finished eating, after they had sung and danced for him, and cleared the table, he took the smoke of one of those pipes, just a little, and with this he fell asleep. (Díaz del Castillo 1982: 184–186)

This passage took on a life of its own during the nineteenth century, when Lewis Henry Morgan, an early American ethnographer who wrote on the Iroquois and has since been credited by the Marxists with independently developing the materialist conception of history, attacked it as being all essentially a lie, a piece of European propaganda to make the achievements of European might more imposing. Bernal Díaz lied when he said the meal took place in a palace; it was a large joint tenement occupied by Motecuhzoma and his fellow householders. He lied when he said that every bowl contained a different dish; all those dishes were really individual servings of the common meal, brought from the common kettle in the common cookhouse. It was the universal custom of the American Indian family, said Morgan, to have one meal a day, breakfast and dinner being characteristic of civilization, a condition to which, for material reasons, they could not aspire. The fact that no women or children ate with the Aztec men was another trait marking their low position on the ladder to civilization, Morgan said. It showed an imperfect appreciation of the female sex, an appreciation which presumably was developed to its highest degree in his Rochester, New York, of the 1870s. In short, historians like Bancroft and Prescott had been deceived in what must have been one of the most massive disinformation campaigns in history, and all the European sources they had read were false (Morgan 1950). Morgan's interpretation was praised by Engels and incorporated into his own work, where it remains as part of the sacred texts of Marxism.

Nobody takes Morgan's revision of Aztec ethnography seriously today, but neither should we accept Bernal Díaz's account uncritically, because there is much in it that smacks more of contemporary European court etiquette than of Aztec practice. As an antidote to his view let us look at two banquets described by Sahagún's native informants, always remembering that these are extraordinary meals that we must use for comparison because we have no accounts by an Aztec informant of one of Motecuhzoma's meals.

The first banquet is a baptismal one and therefore took place frequently, although with different degrees of lavishness. If an infant was born on an auspicious day it was baptized immediately. Those born on unauspicious ones had the situation remedied by their parents, who held the baptismal feast on a more fortunate day. The actual ceremony took place at sunrise, and all the children were invited and fed; unfortunately what they were fed goes undescribed. The elders addressed the mother and the newborn, giving the latter the first taste of the moral lectures and fine oratory that the Aztecs revered so highly.

It is not clear if the feast took place on the same day as the ceremony. Some time on the day of the feast, we are not told when, the guests arrived and were seated in rank order, women apart from men. All of Sahagún's informants were males, high-status males, so our information about women's activities is skimpy and sometimes incomprehensible. The seated guests were each offered a plate with a smoking tube that contained tobacco and fragrances, and sweet-smelling flowers to wreathe their heads, hands, and necks. The food arrived after the guests had begun to smoke and enjoy the scent of the flowers. It came in baskets, some filled with different kinds of breadstuffs and others holding the deep dishes that Sahagún describes using the Spanish word *cazuelas*. This word means both the dish and the food contained in it, a concoction that is usually semiliquid and stewlike, in this case made with meat and fish and, although it is not mentioned because assumed, chile. Another source on baptismal feasts gives the menu as a *mulli* (sauce), or potage, with beans and toasted maize among the ingredients. Before eating every guest took a bit of food and dropped it on the ground as an offering to the god Tlaltecuhtli. After the guests had eaten their fill, the leftovers, as well as the baskets and *cazuelas*, were given to the servers. The end of the meal was signaled by the presentation of chocolate, which every male guest received in a *jícara*, a calabash cup, with a special stirring stick placed across it. Wherever the women were eating they did not get chocolate but what Sahagún called a gruel, almost certainly one of the many Aztec drinks made with maize or other dough, diluted with water and sometimes cooked after dilution to thicken it. It could be varied with a great range of flavorings, and many different sauces could be floated on the surface. The remains of the chocolate, and probably the gruel as well, went to the servers, and the contented guests rested in their seats.

Those unhappy with the hospitality they had received left, angry and complaining. The host was informed of this and had to invite them back the next night to feed them again and make up his deficiencies. Between the two meals, the primary and the propitiatory, there took place what Sahagún said occurred after every banquet, although his informants do not mention it during other banquets. This was when the old men and the old women, who were the only ones allowed to freely indulge in the weakly alcoholic *pulque,* came to be entertained. Depending on availability, which probably meant the season, they were given *iztac uctli,* white *pulque,* made from the sap of the maguey or century plant (*Agave* spp.), which despite being succulent and spiny is not even remotely related to the cactus family. If that was not available there was always *ayuctli,* or water *pulque,* made of honey and water cooked with certain roots. The server put a large vessel of the drink before the guests and then served them in rank order, highest to lowest. If he thought they were not getting drunk rapidly enough, he reversed the order and served the lowest first. When the guests got drunk they began to sing, but never two together, Sahagún said. The others talked, laughed, told jokes, or laughed at the jokes of others. That was the conclusion of every banquet, Sahagún's Aztec informants said.

Baptisms were obviously fairly common. A rarer and grander banquet was given by a well-established member of the merchant caste. It was a once-in-a-lifetime effort, because it was considered a poor thing to die without having made such a splendid gesture, giving lustre to one's name, thanks to the gods, and pleasure to friends, relatives, and the leaders of the merchants. There is a long list of preparations to be made: first of all the purchase of cacao, and the *teunacaztli* (*Cymbopetalum penduliflorum*), the Aztec spice of choice for chocolate, both major trade items which may well have been among the goods imported by the merchant himself. There were other chocolate spices to be bought, and it is significant that chocolate and its spice constellation are mentioned first; it was not just a mere drink to wash down the food. Other shopping had to be done: fowl, crockery, baskets, drinking vessels, chocolate stirrers, and three different kinds of cooking fuel had to be purchased, including one kind of dry cane specifically for providing the heat to steam the tamales.

It was not only edibles, dishes, and fuel that the host had to obtain. He had to recruit his friends and relatives to help serve the meal, as well as singers and dancers to entertain the guests and diviners to predict auspicious days for the festivities. It was not everybody who could be entrusted with gracefully distributing flowers, smoking tubes, food, chocolate, and other drinks, nor could just anybody be asked to receive and seat the guests. The people selected for these tasks had to be well brought up, well spoken and good looking, not mean low people but noble and courtly ones.

The complex etiquette involved in simple acts like giving and taking smoking tubes and flowers reminds us that merchants among the Aztecs were almost a paramilitary force whose visits to distant trading partners often foretold an incursion by the Aztec army. The giver of smoking tubes and flowers mimicked the gestures of a warrior, reiterating the central place of the warrior in Aztec ideology. The smoking tube went from the left hand of the donor to the right hand of the recipient, while the plate that accompanied it went from right hand to left hand, the gestures reproducing the taking of darts and shield by an Aztec soldier. The flowers that went from the left hand of the server to the right hand of the guest were the sword flowers; the ones that went in the opposite direction were called *chimalxochitl,* or shield flowers.

Handing the food around did not seem to have any military significance, but there was a correct and proper way to do it. The food, in this case meat cooked with chiles, was served in an individual deep dish which was to be held in the center of the right hand. Tamales, which were passed around in a basket, were held in the left hand and dipped into the meat with its sauce.

But much had to be done before the food could be served. The festivities began at midnight, with offerings of flowers to the gods and to the drums. At a signal a priest entered and wafted incense to the four directions. Dancing could begin after that, but the merchants did not dance; they sat in their rooms around the courtyard of the merchants' building, which sounds similar in architecture to a caravansary or a Turkish *han,* receiving newly arrived guests and offering them flowers. The dances were performed by senior military men. Before dawn, some of the participants ate small black mushrooms, while others

drank chocolate. The mushrooms were not a culinary item but a hallucinogenic one, causing visions which made some sing, some laugh, and
some weep, as they saw their future foretold. When the intoxication
wore off they described their experiences to the other guests. As dawn
approached songs were sung, and then there was another offering, the
ashes of which were buried in the center of the courtyard so that the
children and the grandchildren of the merchants would be as rich as
their parents and grandparents.

As the sun rose the food was served to all the guests sitting in their
rooms, followed by more flowers and more smoking tubes. Later on,
food was given to the lower-status people who had been invited, as
well as the old men and the old women.

The passage about the activities of the women is unclear, probably
because the male informants themselves were unsure of what the
women were doing. The ladies went to the house of the women, entering five by five, and six by six, each putting maize that they had
brought on a mat and also contributing a mantle made of *ixtli,* or maguey fiber, to the host to help cover expenses. They were given food
but not chocolate; in this case it was replaced by a gruel made of the
seeds of *chía (Salvia hispanica).* Whether these women were the wives
of the male guests, or hired helpers, or the old women previously mentioned, we do not know. We do know that the merchants, who were as
given to moral lectures as their fellow Aztecs, often invoked the elders,
the fathers and mothers of the merchants, so that there must have been
women of considerable status.

That concluded the action for that day, but on the following day,
possibly early in the morning as so many banquets seem to have been
in the Americas, there was more eating, drinking, and handing out of
smoking tubes and flowers. The guests this time were intimates, the
closest friends and relatives of the host, and woe betide him if there
was not enough left over from the first day to serve them and feed
them. If there was enough food, crockery, fuel, and chocolate left over,
that was splendid; it was an omen that the host would live to give
many more such feasts.

But even such a success did not exempt him from the severe lectures
by his elders, the mothers and fathers of the merchants. As always
when there was a possibility that someone might succumb to vain-
glory, the advisability of balance was stressed. The merchant, glowing
with the success of his feast, was warned not to succumb to pride and

sloth and not to give up traveling the weary dusty paths with heavy burdens on his back. This was advice like a rich mantle, said the fathers and mothers; the host should take it and cover himself with it. The banquet of the successful merchant ended on this dampening note. We have no notice of any drinking by the elderly terminating the proceedings, although it may have been such a standard occurrence that it was taken for granted.

Certainly these two Aztec banquets, described by the Aztecs themselves, give us very different pictures from the famous one of Bernal Díaz. Where are all the tables and table linens he speaks of? Where in Bernal Díaz is the major role played by chocolate? What has become of the early morning feasting? It is best to treat the Bernal Díaz account with caution, not with the totally dismissive attitude of Morgan, but questioning some of the finer details of cuisine and etiquette that the Spanish soldier crowding with his fellows into Motecuhzoma's dining hall did not understand and therefore replaced with descriptions of European customs.

There is one very important thing, however, that can be learned both from the conclusion of the Aztec merchant's banquet and the fasts and feasts of Motecuhzoma, and that is the all-pervading dualism of Aztec thought. They were constantly looking at both sides of the coin. When Sahagún's informants write about the merchants and their merchandise in the marketplace they do the same thing: contrasting the good merchant and his or her quality goods with the bad merchants and the nasty stuff they sell. In food the effort was to maintain equilibrium between abstinence and indulgence, and when the Europeans arrived and introduced their meat-heavy diet and new sources of alcohol, the Aztec elders pointed out to them that it was this over-indulgence in meat and drink that was causing the catastrophic population decline. It was equilibrium that was important, good things were a gift of the gods, "so that we would not die of sadness, our lord gave us laughter, sleep, and sustenance" (Sahagún 1950–1982, 6: 93). The Europeans, who tried to aggregate this tradition to their religious fasting and penance as understood by Christianity, had difficulties, because for the Aztecs it was a way to please the gods and earn favors from them, rather than a way of expiating sins, whether of the individual or of humanity.

The belief that life in this world was a ceaseless search for balance and moderation was inculcated by lengthy homilies to the children about, among other things, food and eating. Lectures of this sort were a common literary form among the Aztecs, and many of them have survived.

> Eighth: Listen! Above all you are to be prudent in drink, in food, for many things pertain to it. You are not to eat excessively of the required food. And when you do something, when you perspire, when you work, it is necessary that you are to break your fast. Furthermore, the courtesy, the prudence [you should show] are in this way: when you are eating, you are not to be hasty, not to be impetuous; you are not to take excessively nor to break up your tortillas. You are not to put a large amount in your mouth; you are not to swallow it unchewed. You are not to gulp like a dog, when you are eating food. . . .
>
> And when you are about to eat, you are to wash your hands, to wash your face, to wash your mouth. And if somewhere you are eating with others, do not quickly seat yourself at the eating place with others. Quickly you will seize the wash water, the washbowl; you will wash another's hands. And when the eating is over, you are quickly to seize the washbowl, the wash water; you are to wash another's mouth, another's hands. And you are to pick up [fallen scraps], you are to sweep the place where there has been eating. And you, when you have eaten, once again you are to wash your hands, to wash your mouth, to clean your teeth. (Sahagún 1950–1982, 6: 124, retranslated)

The effect of such teachings continued under the European overlords. Juan de Palafox y Mendoza, bishop of Puebla and viceroy of New Spain during the 1640s, commented on the measured tempo of Indian meals, as well as the scantiness of their food, which gives him the title of his chapter: "Of the Indian's Parsimony in His Food."

> The Indians' ordinary sustenance (and the extraordinary is very rare), is a bit of maize made into tortillas, . . . and they put a bit of water and chile in a mortar of clay or wood, and wetting the tortilla in water and chile, that food is their sustenance. . . .
>
> If at times they eat more than chile and tortillas they are very natural things, roasts, and some dishes of the country, and they usually do it to honor some superior, religious or secular . . . and not to please themselves.

And on other occasions I have seen them eat with great delibera-
tion, silence, and modesty, so that one knows that the patience that
shows in all their habits is shown in eating as well, and they do not
allow themselves to be rushed by hunger or the urge to satisfy it.
(Palafox y Mendoza 1893: 61–62)

What so impressed Palafox y Mendoza as an example of temperance
was the Indians' daily food, which he said would have given Saint
Francis a lesson in poverty had he known about it (1893: 48). The European religious who were contemporaries of Palafox y Mendoza, the
poorest of whom ate several vegetable or fish dishes a day, received
nothing but scorn from the bishop and viceroy. He probably did not
know that before the conquest the Indians practiced fasting, when prescribed by their religious calendar, far more rigorously than what he
had described, which seemed to him to be a fast but was merely the
daily diet.

The simplest fast, and the one used in all three of the culinary cultures we are going to investigate, was to abstain from salt and chile.
Other fasts could include eating "bread" made of maize that had not
been soaked and cooked with lime. Before the New Fire ceremony,
which occurred every fifty-two years, some priests fasted for a year, the
rest of the priests for eighty days, and the lords for eight days. The plebeians fasted too but not, we are told, so rigorously. Durán was horri-
fied by the fact that there were no exemptions from the fasts: children,
pregnant women, everybody had to fast (Durán 1971: 223).

There was a permanent contingent of fasters in Tehuacan. In their
case fasting seems to have been used as a route to visions, in the fashion of the better-known North American vision quests. We have no
knowledge of the visions they received, but it sounds as if in this case
the fasting had a broader purpose than just spiritual benefit to the individual in question.

And the chaplains in like manner were four youths who had to fast
four years . . . Each one was given only a blanket of thin cotton and
a *maxtlatl*. This is a loincloth with which they gird themselves and
cover their private parts. They did not have more clothing than this,
neither by night nor by day, although in winter they found the nights
quite cold and their bed was the hard ground with a stone as a pil-
low. They all fasted four years, during which time they abstained
from meat and fish, salt and chile. They ate not more than once a

day, at noon. Their meal was a tortilla which, it is said, weighed about two ounces, and a bowl of beverage called *atolli*. They ate nothing else, neither fruit nor honey nor anything sweet, except for every twentieth day which were their festival days, like Sundays with us. On these days they were allowed to eat whatever they had . . . The demon appeared to them many times, or so they pretended . . . The great lord of Mexico, Moteuczoma [*sic*], took great pleasure in knowing about the practices of these fasters and about their visions, because he thought their service a very special one and acceptable to the gods. (Motolinía 1951: 125–126)

If food was hedged about with prohibitions, fermented liquor was even more so. There was, of course, no distilled liquor until the arrival of the Europeans, but there were many kinds of fermented drinks. Alcoholic liquids could be made from maize, honey, pineapples, cactus fruits, and many other things. The most important, which we have encountered in the Aztec version of the Aztec banquet, was *pulque,* a name of Antillean origin that replaces the Nahuatl *uctli.* It was made from certain species of the *Agave,* or century plant, or maguey, a spiny rosette-forming plant which is not a cactus, belonging to the Agavaceae family. When, after years of growth, the maguey is about to shoot up a flowering stalk, the bud is cut out and the plant produces great quantities of sweet juice for about two months. This juice, today called *aguamiel,* or honeywater, can be drunk as it is, boiled down to make syrup, boiled down more to make sugar, or fermented into *pulque* or vinegar. *Pulque* could be flavored with many roots and fruit, but the simple version is a whitish liquid with a peculiar but not unpleasant taste. Some of the additives were reputed to make it much stronger, but without them *pulque* contained only a few percents of alcohol.

There are different stories as to who was permitted to drink *pulque*. Cooper-Clark says that it was old men and women over seventy who had children and grandchildren (Cooper-Clark 1938, 1: 98). Motolinía said it was permissible for those over fifty, because that was when the blood turned cold, and *pulque* warmed it and made it easier to sleep (Motolinía 1903: 314). In any case, only a few small cups were allowed. At weddings and certain religious festivals the young were given *pulque;* one feast was even called "when the children drink *pulque*," but it was always in strictly limited quantities. Drinking was acceptable, intoxication was not.

Pulque drinking must have been thought of as plebeian, because

Old Aztec women, those over seventy, were allowed to drink.
From Cooper-Clark 1938, 3: 71 recto.

Motolinía says lords, princes, and warriors made it a point of honor not to drink it, preferring to drink chocolate, which was the prestige drink (Motolinía 1903: 315). Warriors did not all abide by this code, because Sahagún tells us the sad tale of a Tlacateccatl (a corps commander, the leader of eight thousand warriors) from Quauhtitlan, the nobleman Tlachinoltzin:

> He drank up all his land; he sold it all. And when he had come to the end, he went on—he began with his house, on the morrow he would drink up [the value of] the wood or the stones. In this way he would buy *pulque*. When he came to the end [of his possessions], when there was nothing more salable, then his women spun [and] wove for others in order to buy *pulque*.
>
> This Tlacateccatl, a valiant warrior, a great warrior, and a great nobleman, sometimes, somewhere on the road where there was travel, lay fallen, drunk, wallowing in ordure. (Sahagún 1950–1982, 6: 71)

This was by no means the only edifying story of this nature. Teuhchimaltzin was supposed to have visited an enemy court which had no prohibitions on excessive drinking. He waited until midnight, when king and courtiers had drunk themselves into a stupor, and then cut off the king's head and put it into a bag along with some of the king's insignia and jewels, and headed for the border. Another lord killed his elder brother when he found that he had not reformed as pledged from the vice of drunkenness, and concubines met the same fate if they indulged, because some sources say that women were either not allowed to drink alcoholic drinks at all or had to wait until they reached a ripe old age. Even selling *pulque* was a capital offense for a noblewoman who sheltered King Nezahualcoyotl during a period of troubles.

> It happened that he entered the house of a widow, a noble lady, at nighttime, and saw that she had a great vineyard [maguey plantation] not only for herself and for her household, but traded in it, which was a thing prohibited by law and much watched for and punished by the kings who were his predecessors. This so vexed and angered him that he could not suffer it and slew the woman, whose name was Tziltomiauh. He said that although he was fleeing from one particular enemy, who was Tezozomoc, he was not frightened of the commoners of the kingdom, who were those who most destroyed it. The most pernicious thing that destroyed them and made them into beasts, was wine [*pulque*] in excessive quantities, and because of this they who caused the damage must die. (Torquemada 1943, 1: 117)

The laws on the matter were simple and draconian, although the penalties for straying from the path of moderation differed for nobles and plebeians, the latter being given one more chance than the former.

> Thus the drunkard, if he was a plebeian, had his hair cut publicly in the market square, and his house was sacked and torn down, because the law said that he who deprived himself of his good judgment was not worthy to have a house but could live in the fields like an animal; and the second time he was punished with death; and if he was a noble the first time that he was caught committing this crime he was punished with death. (Ixtlilxochitl 1985: 140)

Such affairs of mortals were replayed on a cosmic scale in the encounter between the gods Quetzalcoatl and Tezcatlipoca. The former was the culture hero, the inventor of the arts, the master of all the Az-

ec status symbols, the cacao and cotton, as well as the gold and jade
and fine feathers. He dwelled in Tula at that mythical time when all the
common Aztec crop plants grew to enormous size in those dry cold up-
ands, where even tropical cacao flourished. Tezcatlipoca was the war
god, the god of the sorcerers, the supreme deity, neither good nor evil
but all-encompassing. Together with his sorcerer confederates he prepared a dish for Quetzalcoatl: greens, chiles, tomatoes, green maize,
and beans stewed together. They also prepared *pulque,* which they
blended with honey. The story is a long one, and I will omit the details
of how they gained admission and how Quetzalcoatl ate the stew but
persisted in refusing the *pulque.* Finally the entreaties of the sorcerers
overwhelmed him and he tasted a drop of *pulque,* and then a cup, and
then many more cups, until he was totally drunk. From this fall, and it
does not seem too biblical a term, came his exile from Tula, his depar-
ture to the east, the shrinking of all the gigantic crops to the size we see
them today, the transformation of the cacao trees into mesquite
bushes, and the myth that someday he would come home from the
eastern sea. If one believes that the Aztecs thought Cortés Quetzalcoatl
returned, then Quetzalcoatl's immoderate behavior may be said to
have paved the way for the European conquerors.

FIVE

Aztec Ingredients

What then did the Aztecs eat? Maize was the staple and the focus of a large part of Aztec religion. The cult of the rain god Tlaloc was celebrated so that the rain would fall on the maize, and there was a maize god, Cinteotl, and a maize goddess, Chicomecoatl, as well. Like all staple grains, maize was honored not only on the state level but in the humblest domestic setting.

> When women put maize in an olla they breathed on it first so it would not fear the fire. If maize grains were lying on the ground they should be picked up. "Our sustenance suffers, it lies weeping. If we should not gather it up, it would accuse us before our Lord. It would say: O our Lord, this vassal picked me not up when I lay scattered on the ground. Punish him. Or perhaps we should starve." (Sahagún 1950–1982, 5: 184)

Sahagún describes only eight varieties, although there must have been many more in the vast reaches of the Aztec sphere of influence. The white maize is "our flesh and bones," so that in the theological confrontation between twelve Franciscan friars and some surviving Aztec *tlamatinime,* or sages, that took place in 1524, when the Franciscans gave a quick summary of the biblical story of creation, with Adam being made out of clay, it must have given the *tlamatinime* pause, because in their theology people made of clay belonged to an earlier, inferior creation, and the humans made of maize of the present creation were much more intelligent. The substance of their bodies was described by the Aztecs in highly poetic terms.

The white maize ear—that of the irrigated lands, that of the fields, that of the chinampas . . . is small; it is hard, like a copper bell—hard, like fruit pits; it is clear; it is like a seashell, very white; it is like a crystal. It is an ear of metal, a green stone, a bracelet—precious, our flesh, our bones. (Sahagún 1950–1982, 11: 279)

He goes on to the yellow maize, the reddish, the tawny, the flower (white grain striped with color), the blue-husked, which seems to be especially desirable and revered, the black maize, and the black fly-specked maize, with large, soft, thick kernels speckled with black.

Maize was the staff of life, but several other grains were of great importance. The Aztec tribute lists bear witness. Tribute to the Aztec state could consist of almost anything—military service, military uniforms, labor to cultivate the fields of the state, and goods sent to local garrisons or to the capital. Fine fabrics were prominent in the lists, but beautiful feathers were also important, plus deerskins and live deer. The usual tribute of grain paid by each province was a *troxe* each of maize, beans, *chía,* and *huauhtli,* two grains which will shortly be discussed. A *troxe* was what the Spaniards called the great storage bins that were made of wickerwork and then plastered inside, with a capacity that is estimated between 8,000 and 10,000 bushels. The existence of these containers disproves the contention of many of the sources that the Aztecs knew neither weights nor measures. Weights they may not have known, but obviously measures existed or the tribute lists would have been pointless exercises. The Codex Mendoza gives the total annual tribute as 28 *troxes* of maize, 21 each of beans and *chía,* and 18 of what the editor wrongly calls purslane but is really *huauhtli* (Cooper-Clark 1938: 61). Other foodstuffs that were received every year by the Aztec warehouses included 1,600 pots of agave syrup, 2,200 pots of bees' honey, and 1,600 bales of chiles. There were 160 loads of red cacao, 820 loads of common cacao, 2,000 loaves of very white refined salt for the use of the lords of Mexico only, and 400 loaves of achiote, the oily substance covering the seeds of *Bixa orellana,* which gave flavor and a brilliant orange-red color.

Sahagún describes twelve different kinds of beans, the second tribute seed, but he omits what other authors mention, that the young plants and leaves were also eaten. His description of the yellow bean follows:

> It can be stewed, it can be parched. It is fragrant, savory, pleasing, very pleasing; it is edible in moderation. It causes flatulence in one— it distends one's stomach. Grains of maize can be added. (Sahagún 1950–1982, 11: 284, retranslated)

Sahagún's comment about adding maize to the beans is significant, because the combination was, and remains, a very common one. Whole beans in tamales, mashed beans with tortillas, or just grains of maize in the boiled beans: the original inhabitants of Mexico may have been unaware of protein complementarity on the biochemical level, but they certainly practiced it on the culinary one.

The third tribute grain is *chía* (*Salvia hispanica*). Nowadays it is used to make a refreshing drink by mixing the small black seeds with water and then sweetening and acidulating to taste. Every seed puts out a sort of mucilaginous coating, so that it resembles a very small frog's egg. This property of the seed is apparently an adaptation to growing in unstable soils, anchoring the seed until it has time to put down roots.

The Aztecs used the seeds to make some of the nourishing gruels that were a large part of their diet. Oil expressed from one kind of *chía* was supposed to be excellent for mixing with paint and using as a varnish, as well as protecting the legs and feet of those hunters and fishermen who had to wade in the lake to make their living. As with all vegetable oil in the New World, one must always question how much of such use was pre-Columbian.

The last of the four tribute grains, *huauhtli,* presents us with linguistic problems. To the Aztecs, *huauhtli* was a broad category including the *Amaranthus* and *Chenopodium* species that were used for greens and for seeds. Nahuatl being an agglutinative language, the Aztecs would have specified what kind of *huauhtli* they meant by adding prefixes and postfixes to that word. The Spaniards used *huauhtli* interchangeably with *quelite,* from Nahuatl *quelitl,* "greens of any sort," as well as *bledos* and *cenizos,* both Spanish words that refer only to goosefoot or pigweed, that is to say *Chenopodium* species.

We cannot explain why amaranth seeds had immense ritual significance for the Aztecs. True, some of the species have red seeds and would tint any dough made with them red. It was also the year's first crop, ripening before the maize harvest. For whatever reason many Aztec ceremonies involved making an image of the god with ground amaranth, or maize and amaranth, made into a dough with honey or blood. The image was then worshiped, broken up, and eaten by the worshipers, a practice which the Spaniards regarded as a blasphemous parody of communion. Even private domestic ceremonies required amaranth. When a baby boy was born, a shield and bow and arrows of amaranth dough were made for him to encourage him in manly pursuits.

A particular kind of grain amaranth is still used in Mexico to make a popular sweet called *alegría*. The grains of this amaranth are popped on a griddle and the popped seeds are mixed with syrup cooked to a thread, and then the whole mass is kneaded and pressed into molds. The dish is usually considered to be of pre-Columbian origin, and it could well be, if the original syrup was boiled-down maguey sap or honey.

Confirmation that at least some sort of sugar cookery was known among the Aztecs and their predecessors comes from a scrap of genealogy. This purports to trace the lineage of the last king of the Toltecs, whom the Aztecs considered their instructors in the arts of civilization.

Tecpancaltzin inherited the lordship of the Toltecs, and after ruling about ten years there came a maiden to his palace, a very beautiful maiden, who had come with her parents to bring him some presents, and they even say, and it is found in history, that it was the black agave syrup, and some *chancacas* [either a mixture of grain and cooked syrup, or solidified sugar], sugar from this syrup, as they were the inventors of this, and as something new they presented it to the king, being knights of noble blood and of his own lineage. (Ixtlilxochitl 1975: 274)

The rich oily squash seeds, so much more appealing than the fruit which encased them, were apparently also stuck together with cooked syrup. This process, oddly given by Sahagún's translators as "frying" with honey, makes one wonder what the Aztec word *tzoyonia*, usually defined as "to fry in a pan," really meant (Sahagún 1950–1982, 10: 79).

The four tribute seeds were part of the original inventory of the Aztecs, according to Alvarado Tezozomoc (1944: 8). When they were wandering in the northern desert the men hunted deer, jackrabbits, mice, and snakes and carried with them the seeds of maize, beans, *chía,* and *huauhtli,* as well as squash seeds, chile seeds, and the seeds of *jitomate* and *miltomate.* They released rabbits and jackrabbits on the poor soil along their way and planted maize on the good soils.

By the time the Aztecs were established as the lords of Tenochtitlan and much of the rest of Mexico they had many more varieties of the original foodstuffs and many new foodstuffs as well. Sahagún cannot work up much enthusiasm for one kind of squash he describes, one that was eaten for its flesh:

> It is . . . sweet, pale, tasting of ashes, tasteless . . . stringy . . . It is edible uncooked, harming no one. It can be cooked in an *olla.* It is edible in moderation; it causes one's stomach to swell. (Sahagún 1950–1982, 11: 288)

The variety of squash that provided squash seeds evoked much more pleasurable emotion. Squash seeds were an item of tribute in both pre-Columbian and postconquest lists, and they were used in many more dishes than the sweet one just mentioned.

> I parch squash seeds. I eat squash seeds. I plant squash seeds. I make squash tamales . . . I break the squash open. I remove the squash seeds. I eat the squash seeds. (Sahagún 1950–1982, 11: 288–289, retranslated)

That universal condiment, chile, came in many guises. Hernández describes seven different ones: the *quauhchilli,* the tree chile, which is the smallest and the hottest; the *chiltecpin,* which may seem hotter than the first but loses its fire more quickly; the *tonalchilli,* which is a summer chile; the *chilcoztli,* which tints any food prepared with it yellow; *tzinquauhyo;* and the *texochilli,* which is large and somewhat sweeter and eaten with tortillas. If this last has been smoked and dried for storage it is called a *pocchilli.* The *milchilli* is small and pointed and grows in the maize plot, the *milpa* (Hernández 1959, 2: 136–139).

While the Europeans were marching toward Tenochtitlan they were taunted by their enemies with the possibility of ending up in a pot with salt and chiles and tomatoes, so that we know the combination was popular before their arrival and so it remains.

The chile seller . . . sells mild red chiles, broad chiles, hot green chiles, yellow chiles, *cuitlachilli, tenpilchilli, chichioachilli*. He sells water chiles, *conchilli;* he sells smoked chiles, small chiles, tree chiles, thin chiles, those like beetles. He sells hot chiles, the early variety, the hollow-based kind. He sells green chiles, sharp-pointed red chiles, a late variety, those from Atzitziuacan, Tochmilco, Huaxtepec, Michoacán, Anauac, the Huaxteca, the Chichimeca. Separately he sells strings of chiles, chiles cooked in an *olla*, fish chiles, white fish chiles.

The bad chile seller sells chile [which is] stinking, sharp to the taste, evil-smelling, spoiled; waste from the chiles, late-formed chiles, chaff from the chiles. He sells chiles from the wet country, incapable of burning, insipid to the taste; unformed, not yet firm, immature; those which have formed as droplets, as buds.

The tomato seller sells large tomatoes, small tomatoes, leaf tomatoes, thin tomatoes, sweet tomatoes, large serpent tomatoes, nipple-shaped tomatoes, serpent tomatoes. Also he sells coyote tomatoes, sand tomatoes, those which are yellow, very yellow, quite yellow, red, very red, quite ruddy, ruddy, bright red, reddish, rosy dawn colored.

The bad tomato seller sells spoiled tomatoes, bruised tomatoes, those which cause diarrhea; the sour, the very sour. Also he sells the green, the hard ones, those which scratch one's throat, which disturb—trouble one; which make one's saliva smack, make one's saliva flow; the harsh ones, those which burn the throat. (Sahagún 1950–1982, 10: 67–68, retranslated)

Bernal Díaz del Castillo referred to his rations during the fighting, which must have been very close to the standard Aztec diet, as "our misery of maize cakes, ají or pepper, tunas (cactus fruit) and herbs" (Díaz del Castillo 1982: 376). The green herbs they ate, which included the leaves of *Chenopodium* and *Amaranthus* species, were endless and cannot be described here, but there were also plenty of roots and other plant products. The plant biography section has dealt with the large starchy root of the chayote, from the Nahuatl *chayotli* (*Sechium edule*), in the section on Cucurbits. Another root was the jícama (*Pachyrhizus erosus*), which the sources agree was almost always eaten raw and praised for its cool crispness. Sweet potatoes and manioc were minor players. Gardeners might like to know that the roots of two plants which we think of as decoratives were eaten. The bulbs of

Tigridia pavonia (Nahuatl *oceloxochitl* or *cacomitl*) provided a starchy food which authorities quoted by Santamaría (1959: 176) say tastes like chestnuts, a label which is applied to starchy roots and bulbs about as often as "tastes like chicken" is applied to exotic meat. The tuberous roots of *Dahlia coccinea, Dahlia pinnata,* and *Dahlia lehmanii* were eaten, and the plants were probably domesticated as food sources, not for decoratives. Intrepid and erudite authors of gardening books occasionally try eating their dahlia roots. They do not think highly of them.

The Aztecs used some mushrooms for hallucinogens, but they used others for food. Sahagún's informants are adamant that the six kinds that they list be well cooked, either in an *olla* or toasted on a *comal,* and claim that they are fatal if not so treated. Another edible which may be classed with the mushrooms is *huitlacoche,* the maize smut fungus (*Ustilago maydis*). This is a disorganized greyish mass, glossy outside and black inside when overripe, which grows on maize plants. It is sold in Mexican supermarkets today and imported into the United States at a hefty price, although one can probably find it in the nearest maize field. Any recipe for champignons is suitable, although there are also many indigenous Mexican ones.

The agave (*Agave* spp.) has already been mentioned as a source of syrup, sugar, wine, and vinegar, but parts of certain species were edible. The Tehuacan caves produced quids, ancient wads of fiber left over from chewing roast maguey leaves. The head, the ball-like portion left after the leaves have been chopped off, could be roasted in a pit oven:

> As to the heads, if they are prepared by a competent cook, the slices are so good that the Spaniards relish them as much as they do well sweetened lemon preserves. (Motolinía 1951: 333)

Even if they were not eaten, the maguey leaves could be used to line a pit oven. For this a pit was dug and a great fire was built in it to heat the soil and the rocks. Then the maguey leaves could be arranged between the hot rocks and the food, the food covered with more maguey leaves, and the whole covered with earth and left for the proper period of time. Some species of maguey had leaves covered with a thin membrane, which could be stripped off to wrap meat or maguey worms.

Cactuses also had many edible parts. The young stems or pads of certain species of *Opuntia* could be eaten raw or cooked as greens. Sahagún tells us of thirteen different varieties of *tunas,* the Spanish word for *Opuntia* fruit (Sahagún 1950–1982, 11: 122–124). Some were sweet, some were sour, some could be eaten raw, and some needed cooking. The Europeans took a puerile delight in feeding newcomers the kind of *tuna* that produced brilliant red urine, to the understandable dismay of the unwary eater. The juice of the *tunas* could be used to make wine or boiled down to become sugar. Even the flowers were edible, but that was famine food.

That the Aztecs were great fruit eaters we know from their vocabulary, as well as the lists of food gifts they gave to the Europeans. There is a great proliferation of words for different stages of ripeness: from puckering the mouth, to almost ripe, to fully ripe, to the various stages of decay. Fruit fell into two major classes: *xocotl,* or sour fruit, and *tzapotl,* or sweet fruit.

To supply themselves with animal food, the Aztecs had five domesticated animals as well as all the wild animals that lived in an as yet not overpopulated or polluted New World. The domesticated animals were the turkey, the Muscovy duck, the dog, the bee, and the cochineal insect. The last was a source of dye rather than a foodstuff and was one of the most valuable resources the Europeans found in the New World, ranking right behind gold and silver in export value. It is most familiar to us for the role it played in the American revolution, providing the dye for the garments of the higher-ranking British officers that gave them the name of "redcoats."

The turkey will be discussed more fully in the Maya section, but the reader should be warned here about the ambiguity that exists in the sources, which tend to lump all large birds as "Indian fowl." There were many candidates for this role. Only the turkey was domesticated, but many of the others were raised from poults or eggs. An example of this may be found in *Aldrovandi on Chickens,* a late sixteenth-century Italian work (Aldrovandi 1963). There are several illustrations of "Indian fowl," one of which looks like the fabled phoenix. Another "Indian fowl," the picture of which was given to Aldrovandi by the Grand Duke of Tuscany, affirms its New World origin by a neat vignette of maize in the lower right-hand corner, but the New World fowl is a clearly recognizable male curassow (*Crax rubra*) (Aldrovandi 1963: 386–387). In other words, when the sources speak of "Indian fowl" or even "wattled fowl," both of which are usually translated as "turkey," the identification should be received with skepticism.

It is only in Nahuatl sources that we can be sure we are talking

about turkeys (*Meleagris gallopavo, totollin* and *huexolotl* in Nahuatl). Sahagún has no doubt about the culinary importance of this
New World domesticate. "I eat the wing tips of a turkey; I am given
them. They are fleshless, thin-fleshed, good tasting, very good tasting. . . . it leads the meats; it is the master. It is tasty, fat, savory" (Sahagún 1950–1982, 11: 56, 53). Given the importance of turkeys and
other fowl in the diet, it is not surprising that there was a religious festival honoring them.

> This festival occurred twice a year, every 200 days, so that one year
> it came once, and the next year twice, for this festival the Indians
> saved during the year the eggshells from which the chicks had
> hatched which the fowl had laid. On this day, at dawn, they spread
> them on the roads and streets in memory of the goodness of the god
> who had given them fowl. (Cervantes de Salazar 1914: 59–60)

The quantity of turkeys raised was phenomenal. Motolinía says that
the market of Tepeyacac, just one of the several suburban markets
around Tenochtitlan, sold eight thousand birds every five days, and
this all year round (Motolinía 1903: 332). Matlalaca, the majordomo
of the poet-king of Texcoco, Nezahualcoyotl, sent one hundred turkeys to the court daily, as well as great quantities of other edibles
(Cooper-Clark 1938: 58). They not only were food for humans, but
according to Cortés were also used to feed the animals in Motecuhzoma's zoo (Cortés 1986: 110; unfortunately mistranslated as
"chicken"). Torquemada claims that five hundred turkeys a day went
to the zoo animals (Torquemada 1943, 1: 298).

There is not much material on the care and raising of Muscovy
ducks (*Cairina moschata*). The edible dogs interested the Spanish writers much more. They were not, as many people think, Chihuahuas, or
even hairless Chihuahuas. There existed, among many others, a much
larger hairless variety that nearly became extinct because the Spaniards salted too many of them down in barrels to serve as naval stores.
Cortés, in his Fifth Letter to Charles V, said that they were "quite
tasty" (Cortés 1986: 398).

Dog breeding was a lucrative profession and one that seems to have
been carried out on a considerable scale. Sahagún gives a glowing
prognosis for the fortunate dog breeder who was born on the calendrical day Four Dog:

And thus they said: if he bred dogs, he whose day sign was the dog, all would mate. His dogs would grow; none would die of sickness. As he trafficked in them, so they became as [numerous as] the sands. . . . It was said: "How can it be otherwise? The dogs share a day sign with him. Thus the breeding of dogs resulted well for him." He sold them all. . . . Also owners and breeders of dogs became rich, and the price of dogs was so high, because they were eaten and needed by the people in days of old. . . . When dogs were sold, they seemed to have great jowls and mouths; they were judged, sought after, and coveted; whatever kind would be taken, whether short haired or long haired. (Sahagún 1950–1982, 4/5: 19–20)

It is not just the household pet aspect of the question that makes dogs seem so unappetizing to us today. The thought of eating one of those skeletal creatures that skulk about the foul muddy back streets of backwoods Latin American towns does not stimulate the gastric juices. However, the inhabitants of the Pacific rim have long eaten dogs, and their secret was disclosed by Sir Joseph Banks in his diary of the first Cook expedition to the Pacific. He ate dogs in Tahiti in 1769 and thought very highly of them: ". . . few were there of the nicest of us but allowed a South Sea dog was next to an English lamb" (Banks 1896: 136). Acute observer that he was, he did not think that English dogs would be as good, because the Tahitian dogs had been fed wholly on vegetables during their entire lives. The same seems to have been true of their Mesoamerican fellows. The professional dog raisers probably fed their dogs maize, because there are many West Mexican clay figures of dogs holding ears of maize in their mouths. Motolinía says, "I have seen a dog . . . devour avocadoes with relish" (Motolinía 1951: 280). The Aztec gourmets shopping for dogs in the market probably asked even their most trusted dog dealers searching questions about the diet of the animal in question.

This section dealing with the meat supply is the place to discuss the common accusation that the Aztecs were cannibals on a scale never seen before or since on the face of the earth. Set forth by Michael Harner in 1977, this thesis was that the Aztecs had depleted all their sources of protein and, lacking any large domesticated four-footed animals, the elite were forced to turn to eating the plebeians to survive. We know that the Aztecs sacrificed human beings, although the scale is a subject of dispute, and we also know that some of these sacrificial victims were eaten. The preferred sacrificial victim was a captive, and the still beating heart was offered to the god. The body was then tumbled down the pyramid, where it was seized by old men who cut it up, dividing the limbs among the captors according to a standard formula. The captor took the meat home, had it stewed with maize, and sent it around to friends and relations. Sahagún nearly gives us the recipe for this dish, *tlacatlaolli*, or human stew:

> First they cooked the maize, which was going to be served with the [human] flesh, and they put a little of the meat on the maize, they mixed no chile either with the cooked stuff or with the meat, only salt. This meat was eaten by him who made the banquet and his relations. (Sahagún 1982: 514)

The accounts agree that this was a communion of sorts, unity with the god being achieved by sharing the god's food and eating it with "reverence, ritual, and fastidiousness—as if it was something from heaven" (Durán 1971: 191). The portion of flesh per person was very small indeed, about half an ounce, and some people refused it altogether. Only great warriors, capable of taking captives, or rich merchants who could afford to buy slaves in the market could offer such sacrifices. The very description of the method of cooking, with the absence of chile, should signal to us that this was not an ordinary meal but a religious rite.

Harner was led astray by two factors, one from his own time and one from the time of the conquest of the Aztecs. The period in which he wrote his article can only be called the time of the great protein madness in the United States. Maximizing your protein intake was the ultimate good. I myself heard a distinguished archaeologist say that the measure of a civilization was the quantity of animal protein it provided for its citizens. Today that particular dietary craze lies buried and forgotten beneath all its successors, and we realize that we can get along with a lot less animal protein, and that the Aztecs too probably had enough without resorting to the consumption of humans on a vast scale.

The other factor which produced this view was an unwary trust in the sixteenth-century sources. Written to justify the brutal conquest of an innocent people, they had to demonstrate that theirs was a just war, and one of the best ways to do this was to exaggerate customs that Church and crown found unacceptable. Cannibalism was a perfect stick to beat the Indian with, and certain Europeans seized that stick and belabored the Indian with it for all they were worth. The truth was the loser in the process.

Domesticated animals were by no means the only sources of protein. There was a great variety of edible game, although we might not recognize some of it as such. There were deer, peccary, rabbits, jackrabbits, mice, armadillos, snakes, gophers, opossums, and iguanas. Harner claims that game was almost completely extinct from overhunting in Central Mexico, a view which is flatly contradicted by a description of a great hunt held by Viceroy Mendoza in 1540 which netted thousands of animals of all sorts. Hernández lists many wild birds that could be kept and fattened in cages and the grains suitable for them, although he disdains some of the many birds caught on the lakes because he thought they didn't taste very good (Hernández 1959, 2: 340, 353). Even snakes could be caged and fed, becoming suitable for a lord's table at the end of the process. One snake dish involved cutting off the creature's head and tail and stewing it in *pulque,* producing a strengthening ragout for the elderly.

Perhaps runners brought seafood from the coast to the lords, but there are no reliable accounts of an Aztec post system, as the diverging opinions as to how Motecuhzoma communicated with his ambassadors on the coast show. Certainly dried seafood could have been brought to Tenochtitlan. For the fresh we shall just have to put a question mark.

Lake produce was an everyday resource, at least for the Aztecs. The Europeans were less willing to take it for granted. "At all times the markets are full of a thousand species of vermin, raw, cooked, fried, or toasted, sold especially for the sustainment of the poor" (Clavigero 1780, 2: 217–218). Many people would agree with Clavigero's description of these foods as vermin. One of them was *axayacatl,* or water bugs; and another was *ahuautli,* meaning "water amaranth," probably because of the granular texture, the eggs of the same water bugs. The bugs, members of the Corixidae, or water boatmen, family, were collected in nets, ground, formed into balls, wrapped in maize husks, and cooked. Hernández describes it as a "good, abundant, and not disagreeable food" (Hernández 1959, 2: 390). The bug eggs were collected on loosely twined ropes flung into the lake. They could be made into tortillas or tamales or wrapped in maize husks to be toasted. They were said to taste like fish, or caviar. *Izcahuitli* were tiny worms netted on the lake. When cooked with salt and chile, they became blackish and had the consistency of crushed bread. They were made into tortillas to dry and keep, but they could not be stored for any length of time.

Water boatmen were not the only insects eaten by the Aztecs. Among many others were the maguey worms, the white larvae of *Aegiale hesperiaris* and *Agathymus* species and the pink larvae of *Comadia redtenbacheri,* which still appear in bottles of *mezcal* (an agave-based distilled liquor made by a process different from that used for tequila) to make the tourists shudder:

> On this *metl* or maguey, near the roots, whitish worms generate, which are as thick as the quill of a wild turkey, and as long as half a finger. When roasted and salted these worms are very good to eat. I have eaten them many times on fast days. (Motolinía 1951: 333)

A curious thing has happened in contemporary Mexico, where these insect foods, those of them that have not disappeared due to pollution and overexploitation, have become immensely fashionable and almost nationalist icons. White maguey worms, which live in the *pulque* maguey, now more rarely grown because of the declining consumption of the liquid, are sold for hefty prices per kilo to restaurants that make the availability of these exotic foodstuffs their signature. What could barely enter the back door a few years ago is now food for the top crust that can afford it.

Lake creatures that are more acceptable according to our standards were also consumed. These included several kinds of lake shrimp (*Cambarus montezumae* and *Cambarellus montezumae*), frogs, and a great variety of small lake fish. Not only the frogs were eaten, but their progeny, the tadpoles, as well. Hernández said tadpoles were sold in the market prepared in different ways and that the natives liked them better than turkeys, which they left for the Europeans to eat (Hernández 1959, 2: 391). *Axolotls,* a kind of large larval salamander that never grows up, were also eaten. Clavigero calls them ugly and ridiculous and says that they taste like eels (Clavigero 1780, 1: 104–105).

Perhaps the most famous lake produce used and widely traded by the Aztecs was the edible algae (*Spirulina geitleri*).

> *Tecuilatl,* which is very like mud or slime, grows in certain places in the lake basin of Mexico on the surface where it is collected or swept up by nets, or heaped up by spades. Once taken up and dried a bit in the sun, the Indians shape it into small cakes and put it out in the sun

on fresh green leaves so that it becomes perfectly dry. It is then kept like cheese . . . It is eaten when necessary with toasted maize or with the ordinary tortillas of the Indians. Each source of this slime has its owner, some of whom earn as much as a thousand gold escudos a year. It tastes like cheese, and that is what the Spaniards call it, but less pleasing and with a certain taste of mud. When new it is green or blue, when old it is mud color, green verging to black, edible only in very small quantities, in place of salt or as a condiment to maize. As for the tortillas which are made of it they are a rustic food, which is proved by the fact that the Spaniards, who avoided nothing that would please the palate in these countries, have never brought themselves to eat it. (Hernández 1959, 2: 408–409)

Chocolate will be the last item in our discussion of the Aztec market basket, as it was the last item in Motecuhzoma's banquets, just before the hollow cane full of perfumed tobacco was presented. It is also one of the most complex items to deal with, because it was so much a part of beliefs and practices having to do with the power of the rulers. We come across this in Sahagún, where a paragraph on cacao is tucked away among the metaphors, and the metaphors are "heart" and "blood," in other words the crucial sacrifices which make the sun move through the heavens and keep the earth on an even keel.

This saying was said of cacao, because it was precious; nowhere did it appear in times past. The common folk, the needy did not drink it. Hence it was said: "The heart, the blood are to be feared." And also it was said of it that it was [like] jimson weed; it was considered to be like the mushroom, for it made one drunk; it intoxicated one. If he who drank it were a common person, it was taken as a bad omen. And in times past only the ruler drank it, or a great warrior, or a commanding general, a general. If perhaps two or three lived in wealth, they drank it. Also it was hard to come by; they drank a limited amount of cacao, for it was not drunk unthinkingly. (Sahagún 1950–1982, 6: 256)

Cacao in the valley of Mexico predates the Aztecs. The builders of the great pyramids of Teotihuacan (A.D. 0–650), which tourists go to climb over outside of Mexico City, had a heavy trade with the cacao-producing regions of the Pacific coast of Guatemala, as we know from the trade goods found there. There is not enough preservation in Teotihuacan for cacao beans to be found, but it is tempting to assume that the elegant pottery of Teotihuacan was being traded for cacao. The ninth-century site of Cacaxtla, in the state of Puebla to the east of Mexico City, seems to have been a depot for Maya cacao merchants, who are depicted with their stock in trade in vivid Maya-style frescoes.

Cacao was an innovation for the Aztecs, part of the trappings of power and royalty they acquired when they established themselves in the valley of Mexico. The northern desert wanderers who became the rulers of Tenochtitlan had had no idea of chocolate and its powers during their progress from their mythical homeland, Aztlan, and, as we shall see, with typical Aztec ambivalence, they felt guilty about the addition of this luxury to their cultural inventory.

They may have felt guilty, but this did not stop the Aztec empire from receiving a yearly tribute of 980 loads of cacao. Every load contained 24,000 beans and weighed about fifty pounds. Lest it seem bizarre to count out all those cacao beans one by one, it should be realized that they also served as money. The robbery planned by Pedro de Alvarado and others of Motecuhzoma's warehouse, where they claimed there were 40,000 loads stored in the great willow bins plastered inside and out, so large that six men could not reach around them, was a bank robbery as well as a theft of a valuable commodity.

The cacao bean was a coin, albeit of the smallest denomination, so that it took eighty or a hundred beans to buy a small mantle, or a canoe-load of fresh water if you lived on the salty part of the lake. Being a coin, it was counterfeited. Sahagún has a description of the shady practices of the cacao counterfeiters, who among other tricks filled empty cacao shells with clay or earth. Given the familiarity of the Indians with the concept of coins and of counterfeiting, it is not surprising to find that false European coins were being manufactured very early in the conquest period. By 1537 the first viceroy, Antonio de Mendoza, reported this practice to Charles V in a tone of wry admiration.

I wrote your Majesty that I was afraid, given the ingeniousness and skill of the natives, that they would start counterfeiting coins. Fifteen or twenty days ago they brought me two *tostones de a quatro* [coins], counterfeits that they had made. I ordered all the silversmiths of Mexico City and the guild to be brought here so that I could find out who had made them, but could prove nothing, nor is it possible to know about things of this sort that they do among themselves, nor is it enough to order them to desist. As for cacao, which is a coin used by them, they counterfeit that too, and it looks exactly the same, some grains better and some grains worse, and each one unique. (Mendoza 1864: 193)

Four different varieties of cacao were recognized, and the counterfeiters probably directed their attention to the three that were mainly used for coinage. The smallest bean was considered the best for culinary use. Let us hope that *tlalcacahuatl* beans were exempt from being filled with mud and other indignities. An inferior species, *Theobroma bicolor,* could also be made into a drink, considered fit only for low people; mostly it was given as alms.

It should now be obvious that Aztec cacao consumption was no simple matter of a single substance being utilized according to a single recipe. There were many sorts of cacao and many ways of using it. Most of the cacao was drunk, but we read of the seeds, both raw and toasted, possibly sweetened as well, being eaten, and there are a few scattered references to cacao being used in a solid as well as a liquid state. Whether this refers to eating the seeds or to some now unknown Aztec chocolate confection or dish, we do not know.

To make drinking chocolate the beans were ground on the metate after they had been fermented, cured, and toasted. If the chocolate was for immediate use tepid water was added, and then the mixture was aerated, either with a spoon or by pouring it from one vessel into another. If the chocolate was of the proper kind this produced a head on it, which could be set aside while ground maize and other additions were made to the liquid. The mixture could be beaten up again, and the new head could be set aside and mixed with the old one, all to be replaced on top of the chocolate when the beating process was completed. The frothy head was the sign of quality, and its absence showed that corners had been cut in the preparation.

The seller of fine chocolate [is] one who grinds, who provides people with drink, with repasts. She grinds cacao [beans]; she crushes, breaks, pulverizes them. She chooses, selects, separates them. She drenches, soaks, steeps them. She adds water sparingly, conservatively; aerates it, filters it, strains it, pours it back and forth, aerates it; she makes it form a head, makes it foam; she removes the head, makes it thicken, makes it dry, pours water in, stirs water into it.

She sells good, superior, potable [chocolate]: the privilege, the drink of nobles, of rulers—finely ground, soft, foamy, reddish, bitter; [with] chile water, with flowers, with *uei nacaztli* [*Cymbope-talum penduliflorum*], with *teonacaztli* [*Chiranthodendron penta-dactylon*], with vanilla, with *mecaxochitl* [*Piper amalago*], with wild bee honey, with powdered aromatic flowers. [Inferior choco-late has] maize flour and water; lime water; [it is] pale; the [froth] bubbles burst. [It is chocolate] with water added—Chontal water . . . [fit for] water flies. (Sahagún 1950–1982, 10: 93)

The list of additions to chocolate is awe-inspiring. Sahagún says that the banquet version was usually spiced with *xochinacaztli* or *uei na-caztli* or *teunacaztli*, the ear-shaped flowers of *Cymbopetalum pendu-liflorum*, which Popenoe (1919: 405) describes as tasting like "black pepper with the addition of a resinous bitterness." Clavigero, the Mex-ican-born Jesuit who was exiled to the fogs of Cesena in the Po valley of Italy when the Jesuits were expelled from Mexico in 1767, said that it grew in the hot country, and the flower was expensive and always to be found in Mexican markets (Clavigero 1780, 2: 220).

Clavigero also mentions vanilla and honey as ingredients and *me-caxochitl,* the flowers of *Piper amalago,* a small vine related to *Piper nigrum,* the vine that produces black pepper in the Old World. The leaves of *Piper* species are much used as flavor-adding wrappings in Mexican food today, although the flowers are harder to find. The flower of *Tagetes lucida,* the marigold that has the alternative name of Mexican tarragon and does not smell in the least like our garden mari-golds, was added, and so was the flower of *Bourreria huanita,* which had the Aztec name of popped-maize flower. The latter was mixed with the cacao to perfume it, so perhaps it was kept in a tightly closed vessel with the raw or roasted beans instead of being mixed with the liquid chocolate. Still another flower, and we do not know if it was considered medicinal, or a condiment, or both, was *yolloxochitl,* or heart flower (*Magnolia mexicana*). It was said to taste like ripe melon. The Badianus herbal has it as a cure for sterility and a flavoring for chocolate, and we are reminded of the chocolate which Motecuhzoma took before he went to visit his wives (Anon. 1940: 310).

The seeds of *piztle* (*Calocarpum mammosum*) gave the flavor of bit-ter almond when they were added. Hernández (1959, 1: 303–305) gives four recipes for drinks with chocolate and calls one of them *cho-colatl.* This contains equal parts of the sweet and tasty seeds of *pochotl* (*Ceiba* spp.) and cacao. They are ground, mixed, and beaten and the foam is reserved, a little softened maize is added, the foam is replaced,

and the whole mixture drunk tepid. Hernández warns that it is exceedingly fattening. His other drinks are *atextli,* one hundred grains of raw
cacao toasted and ground, then softened, by which he probably means
nixtamalized, maize as much as can be held in two hands, spiced with
Piper amalago, Vanilla planifolia, and *Cymbopetalum penduliflorum.*
Another Hernández recipe involved the bark of the root of a bush that
was supposed to add a refreshingly bitter taste as well as augmenting
the foam. *Tzone,* the simplest chocolate drink he deals with, is equal
parts toasted and ground maize and cacao, with some softened maize
added to thicken it.

The multiple flavorings of aboriginal chocolate make some of the
seventeenth-century Spanish recipes seem less overblown. For every
hundred cacao beans one of them calls for half an ounce each of the
following: sesame seeds, anise seeds, cinnamon, black pepper, *Cymbopetalum,* vanilla, *achiote* (*Bixa orellana*), and *Piper amalago* flowers.
The fact that the first four spices are Old World and the second four
New World leads one to think that they might be interchangeable, depending on which side of the Atlantic you were on.

Many authors think that chocolate was used with cinnamon in the
New World, and how this mistake originated should be explained
here. There were several spice-producing trees in the Antilles when the
Europeans got there, mostly relatives of the allspice (*Pimenta dioica*),
which is itself a plant of the New World tropics and another flavor that
was added to chocolate. After an initial flurry of enthusiasm they were
judged inferior to the real Old World cinnamon (*Cinnamomum
verum*) or its cheaper cousin *Cinnamomum aromaticum,* which was
also called cassia bark. This is where the trouble arose, because there
were trees of the genus *Cassia,* of the Leguminosae family, in the New
World tropics as there were in the Old. The Spaniards were interested
in *Cassia* because the Old World species provided valuable medicinal
substances, and they exported quantities of New World *Cassia* to
Spain, where it was found not as effective as material imported from
Egypt. What the people who write about cinnamon in the New World
do not realize is that this *Cassia* that grew in the Antilles was not cassia, the aromatic spice, it was *Cassia* the powerful laxative.

To return to the Aztecs and their chocolate: On the one hand it was
considered to have many virtues—according to Sahagún, taken in
moderation "it gladdens one, refreshes one, consoles one, invigorates
one" (Sahagún 1950–1982, 11: 119). He admitted that too much, especially if the beans were underripe, could make you drunk, and some

authors claimed that it was addictive. It is hard to tell at this distance if the intoxicating effect of chocolate was inherent in some native varieties or some method of preparation, or was due to the addition of some psychoactive ingredient, or just the way of the Europeans of describing the phenomenon, unfamiliar to them, that we know as coffee nerves.

Whether women were allowed to enjoy chocolate is unclear. In the descriptions of certain banquets we read of the noblewomen, who ate apart, receiving a gruel of *chía* with a dressing of chile on top while the men were getting chocolate, but whether this practice applied only to certain circumstances or whether the ban was universal we are not told.

True to the Aztec system of thought, there was a negative view of cacao as well as a positive one. The story is told by Durán (Durán 1964: 134–138). The first emperor Motecuhzoma, there being two of that name, sent a delegation to find the original homeland of the Aztecs, the caves and the lakes of Aztlan. By magical means they and their gifts were transported to the land of their ancestors, where the natives were astonished to find that the delegation were the grandsons and great-grandsons of the people who had left Aztlan, whom the immortal residents of Aztlan remembered as contemporaries. The delegation wished to present the gifts they had brought to the mother of their god Huitzilopochtli, the Lady of the Snaky Skirt, Coatlicue, who lived on a hilltop, to which they were guided by an old man.

The old man said, "Pick up what you have brought and follow me."

They put the gifts on their backs and followed the old man, who climbed the hill with ease. They went behind him, their feet sinking into the soft sand, walking with great difficulty and heaviness. The elder turned his head and when he saw that the sand had almost reached their knees he said, "What is the matter? Are you not coming up? Make haste!"

When they tried to do this they sank up to the waist in the sand and could not move. They called to the old man, who was walking with such lightness that his feet did not seem to touch the ground. "What is wrong with you, O Aztecs?" said he. "What has made you so heavy? What do you eat in your land?"

"We eat the foods that grow there and we drink chocolate."

The elder responded, "Such food and drink, my children, have made you heavy and they make it difficult for you to reach the place of your ancestors. Those foods will bring death." (Durán 1964: 136)

Eventually the goddess, the mother of the god, appears and the gifts are presented to her. Notice the mention of chocolate being eaten as well as drunk.

"Tell me, children," said she, "what have you brought me: is it food?"
"Great lady, it is food and drink; chocolate is drunk and sometimes eaten."
"This is what has burdened you!" she told them. "This is why you have not been able to climb the hill." (Durán 1964: 137)

The old man descends the hill, and as he goes down he becomes younger and younger. He points out the virtue of the hill to the Aztec messengers waiting at the bottom and once again tells them the error of their ways.

"We become young when we wish. You have become old, you have become tired because of the chocolate you drink and because of the foods you eat. They have harmed and weakened you. You have been spoiled by these mantles, feathers and riches that you wear and that you have brought here. All of that has ruined you." (Durán 1964: 138)

This deep ambiguity of the Aztecs about their life makes them infinitely more sympathetic to the modern reader. It also illuminates the old cliché of the Aztecs as blood-thirsty militarists as a ridiculous oversimplification, a product of the self-justification of the Europeans which survives because of a darker strain in our own thoughts.

Aztec Cooks and Menus

Sahagún lists the cook along with the spinner, the seamstress, and the physician in his list of occupations for common women.

> The cook is one who makes sauces, who makes tortillas; who kneads [dough]; who makes things sour, who makes sourdough. [She is] wiry, energetic. [She is] a maker of tortillas—a tortilla maker; she makes them disc-shaped, thin, long . . . She makes them into balls; twisted tortillas—twisted about chile; she uses grains of maize. She makes tamales—meat tamales; she makes cylindrical tortillas; she makes thick, coarse ones. She dilutes sauces; she cooks, she fries; she makes juices.
>
> The good cook is honest, discreet; [she is] one who likes good food—an epicure, a taster. [She is] clean, one who bathes herself, prudent; one who washes her hands, who washes herself; who has good drink, good food.
>
> The bad cook [is] dishonest, detestable, nauseating, offensive to others—sweaty, crude, gluttonous, stuffed, distended with food— much distended, acquisitive . . . She smokes the food; she makes it very salty, briny; she sours it. She is a field hand—very much a field hand, very much a commoner. (Sahagún 1950–1982, 10: 52–53, retranslated)

Cooking was part of the education of every girl. The umbilical cords of newborn baby girls were buried under the *metate*, the grinding stone, as the umbilical cords of newborn boys were buried, with a shield and arrows, in the direction from which the enemy was expected. The Codex Mendoza (Cooper-Clark 1938, 3: 60) shows a thirteen-year-old girl grinding maize, surrounded by basic kitchen equipment. Her mother kneels behind her and gives advice, as the speech scroll coming from her mouth shows. The kitchen equipment consists of the *metate*, the three-legged grinding stone, and the *mano*, the roughly cylindrical hand stone. In front of the young lady is an item labeled an *escudilla* in Spanish. In Nahuatl it would be called a *molcaxitl*, a sauce bowl, and in modern Mexico a *molcajete*. It is a three-legged clay dish, the interior of which has been deeply incised with a sharp object before the clay was dry. A small clay pestle, used for grinding the contents of the bowl, is visible above the rim. It is used for making the basic sauce of chiles and water, and all the infinite variations thereon. Below the *molcaxitl* is the *comalli*, the clay griddle, with the three round stones that support it over the fire. The *comal*, as it is called in contemporary Mexico, is almost flat and therefore would be difficult to use for frying even if there had been great quantities of grease to fry with. The three stones made up the hearth, the most sacred spot in the house. They are even named by Cooper-Clark (1938, 1: 91): Mixcoatl (cloud serpent), Tozpan, and Iuitl. The fire god, Huehueteotl, resided among them:

> With him one was warmed, things were cooked in an *olla*, things were cooked, things were toasted, salt[water] evaporated, syrup was thickened, charcoal was made, limestone was fired, things were well fried, things were fried, things were roasted. (Sahagún 1950–1982, 1: 29)

The last item of pottery in the picture is an *olla*, a necked jar with two handles. Cooking in an *olla* is a constant refrain repeated throughout all the food descriptions. This might mean steaming, as when a little water was put in the bottom of the *olla*, then a light framework of sticks to keep the tamales from coming in contact with the water, then the tamales in their wrappers, and the whole tightly covered and set over the fire. Stewing and boiling were also practicable in an *olla*. What Sahagún's translators give us as frying is different from our idea of the meaning, which always involves grease. They have been quoted as describing something frying in syrup, but what would be cooked in this way, and what vessel it would be cooked in, remains unstated.

The last items in the illustration of the girl grinding maize are four

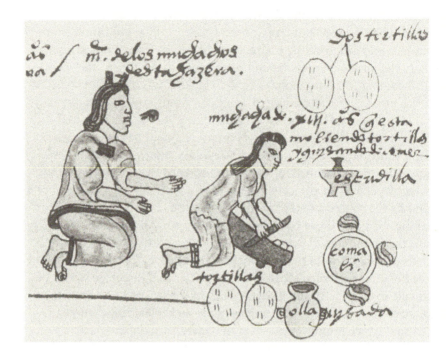

Thirteen-year-old girl grinding maize.
From Cooper-Clark 1938, 3: 60 recto.

tortillas. The two directly below her are presumably to show that she is
now a *tlaxcaloani,* a bread maker, while the two above her head are
the proper ration for a girl of her age. Cooper-Clark (1938: 90) describes a tortilla as being ten inches in diameter and five-eighths of an
inch thick, but, as we shall see, tortillas varied.

It is hard to interpret the rations because we do not know how many
meals there were in a day. Most sources say two, one in the morning
and one in the afternoon; but Alvarado Tezozomoc, describing the
moving of a great stone statue to Tenochtitlan—a statue which at
some times refused to budge, and sometimes spoke, being another of
the prodigies said to predict the arrival of the Europeans—said the
workmen coping with it were fed three times a day; at dawn, at nine in
the morning, and at three in the afternoon (Alvarado Tezozomoc
1944: 495). Nor is it clear if these so-called meals included the consumption of the many gruels which formed such a major part of Aztec

nourishment. If you drank the equivalent of several tortillas-worth of maize dough mixed with water, had you dined or had you just had a drink?

The religious calendar had a marked effect on what people ate and when. We have seen this in the account of fasts, but they provided for feasts as well.

Thus ended the feast, except that for ten days there was eating and banqueting in [the city of] Mexico. Each one of the nearby provinces was obliged to contribute and feed the lords. The Chalcas provided on the first day, the Tecpanecs on the second, others on the third. Thus each had its turn, providing splendid rich foods and drinks: chocolate, *pinole*, great quantities of *pulque*, all striving to give the best. On one day this was done for the princes, on another for the Tequihuas, on another for the Cuachique Otomis. In this way the ten days were spent—eating, drinking and feasting—celebrating the octave of the goddess and her feast. (Durán 1971: 215)

We have one piece of evidence that shows that the cooks for such great affairs were not exclusively female. The Códice Tudela says:

Thus they buried the noble men and noble women that died, with feathers and wrapped in cloaks, and they buried with them two or three or four Indians [male] and Indians [female], or more, as was [the rank of] the lord, and they buried those Indians alive so that they would make food for them where they were going. (Tudela 1980: 283)

It is speculation on my part, but perhaps the males were in charge of the outdoor cooking. It certainly seems likely that men dug the holes for the pit ovens and lined them with maguey leaves, as it seems likely that males did the barbecuing of meat on the *barbacoa*, the framework of sticks over the open fire.

The descriptions of preparing for an Aztec banquet tell us that there were specialist cooks who could be hired. Whether they were professionals, hired for their skill and reputation, or experienced elderly ladies, or perhaps a few professionals organizing the many hands needed is not stated. The court of Motecuhzoma, where meals were served daily to hundreds of people, must have had sizable and efficient kitchens, but all we know about them is that after Motecuhzoma became a captive the kitchen in his palace still functioned, and a file four abreast as long as a "long stone's throw" appeared at mealtimes bearing food to feed him, his lords, and his captors (Cervantes de Salazar 1936: 62).

We have no information on the arrangements inside Motecuhzoma's kitchens, but we have splendid descriptions of the planning of a nonroyal banquet.

Then he who undertook [the banquet] began what now was to be done in his house. The many prepared tamales were specified as to certain sizes. All about in the cities were hired those who made tamales. They went with turkey hens to enter his home . . . He summoned [guests from] twelve cities. (Sahagún 1950–1982, 9: 59)

And then he prepared all the grains of dried maize which would be needed. In wooden bins he put them. And the beans also he piled into wooden bins, and the wrinkled *chía* [and] small *chía* seeds. Using bins he placed about all things required to assist them, that they might not go hungry. . . . And chiles he placed in [containers of] matting; and he laid out salt, perhaps forty or sixty [jars of it]. And he arranged to buy tomatoes; daily he bought tomatoes with perhaps twenty small capes [one small cape = 100 cacao beans]. And then he provided turkeys, perhaps eighty or a hundred of them. And then he bought dogs to provide the people as food, perhaps twenty or forty. When they died, they put them with the turkeys which they served; at the bottom of the sauce dish they placed the dog meat, on top they placed the turkey as required. And then he provided the cacao beans, perhaps twenty sacks of them, as required. And then he provided the chocolate beaters, perhaps two or four thousand of them; then the sauce dishes, the large baskets, the earthen cups, the merchants' plates, the wood, the charcoal. All this he packed into the house. Then he paid for the water which was consumed daily, perhaps three or four boats of it. The value of a boat [of water] was one small cape given [for it]. (Sahagún 1950–1982, 9: 48)

And some plucked and removed the feathers from birds, and dressed them; or slew, singed, and dressed dogs; or prepared and cooked meat, and braised it in pots. Some ground and powdered tobacco and with a heavy straw filled tubes with it. And among the ashes was the labor of the old women. They made tamales using dried grains of maize; . . . they made tamales of meat. Some cooked tamales in an *olla*. Some washed the maize grains which had been cooked in lime. Some carried and drew water, or poured it. Some broke up, ground, and pulverized cacao beans. Some mixed cooked maize with chocolate. Some cooked stews, or roasted chiles—different kinds of chiles. All night they remained there. Vigil was kept. They kept watch. There was constant awaiting of the light. They sat holding vigil and chattering. (Sahagún 1950–1982, 4–5: 123)

Were it not for Sahagún we would have no idea what all these cooks, professional or not, were preparing, except for chance mentions of a dish here and a dish there. Because of Sahagún's all-encompassing curiosity and the diligence of his Aztec students and informants, we know more about the repertory of Aztec cuisine than we do about all but the most recent and most literate societies. It would be instructive to list all the dishes mentioned by Sahagún and then see if we could find as many from the Rome of Apicius, or from medieval Europe.

There is nowhere we can start our survey of the Aztec culinary repertory except with maize products. Even for the lords it was the staple, and the rest was sauce. But among the Aztec elite maize appeared in so many forms that it is hard to imagine them suffering from the monotony which we envisage when told of a culture which has a single staple food and eats it every meal of every day. This is a detailed list which Sahagún gives of the food the lords ate, although I have rearranged it to put the maize products together.

The tortillas which the lords ate every day were called *totonqui tlaxcalli tlacuelpacholli*, meaning white and hot tortillas, and they were folded, arranged in a *chiquihuitl* [container], and covered with a white cloth.

Other tortillas they also ate every day were called *ueitlaxcalli*, meaning large tortillas; these are very white and very thin, and wide, and very soft.

They also ate other tortillas called *quauhtlaqualli*; they are very white, and thick and large and rough.

They also ate some buns that were not round, but long, which they called *tlaxcalmimilli*; they are round and white and a span [eight inches?] long or a little less.

Another kind of tortillas they ate were called *tlacepoalli tlaxcalli,* which were in layers, and they were dainty food.

They also ate tamales of many kinds, some of them white and pellet shaped, neither round nor square, on their top they have a spiral, which is made by the beans with which it is mixed [the layer of beans is rolled in the dough like a jelly roll].

Other tamales are eaten which are very white and very delicate . . . another kind of white tamale was eaten which was not as delicate as the above, they were somewhat harder.

Other tamales eaten are reddish, with a spiral on top, they are reddish because after the dough is made they are kept for two days in the sun or near the fire, and they stir it, and it becomes reddish.

Other tamales eaten were simple or ordinary, they are not very white but middling, and have a spiral on top like the above mentioned; other tamales were eaten which were mixed with nothing at all.

The lords ate these kinds of bread already mentioned with many manners of fowl roast and stewed; some of them in dough, containing a complete fowl, another kind with pieces of fowl in dough, which they call fowl in dough, or cock, with yellow chile.

Other kinds of roasted fowl were eaten; and another roast which was roast quail.

There were also many kinds of tortillas for the commoners.

They also ate a kind of tamale made of maize tassels, mixed with amaranth/chenopodium seeds, and mixed with ground cherry kernel meats.

They ate certain tortillas made of tender maize ears, and another kind of tortillas made of very small and very tender maize ears. (Sahagún 1982: 463–464)

Hernández adds a few details about the more elegant varieties of tortillas that the lords ate.

But for the important Indians they prepared tortillas of sifted maize, so thin and clean they are almost translucent and like paper, also little balls of sifted maize, which despite their thickness are quite transparent, but these things are only for the rich and for princes. The bread they prepare and cook on the *barbacoa* is also not displeasing. (Hernández 1959, 2: 292)

The order of the meals seems to have been tortillas and tamales paired with a sauce first, followed by fruit, which Sahagún says the lords ate a wide variety of, and finishing up with the chocolate. How the lords handled the combination of tortillas and sauce is not specified—in less elegant circles one took a tortilla in the left hand, put the sauce in it, and used another tortilla in the right hand as a spoon. The server also had to observe what seems like a fairly awkward etiquette.

> To carry it one held the sauce dish in his right hand, not holding it by its rim, but only going resting it in the palm of his hand. And there in his left hand he went bearing the basket well filled with tamales. Neither did he take it by its rim; only on the palm of his hand did he set the basket. (Sahagún 1950–1982, 9: 34–35)

The sauce dishes or casseroles contained a wide sample of the animal kingdom, as well as some purely vegetarian mixtures.

> The lords also ate many kinds of casseroles; . . . one kind of casserole of fowl made in their fashion, with red chile and with tomatoes, and ground squash seeds, a dish which is now called *pipián;* they ate another casserole of fowl made with yellow chile.
> They ate many kinds of casseroles, and they ate roast birds . . .
> They also ate many kinds of chile stews; one kind was made of yellow chile, another kind of *chilmolli* [sauce with chile] was made of *chiltecpitl* [a kind of chile] and tomatoes; another kind of *chilmolli* was made of yellow chile and tomatoes.
> They also ate fish in casseroles: one of white fish made with yellow chile and tomatoes; another casserole of greyish-brown fish made with red chile and tomatoes, and with ground squash seeds which is very good to eat.
> They eat another kind of casserole made of frogs with green chile; another kind of casserole of those fish which they call *axolotl* with yellow chile; they also ate another kind of tadpoles with *chiltecpitl.*
> They also ate a kind of little reddish fish made with *chiltecpitl;* they also ate another casserole of large-winged ants with *chiltecpitl.*
> Also another casserole of locusts, and it is very tasty food; they also ate maguey worms, with *chiltecpitl molli* [sauce]; also another casserole of shrimps made with *chiltecpitl* and tomatoes, and some ground squash seeds.

Also another casserole of the kind of fish which they call *topotli*, made with *chiltecpitl* as the above said.

Another casserole they ate was of large fish, made as above.

. . . they ate another casserole made of unripe plums [*Spondias* spp.], with some little white fish, yellow chile, and tomatoes. (Sahagún 1982: 463–464)

The great Aztec markets provided ready-made food and drink as well as the raw materials. There seems to be more emphasis on maize products among the market food and fewer casseroles and sauces, but this may be an illusion. It should be noted before the following passage that there is no gender in the Nahuatl language. Dibble and Anderson, the translators, made the tortilla seller a male because Sahagún's Spanish text had it so, but the illustrations show a woman.

He sells meat tamales; turkey meat packets; plain tamales; tamales cooked in an earth oven; those cooked in an *olla* . . . grains of maize with chile, tamales with chile . . . fish tamales, fish with grains of maize, frog tamales, frog with grains of maize, *axolotl* with grains of maize, *axolotl* tamales, tadpoles with grains of maize, mushrooms with grains of maize, *tuna* cactus with grains of maize, rabbit tamales, rabbit with grains of maize, pocket gopher tamales: tasty—tasty, very tasty, very well made, always tasty, savory, of pleasing odor, of very pleasing odor; made with a pleasing odor, very savory. Where [it is] tasty, [it has] chile, salt, tomatoes, squash seeds: shredded, crumbled, juiced.

He sells tamales of maize softened in wood ashes, the water of tamales, tamales of maize softened in lime—narrow tamales, fruit tamales, cooked bean tamales; cooked beans with grains of maize, cracked beans with grains of maize; broken, cracked grains of maize. [He sells] salted wide tamales, pointed tamales, white tamales, fasting foods, roll-shaped tamales, tamales bound up on top, [with] grains of maize thrown in; crumbled, pounded tamales; spotted tamales, pointed tamales, white fruit tamales, red fruit tamales, turkey egg tamales, turkey eggs with grains of maize; tamales of tender maize, tamales of green maize, brick-shaped tamales, braised ones; plain tamales, honey tamales, bee tamales, tamales with grains of maize, squash tamales, crumbled tamales, maize flower tamales.

The bad food seller [is] he who sells filthy tamales, discolored tamales—broken, tasteless, quite tasteless, inedible, frightening, deceiving; tamales made of chaff, swollen tamales, spoiled tamales, foul tamales—sticky, gummy; old tamales, cold tamales—dirty and sour, very sour, exceedingly sour, stinking.

The food seller sells tortillas which [are] thick, thickish, thick overall, extremely thick; he sells thin [ones]—thin tortillas, stretched-out tortillas; dislike, straight . . . with shelled beans, cooked shelled beans, uncooked shelled beans; with shelled beans mashed; chile with maize, tortillas with meat and grains of maize, folded . . . with chile—chile wrapped, gathered in the hand; ashen tortillas, washed tortillas.

He sells folded tortillas, thick tortillas, coarse tortillas. He sells tortillas with turkey eggs, tortillas made with honey, pressed ones, glove-shaped tortillas, plain tortillas, assorted ones, braised ones, sweet tortillas, amaranth seed tortillas, squash tortillas, green maize tortillas, brick-shaped tortillas, *tuna* cactus tortillas; broken, crumbled, old tortillas; cold tortillas, toasted ones, dried tortillas, stinking tortillas.

He sells foods, sauces, hot sauces; fried [food], *olla*-cooked [food], juices, sauces of juices, shredded [food] with chile, with squash seeds, with tomatoes, with smoked chile, with hot chile, with yellow chile, with mild red chile sauce, yellow chile sauce, hot chile sauce, with "bird excrement" sauce, sauce of smoked chile, heated [sauces], bean sauce; [he sells] toasted beans, cooked beans, mushroom sauce, sauce of small squash, sauce of large tomatoes, sauce of ordinary tomatoes, sauce of various kinds of sour herbs, avocado sauce. (Sahagún 1950–1982, 10: 69–70, retranslated)

This is not all that they sold in the market, but the list grows interminable. There was not only street food in quantity but street drink as well. That class of foodstuff that is extinct in our lives today, the starchy liquid, was sold from shops full of jars large and small, on the streetcorners as well as in the market, according to Cervantes de Salazar (1936: 39). He equates them with the Spanish *mazamorras* and *poleadas,* the gruels and paps and brases which were a familiar part of the European diet before they withdrew to the sick room sections of the cookbooks, shortly before they vanished entirely.

Hernández (1959, 2: 290–291) gives descriptions of a number of variants of *atolli,* many of which must have served as instant meals. Basic *atolli* involved taking eight parts of water, six parts of maize, and lime and cooking them together until the maize softened. This is the standard process of nixtamalization, the way to prepare maize for the manufacture of dough for tortillas and tamales, and it tremendously enhances the nutritive value of the maize. The softened grain was then ground and cooked until it thickened. If a tenth part of maguey syrup was added it became *nequatolli.* For the healthy a bit of green chile could be put on top to "stimulate the venereal appetite." If honey and chile were added partway through the cooking it was *nechillatolli. Iztac atolli* was topped with chile ground with salt and tomato. *Yollatolli* was maize cooked as before, but without the lime. When it was made into gruel it was cooled and diluted and extinguished thirst no matter what the cause. *Xocoatolli* was made of a pound of nixtamalized maize dough which was allowed to stand for four or five days until it developed "an agreeable sourness." Then two pounds of fresh dough were added and the mixture was cooked and diluted and could have salt and chile added. We shall see more of this sort of thing in the Maya area. *Chillatolli* had chile ground with water added partway through cooking. It cured colds. There could be beans in the *atolli* if it was *ayocomollatolli,* which contained cooked whole beans, pieces of dough, and *epazote (Chenopodium ambrosioides).* This last was and is an exceedingly common seasoning in Mexico, considered to be especially compatible with beans. *Tlax calatolli* was made from the soft inner part of thick tortillas which had had their crusts removed and the interior mashed with cold water and then brought to a boil. It was eaten with a spoon. *Tlatonilatolli* had a bit of maize in it, and much powdered chile and *epazote.* It was taken hot and strengthened the entire body. Toasted and ground maize, mixed with cooked maize and chile, was *izquiatolli,* which should be drunk by those who because of a weakness of their heart or dyspepsia are almost always sad. Maize was not an obligatory ingredient. There was *chianatolli, chía* toasted and ground, with water added to taste. It could be taken plain or with chile. An *atolli* of red amaranth with honey was *hoauhatolli.* Then there was *pinolli,* which was ground toasted maize that could be carried about in a little sack by travelers. Adding some *pinolli* to water presented an instant meal. The *pinolli* could then be changed by adding cacao and all sorts of other things.

This short catalog of foods that the Aztecs ate should end, however, on a note which would have been congenial to the Aztecs themselves. At one point the emperor Motecuhzoma II commanded his servants to bring him soldiers' stores, saying that he did not wish to eat the delicate foods eaten by other kings but hard, rough food. Providing such

food was the responsibility of the market people, and according to Sahagún they would have come up with dried tortillas, or *totopoxtli; pinolli,* which in this case was ground toasted maize and *chía* seeds;
dried maize dough, to be diluted with water on the march; and dried
lime-treated maize dough (Sahagún 1950–1982, 8: 69). After all our
lists of luxurious viands the Aztecs would probably have approved of
the chapter on their food ending on a note of austerity.

The Maya and the Explorers

W hen the Europeans arrived in Maya territory, the political situation was quite different from what they were to find among the Aztecs and the Inca. The Aztecs and the Inca were new powers—they had sprung up a century or two before the coming of the Europeans and were still enlarging and consolidating their empires. The glory days of the Maya were long over. More time had elapsed between the collapse of the Classic Maya, between A.D. 800 and 900, and the European conquest than has elapsed between the European conquest and ourselves. The building of great stone temples and palaces, the carving and inscribing of monuments commemorating the triumphs of the rulers, the sophisticated artists who had signed their sculptures and their painted vases—all that was gone. True, there was still some stone architecture, which impressed the Europeans because it was the first that they had seen in the New World, and the Maya could still read and write their calendrical and prophetic books, but it was all on a simpler level.

The Maya at the time of the European conquest were the inhabitants of a group of small city-states, marrying with, and warring with, each other, as their ancestors did a thousand years earlier. The less centralized organization made them a more difficult proposition for the invaders. Among the Aztecs and the Inca, once the ruling families had been eliminated or persuaded to change sides, the leadership for any revolt could only be locally, not nationally, based. If one leader among the Maya changed sides it made no difference to the others, who were probably his hereditary enemies anyway. As a consequence of this, the conquest of the Maya took much longer. The last independent chieftain, Kanek' of Tayasal, did not capitulate until 1697, and there were still major revolts in the nineteenth century which only collapsed because the time came to go home and plant the maize.

Maya speakers lived in southern Mexico, the Yucatan peninsula, Belize, Guatemala, and parts of Honduras and El Salvador at the time of the European conquest. We will deal mostly with those who lived on or near the Yucatan peninsula, because they are the best recorded. The Maya in the highlands of Guatemala and Chiapas were conquered by Pedro de Alvarado in 1523–1524. One of the most brutal of the conquerors, he had no chroniclers among his soldiers. His letters to his superior, Cortés, are exclusively on military matters. What little we know about the contact period highland Maya tends to be later, and therefore suspect. If a bit of material from the highlands fits into my narrative I shall use it, but it will be identified as such.

The distinction made above, between the lowland and the highland, is reflected in the extreme differences among Maya cuisines. No one could think that a Maya living in Yucatan, a limestone plateau just above sea level and with limited water, had the same dietary options as one living in the pine-forested uplands of Guatemala. Even on the Yucatan peninsula, dwellers near the lagoons and salt flats of the coast obviously enjoyed different meals from those inland. We shall see how these regional differences in available foods became political bargaining chips.

The basis of Maya food was maize. It would seem that no one could argue about this when practically every ceremony recorded from birth, when the umbilical cord was cut over a maize cob, to death, when some maize dough was put in the corpse's mouth, involved maize. Yet a fairly sizable academic industry has grown up specializing in denying this fact and putting forward everything from the *ramón* nut (*Brosimum alicastrum*) to root crops, seafood, or orchards of tropical fruit as maize replacements. Obviously these foods were all eaten, but the determination of archaeologists and anthropologists to dethrone maize from its place as the basis of Maya life demands explanation.

Scholars of today would scorn anybody who assumed that the Maya that the Europeans met spoke English, or Spanish, or used the same kinship system used by modern Americans or sixteenth-century Europeans, yet in the field of food they use the categories of the modern Western world without a second thought. Their incapacity to accept a cuisine based on a single staple food is a good example of this.

We do not have a staple food today. Unless one comes from China,

Southeast Asia, or some obscure and archaic corner of Europe, one cannot understand what it means. The carbohydrate-providing staple, often with a name that is synonymous with that for food in general, without which a meal is not a meal, has no place in our thinking. Our usual reaction when confronted with the idea of eating a single substance, every meal of every day, is to exclaim at the desolate monotony of the prospect. But this is the way that most people have lived since the Neolithic revolution made it possible. Rice in the East, wheat in Europe, and maize in much of the Americas; these were the staples. Everything else that one ate was an accompaniment, pleasant but not essential.

On this subject the sixteenth-century Europeans could understand the Maya far better than we can. Their cuisine depended on a staple, wheat, which was made into *pan,* bread. It may have varied in shape and in composition according to the availability of supplies and the depth of the consumer's pocket, but it was all bread, and one prayed to be given it daily. When they got to the New World they realized that the New World staple, maize, held the same position in the life of the inhabitants of the New World that wheat held in their own lives back in the Old World, and that the sustenance, solid or liquid, made of it was bread, with all the emotional baggage that the word carried. Bread did not mean to them what it means to us today, a disposable, dispensable substance. Bread was life itself, and it was anything predominantly made of the staple, not just one kind of grain product. Misunderstanding this has led to many modern misinterpretations of the sources and much unnecessary argument.

It is a pleasure to move from what academics think that the Maya ought to have eaten to accounts of what the Maya ate and shared with their European visitors early in the sixteenth century. The New World had been known for twenty-five years by then, and Spain was well established in the Caribbean and on the mainland of what is now Panama and Venezuela. There were even two shipwrecked Spaniards already living with the Maya in Yucatan. One of them, Aguilar, afterward rejoined his people and provided Cortés with invaluable services as an interpreter. The other, Guerrero, stayed with the Maya and helped to organize their very effective resistance. At the time of the first systematic exploration of the coast of Yucatan, their contrasting choices of allegiance were still several years in the future.

Francisco Hernández de Córdoba set out from Cuba in the spring of 1517. The expedition soon began to need water and asked for it when they met a Maya in a canoe off the island of Cozumel. He gave them some gourds or calabashes full of water, some balls of ground maize, and some maize dough. What the balls of ground maize were we cannot tell for certain, but the fact that they are differentiated from the maize dough implies that they may have been cooked. Perhaps they were one of the many varieties of tamales, nixtamalized maize dough wrapped in leaves and then steamed or baked on or under the coals of the hearth. We do not know whether they were plain or filled, or whether there were other ingredients added to the ground maize. If the canoeist was setting out on a long voyage, they could have been cooked in a way that ensured that they would keep for a week, but Las Casas (1961: 403), who relays all this information to us, gives no details. He is more helpful about the maize dough carried in the canoe. According to him this dough could be made into something very much like several kinds of European gruels, which he refers to by their Spanish names. A *zahina,* an unthickened gruel, could have been prepared by simply mixing the dough with the water which was on board. As we shall see, this was one of the most common Maya ways of consuming maize, strange and unappetizing as it seems to us. The other possibility, a *poleada,* is less likely to have been prepared in a canoe bobbing on the Gulf of Mexico. To prepare this, the dough would have been mixed with water and then cooked, producing a thickened liquid which could range from being a thin porridge to a thick jelly, depending on the proportion of dough to liquid. The first drink mentioned, the one consumed uncooked, is what we shall call by the Nahuatl term *posolli,* remembering that when such terms are used by the sources they are usually not defined. The Nahuatl term *atolli* shall apply to the cooked liquid. There are as many variants of these two drinks as human ingenuity can devise, and the names are used for different variants in different areas. All this notwithstanding, at the first recorded meeting with the Maya, other than that of Columbus, we have been introduced to the Maya staple food, maize, and the two principal ways of eating it, as a solid and as a liquid.

The generous and hospitable Maya were asked to bring more food and more water. Three days later six people returned, bringing in their canoe some maize made into bread and two roasted fowl, the big ones native to that country. This is usually interpreted as the gift of a pair of roasted turkeys, which it may well have been, but for reasons which the next several paragraphs should make clear, we will stick to the vaguer and more general term *fowl.*

There were many large fowl in the tropical New World. Two of them were domesticated: the turkey (*Meleagris gallopavo*) and the muscovy duck (*Cairina moschata*). Others were raised from eggs or chicks found in the wild or obtained by shooting or trapping. They included the curassow (*Crax rubra*), the crested guan (*Penelope purpurascens*), the horned guan (*Oreophasis derbianus*), chachalacas (*Ortalis vetula*), and the ocellated turkey (*Meleagris ocellata*). All of them were referred to by the Europeans as *gallina* or *pavo*, that is to say "hen" or "peafowl." We are not even secure in our identification when our source specifies a *gallo de papada,* a wattled fowl, as the bird presented. Several of the birds listed above could be described as wattled. That is why we shall play it safe and refer to fowl consistently but also give a brief history of the two species of turkey.

The original range of *Meleagris gallopavo,* the turkey we all know, seems to have been north of the Río Balsas in Mexico, that is to say among the mountains of the central plateau. It is a paradoxical creature, being at the same time wild and tame, wary and stupid. People who have lived in its territory in the southwestern United States describe it as aggressively begging to be domesticated, but at the same time it is considered one of the craftiest of game birds. The earliest bones of turkeys that could be considered domesticated were found in Tehuacan and date from between 200 B.C. and A.D. 700. Their use must have spread rapidly, because by the time the Europeans came exploring, turkeys seem to have been available far beyond their natural range. Columbus may have brought them back from the islands on his first voyage, or perhaps he first saw them when he landed in Honduras on his fourth voyage. By 1511 the king of Spain was ordering every ship returning to Spain from the New World to bring back ten turkeys, five males and five females. It was one of the most rapid successes as far as the adoption of New World foodstuffs goes, speedily replacing the tough, stringy peacock as a spectacular dish for banquets.

In 1530, three years after his Protestant mercenaries had sacked Rome, Charles V was crowned Holy Roman Emperor by Pope Clement VII Medici in Bologna. Afterward the princes and prelates feasted inside on elaborate and luxurious dainties, but outside on the square a whole ox was roasted over a great fire for the plebeians. The ox was stuffed with sheep, hares, geese, and *galli d'India,* a term sixteenth-century Italians used for exotic birds like guinea fowl or turkeys. A contemporary illustration of the rejoicing shows what is unmistakably a turkey head protruding from a slash in the belly of the ox. The turkey so quickly became an article of conspicuous consumption that it early attracted the attention of legislators anxious to quell the consumerism of the epoch. As early as 1561, the vote was 60 to 18 in Vicenza, Italy, to exclude turkeys from banquets as being overly luxurious, although wild ducks were acceptable.

Even if the birds roasted for the first Europeans on Yucatan were turkeys, it was probably not the species of turkey we know, *Meleagris gallopavo*. The wild turkey of Yucatan was *Meleagris ocellata,* which had evolved as a separate species while Yucatan was isolated by the sea during an interglacial period. It apparently cannot be domesticated, but it was heavily used all the same. The inhabitants of one residential palace in Mayapán, who lived there a few centuries before the arrival of the Europeans, left trash heaps in which 70 percent of the identifiable bones were those of *Meleagris ocellata.* Some of the bones were larger and stouter than usual, which means that the creatures were probably kept in pens and artificially fattened, even though they must have been raised from poults captured in the forest.

The importance of the turkey to the Maya is underlined by its prominence in the world of ritual. Although it was often replaced by chicken after the smaller and cheaper bird arrived with the Spaniards, the blood, broth, and cooked meat of a turkey were, and still are, important components of the ceremonies for curing, planting, and praying for rain.

Hernández de Córdoba landed and made his way to a village, and the gifts of birds, roasted or boiled, continued. He described the houses as small, with thatched roofs, and standing amidst a great number of fruit trees. The Maya were excellent orchardists, tending a large variety of fruit-bearing trees and even growing the all-important cacao, utterly unsuited to their climate, by planting it in limestone sinkholes, where it could have the soil and the moisture that it needed. In this particular village the Europeans had their meal seated under a great tree, where the son of a lord, and a woman, brought them a boiled bird of the big ones. The side dishes are not mentioned, but if the usual pattern for this sort of entertainment was followed, they would have included several sorts of maize bread and whatever was in season from the fruit trees.

One thing the expedition of Francisco Hernández de Córdoba noticed on the island of Cozumel, and later in Yucatan, may still be seen in those places today by the visitor. It was, and is, an excellent place for honey production. Today the honey is produced by the European honey bee (*Apis mellifera*), but prior to its introduction there were plenty of indigenous bees (*Melipona* sp., *Trigona* sp.) to do the job. Bee yards with thousands of hives are described by early travelers. Hernández de Córdoba was said to have seen many wooden hives and to have been brought calabashes full of white and excellent honey. Honey was one of the principal products of the country and along with locally produced cotton cloth was traded far and wide in Mesoamerica. Among the Maya it was used to sweeten some of the maize drinks, the *posolli* and *atolli,* and to make an exceedingly important alcoholic ritual beverage, *balché.* The fact that a good part of one of the four surviving Maya books, the Madrid Codex, is concerned with bees and bee keeping underscores their importance.

Was this honey used to make preserves or hard-boiled sugar goods? We know that watery honey was cooked to make it more storable, so that combinations like boiled honey and squash seeds or boiled honey and toasted maize might be pre-Columbian. The words of a highland Maya lord on the subject of sweet consumption might give the answer to our question, unless it merely rejects unfamiliar forms of confectionary:

> The chief answered him very quietly "Sir, I thank you, your words are very fine, but I am an Indian, and so is my wife, and our food is beans and chile, and when I want a turkey I have that too. I do not eat sugar, nor is candied lemon peel food for Indians, nor did our ancestors know such a thing." (Remesal 1964: 472)

The expedition continued, skirting the coast of the Yucatan peninsula, until they got near what is today the city of Campeche. They were given another banquet there with a rather different menu, which is not unexpected given the change in scenery between Cozumel and Campeche. There was much maize bread, but also venison, hares, partridges, doves, fowl with wattles "no smaller and perhaps better than peacocks" (Las Casas 1961: 406), fruit, and other things. They went on to Champotón and saw many fowl, but the natives were pugnacious and inflicted a wound on Francisco Hernández de Córdoba which brought his explorations to an end.

When the spring of 1518 came, and with it the traveling season, Juan de Grijalva went out to continue what Francisco Hernández de Córdoba had begun. It was probably Juan Díaz, the chaplain of the expedition, who wrote the account that we have, an account which was popular enough to go through five editions in Europe between 1520 and 1522. There were two in Italian, two in Latin, and one in German, and they are all slightly different. Such bibliographic details are important, because culinary history is a matter of grasping at straws. A sentence or a clause dropped or misunderstood by the translator can make all the difference between the vivid description of a meal and the repetition of a standard formula.

To give an example of the questions raised by the differences between translations, one of the Italian versions of Juan Díaz, the *Littera mādata della insula de Cuba de Indie* (Anon. n.d.), speaks of the "chick-peas they call maize" (294v), or "the native bread which they call maize"(296r), as being consumed in Yucatan. The other Italian version of the same missing original is tacked on to the end of the published travels of Ludovico de Varthema, a Bolognese, in Egypt, Syria, Arabia, Persia, India, and Ethiopia (Díaz 1526). This incessantly refers to the "roots of which they make bread called maize." One would think that by then Juan Díaz would have known the difference between maize bread, made of seeds, and manioc bread, made of roots, but perhaps the translators did not. We will assume that the bread was indeed made of maize, but a doubt always remains.

The *Littera mādata* version of the narrative describes the island of Cozumel as being very pleasant and fruitful, although lacking in gold. They found some "peaches" that weighed three pounds each, although the pounds may have been different from ours. These "peaches" were available on the trees for eight months of the year, and authorities disagree as to what they might have been. *Pouteria sapota,* the mamey sapote, is a possibility, and the papaya (*Carica papaya*) has been suggested. There was an abundance of *pepero,* which is what the Italians of the time called chiles, and also some small animals like rabbits. These have been identified as guinea pigs (*Cavia porcellus*) by some commentators, as squirrels by others, and as *Capromys pilorides* by others still. What were probably sweet potatoes are described by the phrases used all over the New World, namely that they are edible roasted or boiled and taste like cooked chestnuts.

Grijalva and his men sailed on, receiving gifts from the natives of honey, bread, fowl, and game. By the middle of June they were in the Gulf of Campeche, and somewhere on or near the Isola de Sacrificios they enjoyed what must be one of the best-described meals of the conquest. If we allow ourselves to combine the versions of Las Casas and Fernández de Oviedo as published by Ramusio, it becomes so vivid as to be positively mouth-watering.

> Grijalva went out with some of his men, and they found a *ramada* [shelter] made out of tree branches, which was very cool, and the Spaniards put themselves there because of the sun. There were leaves on the ground, and the ground was the table, on which there was a very beautiful mantle. On it were certain well-made clay vessels, like deep plates, full of birds cut up small, with their fragrant broth, like a soup made in a casserole. They had an abundance of maize bread, which was mixed with ground beans, as they make them. The beans are like lupines. There were also various fruits. They offered them some colored cotton mantles, all with great pleasure and happiness, as if they were their own brothers, and among other presents which they usually make to their guests, as we know now, they gave each Spaniard a lit cane, full of fragrant and aromatic things . . . from which they suck in the smoke and it comes out their noses. (Las Casas 1961: 442)

To this Fernández de Oviedo (1985, 5: 818) adds that the broth was yellowish and seemed to have been seasoned with spices. We are not told more about this dish, because, alas, it was Friday and no Christian would touch the bird or its broth. There were also flat round maize cakes, called *pizze* in the Italian text, and probably but not necessarily tortillas. There was also maize on the cob, and it is perhaps the first European encounter with this delicacy.

The different components of this meal will be analyzed later. It is enough to say here that it is in the tradition of the formal banquets held by the Maya, which obligated each and every one of the recipients of the food and other largesse to give another such meal in return. If the original guest died in the interim, his heirs inherited the obligation. There was another type of banquet, which might be called the family banquet, that celebrated events like weddings. These were repaid by an invitation when the guest had a celebration in his own family. The Maya were trying to link the Europeans to themselves by the sort of bonds that the Maya understood. That the guests were oblivious to their social rules did not enter into the calculations of the hosts.

On the following Sunday the Maya and the Europeans ate together again. This time there were no religious limitations as to what could be eaten.

Once the mass was finished they brought certain well made baskets, one with *pasticci* [filled pies] of maize dough stuffed with chopped meat, so that no one could figure out what sort of meat it was. Another basket had maize bread, and there were two others of *tortanelli* [elsewhere identified as tortillas]. They gave it all to the captain, and he gave it out to his companions, so that they could eat. They ate it all, and praised that dish *pasticci*, which tasted as if it were spiced. It was reddish inside, with a good quantity of that pepper of the Indies which is called *asci* [the Antillean term for chile]. (Fernández de Oviedo 1985, 5: 822)

Las Casas (1961: 443–444), retelling this episode, adds calabashes full of well-cooked meat soup to the menu. He says the meat was either fowl or venison. Whatever it was, it was willingly eaten by the guests, who said that it was very good and tasted spiced, which for a European of the period meant the equivalent of high status and high praise.

The Europeans were obviously well pleased with their entertainment. We, benefiting from hindsight, find a notable omission from the food and drink served. It is known that the Yucatec Maya grew cacao in moist shady sinkholes in the limestone plateau of Yucatan. It is known that they drank chocolate: we have a later sixteenth-century record of the trial by the Inquisition of a European who had been seen at a Maya rain ritual drinking *atolli, posolli,* and chocolate. It is known that the Maya used cacao beans as currency, as the episode of Columbus and the Maya trading canoe demonstrates, but it appears in neither of these roles during the visits of Francisco Hernández de Córdoba and Juan de Grijalva. Negative evidence is notoriously slippery to use, but it seems fair to presume that if the Maya had cacao in their possession, they saw fit neither to serve it to the Europeans nor to give them some beans as objects of value. Whether chocolate was drunk only on certain ritual occasions or was just too valuable to squander on bearded strangers must remain unknown.

The last of the first three explorations of Maya Yucatan was that of Cortés, on his way toward the eventual conquest of Mexico. In November 1518 he started collecting supplies in Cuba. Every available male and female Indian was set to making that ideal military ration, manioc bread. In time they made three hundred loads of it, each load weighing roughly fifty of our pounds. Supposedly a load was enough to feed one man for one month. To go with the manioc bread Cortés rounded up all the pigs, fowl, and salt pork he could find. In the spring of 1519, when his 550-man expedition was making the same circuitous tour of the coast of Yucatan that had been made by their predecessors, they too were soon living off the country. The same kinds of foods were given to them that had been given to Francisco Hernández de Córdoba and Juan de Grijalva. Fowl, raw and cooked; bread, not further described; and fruit are mentioned by Cortés as they were mentioned by the first two explorers. When he arrived in the present-day Mexican state of Tabasco he got a new kind of present. Here, in Putun Maya country, he accepted a gift of fifteen or twenty women to cook and make maize bread. In a way this was as significant a break with the world of Europe and the colonized Caribbean as Cortés' burning of his boats, which happened shortly thereafter. Both gestures expressed a cutting of ties, in the field of sustenance as well as in the field of governmental authority.

From here on the Europeans were totally dependent on Indian women to make *nixtamal,* the cooked lime or ash-soaked maize, to grind it, and to make it into breadstuffs. One male who attempted to learn and described his skill, or lack of it, was the Italian, Girolamo Benzoni.

When I was traveling in uninhabited places, by force of necessity, I learned to grind it, so that I would not have to eat it just raw and roast. This grinding is the hardest work, and very tiring, and sometimes when there was little grain I did not remove the skin [pericarp] as the lords do, nor did I grind it very much, because my arms were undone from hunger, and very weak. (Benzoni 1962: 57v)

It was not only amateur maize grinders who found the work painful. Women to grind maize accompanied most military expeditions, but often in insufficient numbers. Almost two hundred years after the landing of Cortés, on a mission to subdue and convert the last independent Maya ruler, Kanek' of Tayasal, every fifteen-man squad had an Indian woman to make the *nixtamal,* grind it, and make the dough into tortillas and tamales. It was just too many mouths for one woman to feed. Valenzuela (1979: 310–311) speaks of the pitiable condition of the palms of the women's hands and the joints of their fingers, raw and festering from the continuous grinding.

These first encounters with the Maya are useful to us, because they show the Maya entertaining people who were initially their guests, not their conquerors. Neither Francisco Hernández de Córdoba nor Juan de Grijalva attempted to make settlements in the Maya area, and even though their welcome was not always friendly, things were a long way from the conquered and conqueror relationship that ultimately developed. That led to the dulling of the European powers of observation and the replacement of witnessed fact with cliché. The Maya are feeble, it was said over and over, because they only eat tortillas dipped in water mixed with ground chile. The first bishop of Guatemala, Francisco Marroquín, may have been the one who started the phrase that was to be endlessly repeated to denigrate the Maya: "Their possessions are but a little maize, a stone to grind it on, a pot to cook it in, a mat to sleep on, and a roof of thatch on four sticks" (Sáenz de Santa María 1963: 168).

EIGHT

Diego de Landa

While the Europeans' accounts of their earliest encounters with the Maya are useful, they are still the descriptions of special meals. To know what the Maya ate as part of their daily lives we must turn to that famous observer of things Maya, Diego de Landa.

Seldom has there been a more two-faced figure. A Franciscan who was named bishop of Yucatan in 1572, late in his life, he incinerated at least twenty-seven Maya books, yet recorded an "alphabet" which provided a vital clue for the recent decipherment of the Maya writings which had escaped his holocaust. His portrait hangs in the vast religious complex which he built on top of an ancient pyramid in Izamal, Yucatan, and shows him with downcast eyes and an attempt at a meek smile, yet he overstepped the limits of his authority to such an extent that he was sent back to Spain to be tried for breaking ecclesiastical regulations. He subjected his Maya flock to hideous tortures, yet left an exhaustive account of their daily life. It is to him that we must turn to find out what the sixteenth-century Maya ate, and how and when they ate it.

Landa starts out with a description of the process for making maize dough. We will start a step farther back, with the storage and processing of the newly harvested maize. The questions of different degrees of storability were among the many factors which the Maya farmer juggled when selecting the varieties to plant. Once the correct balance of maize strains had been planted and all the work and attendant ritual of clearing the ground, sowing, weeding, and harvesting had been completed, how was the maize to be kept until the next harvest? Landa tells us that it was kept in underground places, but like many of Landa's statements this has been ignored, or contradicted, by people who thought they knew better.

These underground places that Landa speaks of are probably the bottle-shaped *chultuns,* or pits, excavated in the soft limestone of the Yucatan plateau. Modern investigators think them unsuitable for maize storage because they have dumped maize, of unspecified varieties, into them, and within a few months the maize was moldy and inedible. Had they done their digging in the archives they would have discovered many better strategies to adopt, for long-term food storage, especially in the tropics, has never been a simple matter.

Many sources speak of the maize as being smoked, sometimes for weeks. The Maya used smoking to preserve many things, including chiles, meat, and fish. Given their intimate knowledge of their environment, they probably knew different plants that gave smoke of different qualities, both for flavor and for preservation. Storability could also have been improved by sprinkling sand or lime between the food to be stored. Finally we have the possibility that herbs with insecticidal qualities were interspersed with the maize, the way that *muña* was used to help preserve potatoes in Peru. The technique was used in the Maya area by employing a leaf of *Luehea speciosa* (Maya *kazcat*), a plant of the Tiliaceae or linden family, to store with chiles, according to Roys (1931: 254), probably to keep Maya chiles free from attacks by chile moths, a fluttering pest that anyone who has ever hung a decorative or culinary *ristra* of dried chile peppers has probably encountered.

More evidence of such practices among the Maya is shown by the description of the visit by four highland Maya lords to Prince Philip of Spain, then acting as regent for his father, the Emperor Charles V. The four K'ekchi presented many gifts to the Spanish court on February 4, 1545, even though what most struck Philip was the scantiness of their garments, given the rigors of winter in Madrid. The offerings included vessels of beaten chocolate, presumably prepared on the spot, and the earliest documented appearance of chocolate in Spain, many kinds of chiles, beans, and maize, but also fine textiles packed in wooden boxes and layered with herbs. The herbs were thrown out as being just packing material, but the author of the article on this visit, Estrada Monroy (1979: 195), claims to have discovered sixteenth-century documents in Guatemala preserved from pests and dampness by what might be the same herbs, although he does not identify them.

Other uses have been suggested for *chultuns.* They are said to have been wine cellars, one supposes for the storage and maturation of rare vintages of *balché* and other local brews. All the records that we have speak of *balché* as being a simple preparation of water, honey, and strips of the bark of *Lonchocarpus longistylus,* a member of the genus of trees that produces the fish poison *barbasco* and rotenone. The bark strips are reused, thus making sure that the correct yeast culture finds its way from one batch of *balché* into the next. The ingredients are mixed in a large wooden trough, or even a canoe, a few days before the *balché* is required for a ceremony. Recent Lacandon ceremonial practices required every last bit of *balché* to be consumed before the rite ended, eliminating the need for anything elaborate in the way of storage.

Various beers, mostly maize-based, were also made by the Maya. The foaming substance seen in the Maya trading canoe by Columbus probably fell into this category. If the *Rabinal Achí,* a highland Maya drama, is correct and not merely metaphorical, there once was an extensive range of alcoholic beverages to choose from:

> There are twelve drinks here, twelve liquors to intoxicate, of the ones called Ixtatzunun; sweet, refreshing, cheering, pleasing, tempting; of those which are drunk before going to sleep, here within the vast walls, in the vast fortress; drinks of chiefs. (Anon. 1979: 51)

Admittedly the Maya have undergone considerable cultural impoverishment, and the Spanish priests were especially diligent in trying to eliminate alcoholic drinks and the ritual drunkenness which resulted from their use. They assumed that these drinks led to reversions to idolatry, and smashed the vessels in which they were brewed when they could find them. A tradition of aged fermented drinks may have been lost as a consequence of this destruction.

If there is little to justify identifying *chultuns* as wine cellars, there is less to support the suggestion that they were cool cellars for the storage of Maya pickles. Given a warm climate, with crops ripening around the year, preservation techniques for fruit and vegetables do not need to be as complex as they are in colder places. There are a very few mentions of pickled fruit; Roys (1931: 223), for instance, speaks of the pickled fruit of *Parmentiera edulis,* but I suspect this is a postconquest introduction. Certainly there are no words for pickles or pickling in any of the early dictionaries, and none of the early travelers mention seeing, eating, or smelling such things. In fact, pickling, in the dictionary sense of preservation in brine or vinegar, seems not to have existed in the preconquest New World. Many things might have been kept in *chultuns,* but crocks of pickles were not among them.

Once it was decided to use the maize stored in the *chultun* or some alternative form of granary, nixtamalization was usually, but not always, employed. There were variations even within the process of nixtamalization. Not all of the lime in the Maya area was suitable for this purpose, and sometimes a substitute had to be made by burning the shells of freshwater *Pachychilus* snails. Lime could also be replaced by wood ashes, producing a maize drink that had special religious significance in certain Maya communities.

Landa prefaced his description of making maize dough by saying that the dough was made into both food and drink, and "drinking it as they do it serves them for food and drink" (Tozzer 1941: 89). According to Landa, two of the three daily meals were composed of maize drinks made of nixtamalized maize dough. In the morning they were drunk warm, with a little ground chile thrown on top. Leftovers of the morning meal, with cool water added, were the midday meal. Soups and stews were for the evening. "Bread" was made twice a day, which is puzzling because there is no mention of solid breadstuffs being eaten twice a day. Perhaps by making "bread" Landa meant the grinding of maize. In that case it could well have been done twice a day, once early in the morning, to provide the daily gruel, and again in the late afternoon, to make some sort of tortilla or tamale to go with the evening meal.

Gaspar Antonio Xiu gives exactly the same scheme of two liquid meals a day and one solid one (Xiu 1986: 62–63). He specifies the evening bread as tortillas and gives much more humble menus, not mentioning any soups and stews. There was sauce of ground chiles and water to wet the tortillas, and sometimes some black beans, but meat and fish were eaten only on holidays. Archaeological evidence shows us that meat and fish were high-status articles of diet going all the way back to the Classic Maya.

If these two Maya meal schedules are to be trusted, Maya women were considerably freer than women in highland Mexico, where large quantities of labor-intensive tortillas were demanded at every elite meal. Not only did the maize have to be freshly ground, but the tortillas had to be hot off the *comal,* or at least warm. No wonder that when European bread was introduced to the highlands of Mexico, conservative elderly Aztec men grumbled that without maize grinding the women would be up to who knows what sort of deviltry.

When Landa begins his dish-by-dish description of Maya sustenance, after he speaks of nixtamalization, he speaks of *posolli*. He does not call it this; in fact he gives no native names at all; but the text makes it clear that that is what he is talking about. We shall call it *posolli*, not the Maya *keyem*, although *posolli* is originally a Nahuatl word which has been used for many different dishes.

Landa says that *posolli* is made of half-ground maize, which is hard to interpret if the routine of turning the cooked, pericarpless, washed maize into maize dough is not familiar. The prepared maize is ground once, ground again, and then ground for a third time. After the first grinding the maize is fit to be made into *posolli*, after the second it may be made into tortillas, and after the third grinding it is smooth enough to be made into *atolli*. Thus we can reinterpret Landa as meaning that the maize for *posolli* was one-third ground, having had but one of the standard three passes over the metate. This dough could be mixed with water to form one of the seven maize drinks that begin Landa's Maya menu. He goes on to say that great balls of this dough are given to travelers and that it lasts for months, merely becoming sour. Hernández de Córdoba's Maya boatman and his ball of dough come immediately to mind. Landa's statement is a summary dismissal of one of the most interesting food discoveries of the New World, a discovery probably made, and certainly heavily used, in the Maya area.

Landa omitted one vital fact, namely, that this dough was kept in a container set aside for that purpose or wrapped in leaves that had been used for wrapping sour *posolli* before. This provided a continuous culture, in this case a highly complex one, a whole sequence of bacteria, yeasts, and molds that worked on the maize dough. This soured *posolli*, which stands in roughly the same relationship to nixtamalized dough as yogurt stands to milk, has been shown to be nutritionally superior to untreated maize (Ulloa and Herrera 1986). Apparently some of the bacteria are nitrogen fixing, and experiments comparing the growth of laboratory rats fed on maize and those fed soured *posolli* found that the latter did better.

The sour dough, which many early authors did not differentiate from the unsoured, was usually mixed with water and drunk. Following a common New World pattern, plain water was rarely drunk without additions. Captain Dampier said that the soured kind had a "sharp pleasant taste" and, as a typical Englishman, gave the drink a nickname. We call it "poorsoul," he said (1906, 2: 209). According to him, when the natives entertained they added honey to it, but their culinary ambitions went no higher. In other places cacao was ground with the dough, which an appreciative imbiber said made the drink into another and higher thing. Other additions were toasted and ground *sapayul* seeds (*Calocarpum mammosum*), which were oily and gave a flavor of bitter almonds, or green maize.

Posolli, soured or not, is still very much in use, sometimes to the total exclusion of any other food or drink. It is the food of the very poor, being economical of firewood, on top of its many other virtues. *Posolli* and greens are today considered Indian food and therefore to be shunned by those who wish to repudiate their Maya ancestry. To fit in with modern *ladino* society one must shun maize drinks, increase the use of grease, and tomatoize one's diet.

In the past, this drink was not, as it is at present, something to live down. Among the Huastec, a baby girl was given a bracelet of the bark of the hog plum tree (*Spondias mombin*) so that her dough for *posolli* might sour in one day, rather than the usual three. At the other end of the life cycle, the Chamula fill the mouth of the dead person that they are taking to the cemetery with *posolli* because, they say, in life, when they are tired, they sit by the side of the road and drink *posolli*. The veneration of *posolli* reaches a climax among the Lacandon, once supposed to be the direct descendants of the Classic Maya and now, less romantically and more realistically, considered to be the heirs of those Maya who, as Dampier (1906, 2: 211) said, found the impositions of the Europeans past all bearing and marched off into the jungle, whole villages at a time.

The Lacandon, for whom *posolli* was a food of major importance, offered it to their gods along with *balché,* sprinkling drops of *posolli* to the four directions before eating. Their saying was, "If there are no women, there is no *posolli;* if there is no *posolli,* there are no gods; if there is no *posolli,* there is no sun" (Soustelle 1959: 170).

Landa's statement about *atolli* (again we use the Nahuatl word) shows that we are correct in our supposition that *posolli* was made of maize ground once, because he says that *atolli* was made from the finest ground maize, probably that ground three times. Using the model of the almond milk that he must have known in Spain, Landa says that a milk was extracted from this most finely ground maize, by which he must mean that it was mixed with water and then strained, so as to remove the coarse bits of unground material remaining.

Today these leavings, sometimes called bran, are given to the domestic animals. In a way this was also done in the past. One version of the Maya burial ritual had the dead person buried with *atolli* for personal sustenance during the trip through the underworld; maize leavings, or bran, to give to the animals that had been killed for meat, so that they would not hurt the dead person; and tortillas for the dogs that had been eaten, so that the deceased would not be bitten by them.

After the bran had been removed, the milky part remaining was cooked until it thickened, when it could be served hot for the morning meal. Landa calls it a sort of porridge, but sometimes it may have been a rather thin porridge, because there is a colloquial expression in that part of the world for deception—to give *atolli* with your fingers.

Atolli is basically distinguished by the cooking of the maize after it has been ground and diluted with water. It may be made of young maize that does not need to be nixtamalized to be softened to grinding consistency, and subsequently thickened by boiling. This was a great delicacy, and it could be improved by adding whole grains of young maize, so that there would be something to chew on. Young maize *atolli* was considered sufficiently cooked when a drop of it did not dissolve in cold water. Available only during a brief period of the year, it was often drunk from special vessels or used as an offering.

Like *posolli, atolli* could be soured, and it could be soured during many points in its preparation. One method was to soak the hard, ripe maize, without adding lime, for many days until it almost dissolved of its own accord. Alternatively it could be soaked, ground, and then left to sour before boiling. Souring could also take place after grinding and dilution. One recipe divides the ground maize dough mixed with water into two equal portions, one of which is boiled and then added to the unboiled portion and left to stand overnight. The next day the mixture is boiled again. The taste of the resulting substance is said not to be noticeably pleasant. Even young maize *atolli* could be soured.

Of course *atolli* could also be varied by adding other ingredients. All the American basics were so used. Chile was indispensable, but there were also beans, floated with their broth on top of the *atolli,* and ground toasted squash seeds to mix in. The marigold species *Tagetes lucida,* which is said to smell like cinnamon, could be added, as well as other fragrant species of *Tagetes.* The various root crops, previously cooked and mashed, were stirred in, either to add their distinctive taste or to stretch out the maize supply. Sweet potatoes are especially mentioned for this use.

Another technique used to vary the flavor of Maya maize drinks was to toast the maize at some point. A toasted maize powder used by voyagers will here be called *pinolli,* again from the Nahuatl. To make it the maize grains were parched, which made them easier to grind, then ground; or maize bread or dough was toasted and then ground. It could be eaten as it was, which made it hard to talk, because the *pinolli* was so dry, or mixed with water and then boiled, which would make it a form of *atolli,* by our definition.

Those on the road were unlikely to use much *atolli,* because to make it one had to carry a clay or metal vessel. At least one Spanish force is recorded as forgetting this item, which condemned them to a severely limited diet until they found some ancient Maya pots buried under a tree. Individuals, to avoid having to carry the heavy and bulky cooking pots, eschewed *atolli* and mixed their *posolli* and *pinolli* with water in their light, almost unbreakable calabash cups, leaving the cooking of *atolli* for the home fires. The calabash cups, or *jícaras,* were so much a part of their owners' lives that they were buried with them.

There were also more complex *atollis,* which may be derived from European flour- or bread-crumb-thickened soups and stews, or may have been made for ceremonial purposes in Classic Maya times just as they are today. Whole turkeys are cooked in *atolli* today in the highland Maya villages of Guatemala for confraternity celebrations. We also read of an *atolli* with little balls of maize dough added to it, and an *atolli* with fruit in it. Was this what displeased Benzoni so when he saw it for sale in a market in Guatemala? He describes it as cooked "figs" dressed in a thoroughly mixed drink and said that it made him want to vomit (Benzoni 1962: 109).

Basically bland and acceptable to the Spaniards because of its kinship with their gruels, *atolli* did not suffer the banishment to the diet of the Indian poor and lowly that *posolli* did. The Blessed Pedro Betancourt of Guatemala, who died in 1667, went about his hospital with a vessel of *atolli,* which he frequently ladled out for the sick. Such was his sanctity that when a malicious devil made the vessel fall, not a drop of the *atolli* was spilled. Late one night, when an ailing woman in a distant suburb had confessed to a desire for a sip of *atolli,* he miraculously appeared on her doorstep, carrying his *atolli* vessel. Neither the lateness of the hour nor the distance had prevented him from coming to satisfy her longing.

Landa does not mention the third class of maize drinks. This may be explained by the fact that today *saka* or *zaka* is exclusively consumed during ceremonies. Either the existence of this component of pagan rites was concealed from Landa, or he did not bother to distinguish it from the previously described drinks. What makes this drink unlike the others is that it is made of maize which has not been treated with lime; in other words, it has not undergone the nixtamalization process. Sometimes the maize is barely soft enough to grind, so that the drink is said to be rather sandy in texture, although it keeps better. As usual, there are innumerable local variations, adding cacao, or honey, or other ingredients which would seem to compromise the whiteness that is promised to us by the name *saka,* or white water. This stress on whiteness is reflected in one of the many Maya food riddles, one which is sometimes translated as applying to *atolli* as well as to *sacab,* another name for the white liquid:

> "My son, bring me your daughter, she of the white face, so that I may see her. She of the handsome white headdress, of the knotted hair, I desire her." "It shall be done, oh father!" What he is asking for is a white *jícara* full of *sacab,* the water of maize without lime. (Barrera Vásquez 1985: 142)

White maize liquid shares with cacao the honor of being the first foodstuffs to have their names read from the hieroglyphs on the Maya vessels that were buried with the noble Maya dead during the Maya Classic. The glyphs for *sac-ul* have been found on globular vessels, apparently the shape used by the Classic Maya when they wished the liquid enclosed to stay cool. This is translated as white *atolli,* although sixteenth-century Maya dictionaries specifically say that *ul* is not any old *atolli* but that made of young maize. If it was young maize *atolli* that was being buried with the dead, it would explain why vessels for *sac-ul* are so much rarer than vessels for chocolate. Only those who were buried at the time of new maize could carry *sac-ul* on their journey to the underworld, while cacao was available, at a price, at any season.

Chocolate drinks are the last drinks to be mentioned by Landa. But we know that the Maya were consuming chocolate long before Landa, because we can read the inscriptions on the rims of the vessels that they drank it from. Chocolate was obviously of great importance to the Classic Maya, because they took their elegantly painted cylindrical clay chocolate vessels with them into the darkness of the tomb. One of these vessels has a scene of chocolate preparation painted on it, with a buxom young lady pouring the contents of one cylindrical chocolate vessel into another such vessel standing on the ground. We have seen this method of raising a fine head on the chocolate among the Aztecs, and here we see it among the Maya almost a thousand years earlier.

If there are any Maya chocolate recipes in hieroglyphic writing on the vessels, they have yet to be found and translated. We may be sure that there were many ways of consuming it, allowing us to reinterpret the recent analysis of the residue in five Maya vessels found with a burial in Río Azul, Guatemala. Laboratory tests showed that one contained both theobromine and caffeine, alkaloids present in cacao. Three had traces of theobromine, while the last had no trace of any cacao component. This was said to mean that one vessel certainly contained chocolate beverage, three may have, and the last one certainly did not (Hall et al. 1990). It could just as well mean that the dead person had been supplied with three different drinks to take to the other world. He had one container of strong chocolate, three of a milder chocolate, and one which held something else entirely.

To get an idea of the diversity of chocolate recipes which might have filled the Classic Maya chocolate vessels, we must go back to our sixteenth-century sources. Landa says that chocolate could be added to *pinolli,* the toasted maize powder carried by travelers, as an alternative to chile. He also speaks of a drink of ground maize and chocolate which he says is foamy and used by the Maya to celebrate their feasts. We are granted no further details and are left to wonder if this was *atolli* with chocolate, *posolli* with chocolate, or something else. His last drink is made of cacao butter, extracted by beating the ground cacao beans with water. The Spaniards consumed this substance with sugar and cinnamon or added it to their chocolate. That may not have been aboriginal, but the maize drink which Landa mentions that had cacao butter added to it, which he said was highly thought of, probably was. Van Houten's nineteenth-century discovery that cacao butter could be removed from one set of chocolate preparations and added to another set to enhance flavor and eating qualities was being used on cacao's native soil several hundred years before the Dutchman thought of it.

Classic Maya chocolate preparation. From a Maya vase in the
Princeton Art Museum. Drawing by Diane Griffiths Peck.
Courtesy Michael D. Coe.

Landa does not give us the full repertory of chocolate drinks; in fact, he leaves out the principal chocolate drink, which was the one that probably had the most religious significance to the Maya. We must go to another source to find the contents of true Maya chocolate. Notice that it is taken hot.

As well as being currency the cacao is eaten toasted like toasted chick-peas, and it is very good thus. They make many drinks of it, and they are very good, some of them drunk cold, and some hot, and among them is a very common one, called chocolate. It is made of the aforementioned cacao ground, with honey and hot water, other mixtures and hot things being added. This drink is very medicinal and healthy. (Ciudad Real 1976: 182–183)

Chocolate drunk with honey, chile peppers, or plain with water may be passed over as standard preparations all over Mesoamerica. Some interesting and uncommon fragrances were added among the Maya. One such addition was *achiote*, a red paste made from the outside coating of *Bixa orellana* seeds, growing on a handsome shrub with decorative flowers that is still planted in tropical dooryards. The coloring matter was used to tint butter in northern climates, as well as human bodies in warmer ones. The original "redskins" may have been so called not because of their complexion but for the color of the *achiote* applied to their skins. The addition of *achiote* to cacao made it a brick red color and may have been a way of making the chocolate into surrogate blood, blood being a vital component of the Maya state religion. This tie between *achiote* and chocolate is expressed in a rather cryptic fashion by another Maya food riddle, which also features the cardinal (*Cardinalis cardinalis*), a well-known red migratory bird that occurs in the northeastern United States and has a prominent crest which it can raise and lower, a metaphor for the precious chocolate foam.

"My son, bring me four Chac Dzibzib, cardinal birds, those that are at the entrance of the cave, and bring them standing on my precious foodstuff. Let their crests be reddened, and let them be raised on my precious foodstuff when you come before me." "It shall be done, oh father." What he asks for is *ciui*, achiote paste; the crests of which he speaks are the foam of the chocolate, and his precious foodstuff is cacao that has just been ground. (Barrera Vásquez 1985: 139)

A chocolate condiment not encountered previously is *Quararibea fieldii* or *funebris*. This last, according to Schultes (1956: 249), can taste like slippery elm, curry, or licorice. There was also the ground seed of *sapayul* (*Calocarpum mammosum*) that could be added.

The ritual importance of chocolate drinks continues to this day, although we might not recognize them as chocolate. According to Popenoe (1919: 407), one such drink, *batido,* then used in the highlands of Guatemala, was a murky, oily liquid with only the slightest chocolate taste. The recipe he gives, one teaspoon of chocolate paste to one cup of water, certainly could not be expected to produce full-bodied flavor.

Aside from *Theobroma cacao,* there was also its relative *Theobroma bicolor,* known as *pataxte.* The large flat beans were sometimes eaten raw, and it was claimed that the use of the beans in drinks led to rashes and diseases, at any rate among non-Indians. While cacao was taken up and embraced by the invaders, *pataxte* remained an Indian drink. Mixed with *Theobroma cacao,* however, it produced an extra fine head of foam.

NINE

Solid Maya Breadstuffs

After having described the many maize-based drinks, with and without cacao, Landa gives but a paragraph to "bread." He tells us that there were many different kinds available and they were all better hot than cold. Modern scholars noticed that tortillas were not mentioned, being unaware that Landa's use of "bread" could refer to both tamales and tortillas; and from this they invented a confrontation between the two forms of breadstuff which never existed.

The whole issue is a spurious one, because, as we shall see, tortillas and tamales are made of the same dough and intergrade to such an extent that it is sometimes difficult to recognize which of the two has been produced from a particular recipe. The reason for the debate, besides ignorance of matters culinary, is that partisans of the Maya consider tamales to be indigenous and the tortilla to be an import from highland Mexico, along with such unpleasantness as human sacrifice, warfare, and idolatry. However, the old picture of the Classic Maya as peaceful and philosophical agriculturalists, passionately interested in time, the stars, and the calendar, has faded, to be replaced by a new vision of small warring city-states quite capable of savage warfare and bloody sacrifice without outside stimulus. Whoever they were, philosopher farmers or princely warriors, we can only speculate about which maize breadstuffs they consumed when they were not consuming maize as a liquid. It is fair to suppose that they had a great range to choose from, which I will illustrate with examples taken from various periods and places of Maya history.

There are a few indications that tortillas as we define them—thin flat round cakes of dough made of nixtamalized maize toasted on a *co-mal*—were not always used in the Maya area. If we take the presence of *comales,* the flat clay griddles on which the tortillas were toasted, as a diagnostic trait, we find them absent in much of the Maya area, although present on the east coast of Yucatan, at the site of Copan in Honduras, and in the highlands of Guatemala. In the latter area, we have an account of a riot that began when a soldier of a prince of Quiché tried to take the tortillas of a woman who was selling them in the marketplace. It is also said that one Maya group, the Manche Chol, did not know how to make tortillas and had to be taught by the missionaries. Previously they had consumed all their maize in liquid form.

If we define a tortilla as just a round thin cake of maize dough, however toasted, the *comal* becomes a less significant diagnostic feature. There are many words in Maya dictionaries for tortillas, usually described as rather thick, round cakes toasted directly on or under the coals or ashes of the cooking fire. This must seem impossible to the Western scholar, ensconced in an armchair or in a jungle camp. It also seemed impossible to travelers in colonial North America, who barely disguised a grimace of disgust as they saw their maize bread being put, raw, into the ashes of the fire. But with the next sentence the grimace was wiped off their faces. They describe the hostess retrieving the baked bread a short while later, brushing it off, and presenting it to the guests. And, the guests exclaim, how very clean and nice it was!

The *Popul Vuh* (Tedlock 1985), the Maya book that is called the "Bible of Mesoamerica," gives us a clue to another possible method of toasting tortillas without a *comal.* One of the many tests to which the hero twins are subjected in the underworld is to sit on the hot seat, a heated stone slab for cooking (Tedlock 1985: 136). Archaeologists have not reported on the presence or absence of suitable stone slabs in the way that they have reported on the absence or presence of *comal* fragments, because it would indeed be difficult to distinguish such a slab from an uncarved stela or a piece of building material. It would have been necessary to have a suitable source of stone within carrying distance, because not all stone behaves properly when subjected to the heat of a cooking fire.

Such slabs were mined, shaped, and meticulously smoothed and seasoned, with accompanying religious observances, during the period that Frank Cushing (1920: 317–343) was observing the Zuñi of New Mexico in the early years of this century. In the case of the Zuñi, the slabs were used for the preparation of the staple *piki,* a papery thin maize bread. I am not suggesting that the Maya made *piki* bread because the Zuñi do so, merely that the use of properly prepared stone slabs for cooking maize bread is not unknown on this continent.

However the bread was prepared, whether on a stone slab, on or under the ashes of the cooking fire, on a *comal,* wrapped in leaves and steamed, wrapped in leaves and toasted on the *comal* or on the coals, or any other method, it was the composition of the dough which was the most important matter. Here, as in our discussion of maize drinks, we must start with the maize, and first of all with the young green maize. Any sort of bread could be made out of it, although it had to be at the proper degree of ripeness or the mixture would be too watery to hold together. Maize at the right point of ripeness needed no soaking or boiling; it could be ground and prepared immediately. There were maize varieties planted especially for making young maize breadstuffs, but the period during which any sort of maize is at the correct stage of ripeness is limited, and young maize bread must always have been a rare delicacy, available only during a brief season.

The main crop maize, the hard, ripe dry grain that was stored to carry the Maya through to the next harvest, was usually made into dough by the *nixtamal* method. English and American writers commonly write of this dough as being composed of "corn meal," which it is not. Corn or maize meal, however familiar it may be to us, barely existed in Mesoamerica, and it is not hard to see why. Unparched, unpopped dry maize would have been next to impossible to reduce to flour or meal by pounding. Softening it up with lime soaking and boiling was a much easier way to make it into a manageable dough, as well as a more nutritious one.

Once the *nixtamal* was ground, the bread maker had many choices. Seasonings could be applied to the dough or mixed into it. Maya cooks mixed chiles with their maize dough, as well as ground toasted squash seeds, honey, and *achiote.* Especially common, and often used for ceremonies, were bread doughs that incorporated beans. The beans, usually the small black Maya beans, could be added cooked whole, cooked and then ground to a paste, or used partially ripe and whole, like shell beans. In the last case the dough could only be used to form tamales, because they had to be cooked for a long time—otherwise the beans remained uncooked.

All these recipes, except the last, produced a dough that was suitable for tamales, tortillas, or intermediate forms. Some recent ethnographic descriptions and recipes for making tamales have the dough being recooked at this point, with the addition of water or broth. Other modern variations on tamale dough include adding up to half the weight of the dough of lard, the mixture then being beaten until a small blob floats on water. The latter elaboration and probably the former as well are demonstrations of the influence of the European cuisine on the indigenous one.

Plain or with additions, we have arrived at a dough which is suitable for making a great variety of edible objects. If we choose to go the tamale route, the dough, plain or with a filling, can be wrapped in leaves preparatory to cooking. Today the choice tends to be between the leaves of bananas or plantains, or maize husks. In earlier times many other leaves were used, some of which, like the leaves of some kinds of avocados and the leaves of *Piper* species, contributed their own flavor to the finished product. Gathering leaves in the forest was a male task. If he came back with suitable leaves, then tamales were made; if not, another form of breadstuff was substituted. In the highlands tamale-wrapping leaves were mostly available during the rainy season, thus adding another dimension to the maize consumption question. Discarded tamale wrappings form a conspicuous part of street and roadside scenery in Mexico and Guatemala today, but their grease-soaked and tomato-stained appearance shows how far the contents have departed from the original.

A plain tamale could be wrapped and tied with no further ado. If different kinds of tamales were being steamed in the same pot they could be identified by distinctive manners of wrapping and tying. Filled tamales were constructed in at least two ways. The filling could be simply placed in a depression in the dough, which was then sealed with more dough, or the dough could be spread on a piece of fabric, the filling spread on the dough, and then the whole thing rolled up like a jelly roll, using the fabric to help in the process. Sections of the roll could then be cut off, wrapped in leaves, tied, and cooked. Paintings on Classic Maya vases show us plates of round objects with dark spirals on their upper surfaces, exactly the pattern one would expect on the cut top of a tamale filled in this fashion. Other possible breadstuffs shown in Classic Maya vase paintings include a dish of oval objects, some white and some yellow, which are roughly the same size as the attendant servant's hand. Today tamales are always served with their wrappers, but this may be because postconquest additions like lard and broth make them too sloppy to be served conveniently without them. Perhaps the white and yellow objects are firm tamales, made of white and yellow maize dough. It is not likely that they are tortillas, because they are not depicted the way a stack of flat objects would be shown.

The choice of tamale fillings was endless. The same bean preparations that were mixed with the dough could be used to fill it, as could ground toasted squash seeds, meat, fish, and fowl stews, squash flowers, the fragrant white flowers of the *loroco* (*Urechites karwinskii*), and all the many greens used by the Maya, especially *chaya* (*Jatropha aconitifolia*) and *chipilín* (*Crotalaria vitellina*). Landa mentions special breads for offerings made with egg yolks, deer hearts, or quail, and some made in the shape of a heart. Other sources describe a tamale filled with egg covered with squash seed sauce, which was then wrapped in a *chaya* leaf, and a tamale filled with a dove breast. They could also be stuffed with squash seeds and black beans, or *chaya* and black beans, or beans and the leaves of one of the many *Piper* species. Whole birds were covered with dough, wrapped in a mat, and cooked in a *pib,* or pit oven. This dish had a sinister significance, according to Cogolludo's description of a seventeenth-century missionary expedition.

> This chief was called Don Pedro Noh, and he spoke our Spanish tongue very well. He seemed to have good intentions toward the religious, to whom he brought some food, among which was a fowl covered with dough. This turkey so treated our Indians took for a bad omen, saying that it was a sign of war, and that they did not wish peace. (Cogolludo 1954–1955, 3: 267–268)

Once the tamale was filled, if it was going to be filled, and securely wrapped and tied, it had to be cooked. Today in some parts of the Maya area there are globular vessels called *tamaleros,* with a small top opening and a tightly fitting lid. They come in different sizes, from the one that will cook enough tamales for a small family to the one that will hold hundreds of tamales, enough for a village feast. A small quantity of water is put into such a pot, and a framework of sticks is constructed in the pot, so that the tamales are held above the water and steamed, not boiled. The fragments of Maya domestic pottery containing boiler scale which have been found in Belize might be taken as confirming the steaming of tamales there by the Classic Maya.

Steaming was not the only way to cook the tamale in its wrapping of leaves. It could be put on the heated *comal* and turned until it was heated through. Cooking under, in, or over the hot coals and ashes of the cooking fire, all were possible. The *barbacoa,* the framework of sticks that held objects to be cooked and smoked over a fire, could also be employed. For the larger versions especially there was the *pib,* the oven that was a hole excavated in the ground with a fire built in it to heat the earth and the stones. After the fire had burned down, this oven was loaded with food to be cooked and then sealed with leaves and earth, to be left until the fragrance signaled that it was time for the food to be unearthed.

A special bread, described ambiguously as being made of tortillas or tamales but more probably made out of the dough that is the basis of both, is still made today for the *chaachak* ceremony, as an offering to the rain god Chac. This bread is a many-layered construction of maize dough with ground toasted squash seeds, or ground black beans, between the layers. The Maya heavens are believed to consist of thirteen layers, and the layers of bread imitate the construction of the heavens. The dough is made by the women, but the actual bread is put together by the *hmen,* the leader of the ceremony. When it is assembled he jabs his fingers into the soft surface and pours *balché* into the resulting holes. Then the whole thing is wrapped up and placed in the *pib,* which has been dug and heated for the occasion. In some performances of these rites this special bread was shared among the participants after it was cooked. In others it was mashed with the broth resulting from the cooking of the sacrificial turkey and then consumed as a form of maize drink.

For travelers special tamales were prepared which we are told could keep up to twenty days. Some of these long-keeping provisions were large plain tamales, shaped like our loaves of bread, which were then sliced and the individual slices warmed on a heated *comal* or on hot stones. Another sort of traveler's stores was eaten by Tomás de la Torre after his shipwreck:

> Because we were hungry the Indians gave us some of their bread, which was lumps cooked in water, strung on a string like a rosary, black and hard and tasteless, and this was like ship's biscuit for the Indians when they travel. (La Torre 1944: 149)

Maize dough that has been made into *nixtamal* by cooking with an extra amount of wood ashes produces tamales that have a hard skin when dried. These were used as storable supplies in Guatemala and may have been something like the "rosary beads" eaten by Tomás de la Torre.

The tortilla end of the range of edibles that may be made from maize dough is as varied as the tamale end. Today the tortilla is made large or small, thick or thin, depending on family size and taste. Families with many adolescent males tend to prepare large thick tortillas. The tortillas are cooked on the *comal,* but they could also be cooked in the other ways that we have described or folded into leaves and placed directly on the heat source.

Baer and Merrifield (1971: 187–190) give us four different kinds of tortillas, each used and appreciated for their distinctive qualities by the contemporary Lacandons. The first are what we would consider to be the standard tortilla for the Maya area, shaped on a leaf and toasted on a lime water–brushed *comal* so that they puff up briefly, the way proper tortillas do. The second are sourdough tortillas, made of maize dough that has stood overnight and does not puff up when toasted in the way that the first kind does. The third kind is the young maize tortilla, and the final kind is shaped by the two-handed Mexican technique—it is smaller and thicker than the others. Other authors tell us that Lacandon cooked tortillas could be coated with bean paste and then more maize dough and toasted again.

Tortillas were made into travel provisions by drying in the sun or toasting on the fire again. Baer says that the Lacandon prefer the sourdough variety for this treatment, because it becomes crisp when toasted. If the product was not crisp it could be ground and drunk with water; in other words it could be made into a maize drink. This seems like a good idea when you read Valenzuela's (1979: 312) recommendation for jaws with teeth of steel to cope with travel provisions like these.

The most interesting thing about a tortilla is what may be wrapped in it and what it is dipped into. It is rarely eaten without accompaniment, at the very least a sauce or a bean dish. The simplest sauce was ground dried chiles and water. From this humble ancestor comes the line which terminates with the trendy *salsas* beloved of a certain school of today's chefs. But even the original inventors of tortilla-dipping sauces varied them when they could. The ground toasted seeds of large and small squashes, always carefully differentiated by the Maya, could be added to the basic chile water, or you could mix *epazote (Cheno-*

podium ambrosioides) with water and then add ground toasted squash seeds to the flavored liquid. A member of the laurel family, *Litsea neesiana,* could step up the taste, as could *Lippia mexicana,* also known as Mexican oregano. Even better, however, than dipping your tortilla into one of these sauces was dipping it into, or wrapping it around, one of the meat, fish, or fowl dishes next to be described.

TEN

Maya Flesh Food

Meat, fish, and fowl, or flesh, as they will be referred to for the sake of conciseness, were not ordinary food for the ordinary Maya either recently or in the remote past. When the meat-eating Europeans arrived, they described Maya life as perpetual Lent. Landa, who devotes pages to maize foods, skips over the flesh stews in one sentence, saying that they were eaten in the evening and were replaced by greens when the flesh was not available (Tozzer 1941: 91). Gaspar Antonio Xiu (Xiu 1986) does not mention flesh dishes at all. In all but one description of Maya food, the quantity of maize dishes given far outnumbers the dishes incorporating flesh. The one partial exception speaks specifically of elite diet, and the exceptional quality of elite menus is confirmed by other evidence.

The foods of the lords were male and female turkeys and deer, which they ate with maize tortillas, and usually beans which are like habas [European *Vicia faba*], and some greens produced by a tree which they call *ehay* [modern *chaya, Jatropha aconitifolia*], which is like a fig tree, and even the leaves look like it except that they are smaller, these greens cooked are their main sustenance, and even the Spaniards have put them in the pot when they lack cabbage, and very good they are. (Anon. 1898: 163)

There is a source of information on flesh consumption that is lacking for the consumption of maize, fruit, greens, and beverages. These are the archaeologically recovered animal bones from Maya sites, which not only give us a list of species eaten but also indicate cooking and butchering practices. Using the new miracle of carbon pathway analysis, both the human and animal bones can also tell us about the food that nourished them when they were covered with living flesh.

Carbon pathway analysis gives us the earliest dated indication of what the Maya ate. The bones of a male and a female, buried in graves with elite grave goods in Lamanai, Belize, during the Early Classic (A.D. 250 to 600), reveal that the elite male had enjoyed an unusual amount of seafood, even though maize was the cornerstone of his diet (White and Schwarcz 1989). The elite woman had not had the seafood but had, like the male, enjoyed an exceptionally varied diet as far as greens went. It is nice to have hard science prove the obvious, variety being characteristic of elite diets the world over. Considerable effort must have been expended to provide the male with his seafood, because the site of Lamanai is well inland, far up the New River. There are no impediments to navigation on the New River, and a small Maya port exists at the site, so that the fish may have arrived there directly from the sea, or they may have been brought in one of the many preserved forms of fish available to the Maya. The high status conferred by the eating of fish among the Maya is substantiated by a much later piece of vituperation from the highlands of Guatemala, in which one lord is abusing another:

What good is that [Istayul]? He only eats maize and water to grind *nixtamal*, he only eats the dregs of cacao and flies. However, [my food] is not like this. I am brought fish and little fresh shrimp. (Carmack and Mondlock 1983: 194)

Because seafood was high-status nourishment, it gave the Maya lords another chance to exert political pressure on each other. Landa (Tozzer 1941: 40) tells us that the Chel, who lived on the coast of Yucatan shortly before the conquest, would refuse to trade salt and fish to the Cocom, who lived inland. The Cocom took their revenge by refusing to allow the export of game and fruit to the coast.

Even when the archaeological evidence agrees neatly with the documentary, it is always at best a mere sampling of household debris, from which cosmic conclusions tend to be drawn. Given chance and the vagaries of individual taste and family custom, the remains of a few meals of a few households should not be taken to stand for the whole picture. The remains of last night's dinner should not be taken as standing for the totality of all nights' dinners.

This should be taken into account when we look at the other archaeological data on flesh consumption. Hamblin (1985) reports from the island of Cozumel, where we saw the first Spanish meetings with the Maya taking place, that both species of turkey, *Meleagris ocellata,* the ocellated turkey, and *Meleagris gallopavo,* the domesticated turkey, were eaten, which is unusual, because only the former is commonly found on the nearby mainland of Yucatan. Most of the bird bones, and the fish bones as well, were not darkened by exposure to extreme heat, which means that they were cooked in liquid. Both the chile and water dipping sauce and *atolli* were used for such liquids or stocks. Crab carapaces, turtle shells and bones, and iguana bones were all heat darkened and therefore must have been cooked over the open fire.

The iguana has yet to be described in this book. There are two species of them: the green iguana (*Iguana iguana*), which despite being a reptile spends a good deal of time over and in the water, a habit which led to it being officially proclaimed a fish by the Roman Catholic Church and therefore permissible food for periods of abstinence from meat, like Fridays and Lent; and the black iguana (*Ctenosaurus pectinata*), a more terrestrial creature which some people consider superior eating. They can be captured and kept for long periods of time without feeding, a convenient way to have a supply of fresh meat on hand. They also produce delicious eggs, leathery-shelled oblong capsules consisting entirely of yolk. It was one more new creature for the Europeans to assimilate into their culinary scheme of things and their religious practices.

There was nothing to eat but iguana, which the Spaniards have designated fish, and the bishops together confirmed them in that name . . . the taste everybody finds in them is more like that of a very good rabbit . . . it is an ugly beast but very tasty once you get over your disgust at eating it, and when we eat it now we think of it as holiday food. The Father Vicar refused to eat it, remaining hungry rather than lift such a thing to his lips. (La Torre 1944: 169–170)

Iguanas were eaten in Mayapán, a very late preconquest inland site, but the majority of the bones found there came from the white-tailed deer (*Odocoileus virginianus*), the brocket deer (*Mazama americana*), the peccary (*Tayassu pecari*), and the dog. The ocellated turkey was the only large fowl utilized.

Carbon pathway analysis tells us that the edible animals were fattened on maize, although in the case of the deer and the peccary we do not know whether the maize was fed to them or whether they just went and robbed the ripening fields. In certain parts of the Maya area dogs were fattened on maize before they were eaten. Landa claimed, probably expressing European prejudice, that dogs had been eaten in the past, but that in his day the practice was considered shameful. However, another more broad-minded European compared the taste of their meat to that of roast suckling pig.

Other animals used were the spider monkey (*Ateles geoffroyi*) and the howler monkey (*Alouatta villosa*), highly popular among the recent Lacandon, who ate them roasted. Tapirs (*Tapirella bairdii*) and manatees (*Trichechus manatus*) were salted and dried when they could be caught. The Europeans spoke with satisfaction of the great quantities of fat which could be extracted from the manatee, but given the Maya aversion to fat, one must wonder what they did with it. If the behavior of their neighbors is any evidence, they probably rubbed it on their skin.

A special case was the armadillo (*Dasypuz novemcinctus*). The animal was supposed to have a peculiar and unpleasant taste when roasted, which was remedied by adding *Cordia globosa*, a member of the borage family, as a condiment. Armadillos were believed to be occasionally poisonous. Some authors asserted that there was a poisonous species and a nonpoisonous one, while others claimed that it depended on the recent diet of the armadillo in question. The ambivalence continues to this day, with armadillos being looked at askance because of the habit they are supposed to have of tunneling through graveyards and eating the corpses. For the original inhabitants of the Maya area the dubious habits of armadillos, and the subsequent risk of being poisoned, were no reason to refrain from eating them.

The freshwater streams and lakes provided other foodstuffs. Freshwater snails (*Pachychilus* spp.) were eaten with mashed root crops at the time of the Soustelles visit in the 1930s and are mentioned in the diaries of earlier explorers of the area (Soustelle 1937). The fact that snail shells could be burned to provide the lime needed for *nixtamal* suggests that an absence of snail shells does not mean that they were not eaten. Other riverine creatures consumed included frogs, one species of which, the *uo* (*Leptodactylus* spp.), was supposed to be another source of fat, and the river turtles.

How were all these creatures eaten? The first pair of twins in the *Popul Vuh*, the father and the uncle of the ones who encountered the hot seat, tempted Earthquake with a roasted fowl:

> The human heart will desire a bite of meat, a meal of flesh . . . Then they roasted the birds and cooked them until they were brown, dripping with fat that oozed from the back of the birds, with an overwhelmingly fragrant aroma. (Tedlock 1985: 101)

The *Popul Vuh* does not tell us how this tempting fowl was roasted, but it was probably on a *barbacoa,* a framework of sticks over a fire. Meat was often roasted this way immediately after the hunt to preserve it for the long hot trip back to the hunter's home. The catch was divided on arrival, with a portion going to the lord and other portions to the hunter's neighbors and kin. It was a neat way to avoid an oversupply of meat in one house while there was a dearth next door. Presumably on days when the recipients were fortunate in the hunt, they returned the gift. For longer storage the meat was reroasted daily. Gage said that it was "as hard as a stone" (Gage 1958: 223). When the time came this stonelike object was boiled to make it edible.

In the division of the large game, the haunch was considered the choicest portion. It was the gift for the lord and, in the highlands, for the potential father-in-law. In the latter case the complete offering was a peccary haunch, accompanied by *atolli,* guacamole, and a calabash full of small tamales wrapped in two specific kinds of leaves. Haunches of meat were also most acceptable offerings to the gods, along with boiled fowl. Neatly trussed haunches appear in the surviving Maya books in the lists of offerings, placed in flaring-sided flat-bottomed dishes. A haunch of meat, actual or simulacrum, even appears as part of the headdress of a lord on one carved stone monument. These books list another offering, a small bit of turkey meat sitting on a dish of dog meat, which seems to us to be cheating the gods. The Europeans commented on the fact that bird breasts were not considered anything special and were divided up along with the rest of the bird instead of being reserved for the authorities.

As far as we know, the offerings were all fresh meat. There was much preserved meat produced, including turtle, crocodile, and iguana, but it seems to have been for domestic use only. The roasting and reroasting techniques already described could be supplemented by salting. The salt came from the salt works along the coast and from at least one famous salt spring inland. The flesh was cut into strips, and then the strips were put into a vessel of salt. After the salting the flesh was put in the sun to dry and then smoked. Coils of this flesh were hung up on the smoky rafters of the kitchens, and bits of it were cut off and used to give savor to broths and stews. This particular recipe might be of European origin, as the product is usually called by the Spanish name *tasajo*. However, Landa's (Tozzer 1941: 190) testimony about fish preservation seems to guarantee that all the techniques are pre-Columbian. According to him seafood was salted, sun-dried, or roasted, the method depending on the species being processed. Another source mentions slices of ray being prepared with salt, while small fish were strung on straws and dried whole before the fire. Little fish (*Heros nigrofasciatus* and *Fundulus pachycephalus*) from the lakes of highland Guatemala were roasted or smoked and packed into hollow reeds. So packed, they were traded all over the highlands. Given their diminutive size, they must have been more of a seasoning than a staple, perhaps a sort of Maya anchovy.

Evidence for the existence of a Maya salt fish industry, as well as a trade dealing with preserved fish, comes from the corruption trial of the *alcalde mayor* Diego Quijada, held in Yucatan in 1565. He was accused of illegally accepting not only 7,866 eggs, 1,850 large native fowl, and 403 iguanas, but also "five loads of dry fish, of the kind the Indians use" (Scholes and Adams 1938: 237).

If the flesh was not roasted or prepared for storage in some fashion, it could always be wrapped in leaves and then cooked either on the *comal,* in the *pib,* or on the coals. The account of the expedition to conquer Kanek', which has been previously quoted, describes this sort of light quick meal on the march. One wishes they had more to say about the tamales, who had made them, and when:

> They got from the river some little fish they call in their language *chilan,* as small as those in Lake Atitlan [Guatemala], and wrapping them in some palm leaves they put them for a bit in the ashes, and everyone got one tamale and three of those little fish. (Valenzuela 1979: 41)

The nearest thing that we have to a conquest period Maya meat recipe is given to us in the notes to Tozzer's edition of Landa (Tozzer

1941: 144). It is a stew of venison in *chacmole,* which is a sauce of *achiote,* chile, allspice, and tomato, and it was an offering to the gods. Allspice, the unripe fruit of *Pimenta dioica,* is one of the many terminological traps ready to catch the investigator of New World food. By convention, in Spanish, *pimenta* refers to allspice, also called Jamaica pepper, while *pimento* refers to *Piper,* or black pepper, but the question is, do the sources adhere to the convention? Nor do we know if the tomato in this recipe is *Solanum lycopersicon* or *Physalis,* although given the lowland source of the recipe, the former is more likely than the latter.

Nearer to our own time, most of the stews are thickened with maize dough. This makes a dish known as *pulique* in the highlands of Guatemala or *kool* in Yucatan. Another name for these dishes can be the name of the flesh plus "in atolli." Turkey in *atolli* is a dish for great festivals in the highlands, and highland hunters also eat a ritual dish cooked in this way containing the organ meats of a deer. Sol Tax, in Panajachel, on Lake Atitlan in Guatemala, came across a dish where fish was cooked in this manner, with the addition of beans, *achiote,* and chile (Tax 1950). It is possible that the offerings listed in the Madrid Codex, dishes of deer and maize or iguana and maize, might have been deer meat or iguana meat cooked in *atolli.*

Many other seasonings were used in the stews, starting with *epazote* (*Chenopodium ambrosioides*). Standley (1946) condemns both *epazote* and *Eryngium foetidum* as having "incomparably vile odors," although the odor of the latter is no viler than, and is in fact very similar to, that of coriander greens. *Eryngium foetidum* is a latecomer to the conquering parade of New World plants. It is used widely in tropical Asia and Africa but only came into the United States recently, via Vietnamese markets, although it originated next door in Mexico and Central America. Other flavors familiar to us, although from sometimes unfamiliar plant sources, were contributed to Maya food by the garlic vine (*Cydista aequinoctialis*), a wild onion (*Allium kunthii*), and *Pectis linifolia,* an anise-scented member of the Compositae.

The Maya, like the Aztecs, had no objections to eating insects, and if they do not seem to have done it quite as much, it is probably because we simply do not have as much information. From ethnographic studies we hear of large grubs being extracted from rotten trees, toasted on a *comal* with a pinch of salt, and then wrapped in a tortilla and eaten. They are said to be "buttery." Other sources speak of dragonflies being strung on a slender stalk and toasted over a fire.

The Maya were accused of eating human flesh, and like the Aztecs, the conquest period Maya certainly did, but again it was for ritual purposes, not as ordinary food. Reverend Father Francesco of Bologna wrote Pope Paul III in the 1530s saying that the arms and legs of sacrificial victims were given to the principal chiefs, "who ate them with joy and respect, saying they were the relics of saints" (Díaz 1838: 215). The *Littera mãdata* (Anon. n.d.: 298r) is even more precise and says it was only the calves of the sacrificed captives' legs that were given to the victorious rulers to eat: hardly articles of daily diet.

Maya Produce

If there was no meat or fish or fowl, no frogs or iguanas or turtles, if none of the things that we have been talking about in the flesh section were available, a situation which seems to have been more common than not among the ordinary Maya, there were always plant foods to fall back on. Landa said that when there were no meat stews to go with the "bread," the subsidiary dishes were made of vegetables and chile. The term "vegetables," however, is a category that is found neither in botanical nomenclature nor among the Maya.

The Maya languages divide up the edible world in quite a different fashion from English. For example, in Tzeltal (Berlin 1967) the verb "to eat" is used only when asking the question "What are you eating?" Otherwise the verb differs according to the substance being eaten. One verb is used for things that are chewed and the pulp spat out, as is done with sugar cane and maize stalks. Another verb is used for eating things that melt in your mouth, like candy. If we knew what this verb referred to before the conquest, we might be able to solve the riddle as to whether or not the Maya made sweets with their honey. Still another verb is used when bread, in the broad sense, is being eaten, and yet another for the consumption of meat, mushrooms, and chile. Finally, there are two verbs the use of which depends on the texture of the matter being eaten. Mushy, gelatinous, overripe, and overcooked things (for example, brains, bananas, and avocados) are in the first category, although they might also belong in the last category. The last category is for discrete, firm objects, among them young maize, popped maize, beans, and squash seeds. Other Maya languages treat the comestible universe in roughly the same manner.

Prominent among Maya produce were the root crops. Three of them are mentioned in the riddles asked in the *Book of Chilam Balam of Chumayel* (Roys 1933: 96). When asked to bring a bone of his father, buried for three years, the answer is for the youth to bring a manioc root baked in a *pib*. There was no need for time-consuming grating and squeezing, for only sweet manioc was grown in the Maya area. Nor are there any specific recipes for manioc. Most authors speak in general terms of cooking roots on the coals, in the *pib*, or by boiling. Another root is given a more specific treatment in a riddle:

Son, bring me a stone from the burned over land, it is burning hot. Bring with it the liquor to extinguish it, so it will crack here before me. (Roys 1933: 97)

This commands the bringing of a tuber of *macal* (*Xanthosoma nigrum*), an American genus of aroid that could be used for its edible leaves and shoots, as well as its tubers. The *macal* in the riddle should be hot out of the *pib*, and it should be extinguished with clarified honey.

Two other riddles are about the jícama (*Pachyrhizus erosus*). In the answer to one riddle, they are the yellow and white things plugging up the bottom of the well. Perhaps the round yellow and white objects painted on that Classic Maya vase are not tamales at all but yellow and white jícamas. The other riddle describes the jícama as a woman's very white and well-rounded calf and speaks of tucking back the skirt from her white and well-rounded calf, which is a metaphor for peeling the jícama.

For some reason, sweet potatoes (*Ipomaea batatas*) get no riddles, but they are the fourth of this tetrarchy of root crops. They are mentioned as being boiled in their skins and then eaten with honey, or being stewed and flavored with *Clerodendron ligustrinum*. Usually they seem to have been cooked and mashed and then used as extenders for maize, either in bread or in drinks. This practice was especially common just before the maize harvest, when maize supplies were at their lowest.

When there were famines, because of crop failures, locust plagues, or incursions of great flocks of hungry birds, wild roots had to be gathered in the forest. One of them, the wild jícama (*Calopogonium coeru-*

leum), was used as a symbol for famine in the prophetic books. Another such famine plant was the *ramón* (*Brosimum alicastrum*).

Gaspar Antonio Xiu (1986: 62–63), who does not even mention flesh in his quick sketch of the Maya diet, does not mention root crops either. For him the evening tortillas are accompanied by *buul,* the Maya black beans, poetically disguised in the riddles as "a basketful of black birds" (Roys 1933: 96). Xiu speaks of them as a replacement for chiles, but it is more likely that the two were combined. The accepted wisdom was that tortillas and beans were boring; it took chile to make the saliva flow. The beans, the black *buul,* the larger light-colored *ibes* (*Phaseolus lunatus*), or other varieties, could be cooked in plain water or water in which toasted or untoasted chiles had been steeped. Such a chile "stock" might be called the basis of the cuisine, so frequently does it turn up. It is everything from the tortilla accompaniment of the very poorest peasant to the liquid for cooking the turkey for the greatest celebrations. There is even a reference in the *Popul Vuh* (Tedlock 1985: 129), where the grandmother grinds chiles and mixes them with broth, and the broth acts as the mirror in which the rat on the rafters is reflected for the hero twins to see.

Boiled beans could be thickened by adding maize dough and then flavored with chile and *achiote* to make a variety of *pulique.* If there was no flesh to cook in *atolli,* beans could be used as a substitute. Another popular combination was beans and ground toasted squash seed, with or without the addition of chopped native onion greens. A mixture of ground cooked white *ibes* beans and ground squash seed could be dried by dropping hot stones into it, after which it could be stored and later reconstituted by adding water. The same white beans, cooked, could be dressed up by adding an equal weight of ground squash seed, along with chile, *achiote,* a small piece of maize dough, and some hog plums (*Spondias* sp.).

The favorite flavoring for beans was *epazote* (*Chenopodium ambrosioides*). Some people disapproved of adding more than one kind of greens to a dish of beans. Among permissible greens to be added were the shoots of *chayote* (*Sechium edule*) and *chipilín* (*Crotolaria* sp.). Tortillas were eaten with beans not only for gastronomic and nutritional reasons but also for practical ones—they were handy for scooping the beans up to eat.

There was also a kind of bean that could be gathered ripe, together with its dry pod, and stored. When the time came to eat it, boiling water was poured over the bean-filled pods and they became moist and edible. These beans were served with *iguaxte,* a sauce of ground toasted squash seeds and tomatoes. The whole young bean plant could be boiled, dried, and kept for future use, or the leaves and the flowers could be eaten as greens immediately.

The use of all parts of a crop plant is typical of New World foods. Not only maize and beans but also the *Cucurbita,* the squashes, were totally exploited in this fashion. The young fruits were boiled or cooked in a vessel in the *pib,* alone or with other ingredients. The flowers and young shoots and greens were eaten, and the leaves could be used to wrap other foods. The mature fruit of the hard-shelled varieties were boiled or baked in the *pib,* although one was warned not to bake them whole, lest they explode. Pieces of hard-shelled ripe squash could be slowly cooked with honey, making a sweet which is still used today in Guatemala for special occasions.

A glance over the preceding pages will reveal that the most important edible portion of the squash was the seed. The two kinds of edible squash seeds, the large ones and the small ones, could be eaten as they were, or toasted, or ground either raw or toasted. Today a type of praline is made by pouring sugar cooked to the proper consistency over the toasted seeds, adding one more possibility, if made with honey, to our list of pre-Columbian sweets. Ground toasted squash seeds and ground chile, mixed together, were used as a relish. The same seeds, ground and mixed with *achiote* and salt and some liquid, made a sauce for fish or venison. Ground beans and ground toasted squash seeds could be made into a drink.

There were many other greens, some of which were eaten raw. In the morning, the men went to their maize fields carrying tortillas, chiles, and salt, ready for whatever greens they could find. One green that cannot be eaten raw has nevertheless caught the fancy of Yucatec writers today. This is *chaya (Jatropha aconitifolia),* which the Europeans compared to cabbage but said was not as tasty. *Chaya* is a member of the Euphorbia family and, typically for a Euphorbia, contains a milky juice. The leaves are also very prickly. *Chaya* leaves must be picked young and pressed to be edible, but once so treated they may be cooked alone, used as stuffing for tamales, or put in a simmering stew pot.

A green for the very poor was purslane *(Portulaca oleracea).* This succulent little plant originated in the Old World but must have made the trip across the Bering Strait, or whatever was there at the time, with the ancestors of the American Indians or on some animal's muddy feet. Its seeds are found in cultural deposits in Salts Cave, Kentucky, dating back to the first millennium B.C. (Chapman, Stewart, and Yarnell 1974). It therefore comes as no surprise to find the Maya eating this stubborn and ineradicable garden pest, which prompted a despairing Charles Dudley Warner to say that what one needed to be a gardener was to have a cast-iron back, with a hinge in it!

There were many other greens available to the Maya. One author said that they would eat anything that didn't smell bad to them. As in Mexico, the young pads of certain species of *Opuntia* cactus provided a slightly mucilaginous vegetable, and the *chayote* (*Sechium edule*) gave of its watery green fruit, shoots, and large starchy root. There were also the bitter greens of certain species of *Solanum,* and *Calandrina micrantha,* although in certain areas the former were considered poisonous.

Another resource, especially in the rainy season, was mushrooms. They were boiled, roasted, or cooked in tamales, and as we have seen they were terminologically considered meat. The hallucinogenic mushrooms were added to sacred drinks. Once again we are awed at the extent of the knowledge of their environment that the Maya possessed and the amount of perilous exploration that must have gone into the accumulation of this body of wisdom.

The earliest explorers tell us that the Maya settlements were full of fruit trees. One of the cruelest things the Europeans did to consolidate their conquest of Yucatan and ensure the propagation of the faith was to force the Maya to leave their villages and move into compact, grid-patterned towns in the shadows of the newly built churches. The old settlements were burned to the ground and the orchard trees were cut down. The Europeans said that the Maya died of sadness, and while newly introduced diseases certainly played a part, the diagnosis was at least partially correct.

Before this policy was enforced, fruit, along with fowl and bread, was brought by the Indians to the Europeans as a gesture of welcome. Among the fruits presented to the early explorers on the coast of Yucatan were pineapples (*Ananas comosus*) and sapote (probably *Pouteria sapota*), although they are rarely precisely described. There was the papaya (*Carica papaya*), the related *Jacaratia mexicana,* and many species of *Annona.* The Europeans ate one species of *Annona* in Yucatan which must have been taboo in some fashion, because the Maya were astonished to see it being eaten. Perhaps it was the species that was believed to cause chills and fever. At any rate it earned the Europe-

ans the nickname of "annona eaters," a word used in Guatemala today as an epithet for a coward. The *chico zapote,* the fruit of *Manil-
kara zapota,* the tree that produces the sap that used to be made into
chewing gum, was a delicious morsel, although we have no evidence
that the Maya chewed the gum the way the Aztecs did. The fruit of a
species of *Lucuma* was considered inedibly fermented when ripe and
because of this was picked green and ripened in hot ashes. Cactus
fruits were not ignored, both *Opuntia* fruit and *pitahayas,* the fruit of
an epiphytic cactus, being utilized. *Parmentiera edulis* fruits were
eaten by the Europeans sliced like cucumbers, with salt, and by the
Maya with honey. The Maya also used avocados (*Persea* sp.), either
sliced raw and wrapped in a tortilla or put in the stew after the stew
was cooked, so as to avoid the bitter flavor avocado gets when heated.
Other fruits were eaten in *atolli,* with honey, or dried.

The Europeans justified the chopping down of the orchards by saying that the fruit was used to make intoxicating drinks in which the
devil lurked to turn into snakes and worms that gnawed at the souls of
the Maya. They were pleased to find, or pretend to find, some of these
snakes and worms when they overturned the containers of fermenting
liquids. The Maya defended their drinking, and particularly their use
of *balché,* saying that it was a healthy purge. They blamed the decline
in their numbers on the prohibition that the Europeans put on the use
of *balché.* We have no information on the other fruit beers, but *balché*
was apparently stepped up with hallucinogens like *Datura, Psilocybe*
mushrooms, and *Nymphaea,* the water lily. It must have been additions like these that led the Europeans to consider these drinks incredi-
bly intoxicating and linked with the infernal powers.

This brings us to the end of our survey of Maya foodstuffs and the
use they made of them. It is admittedly an artificial construction which
combines the sparse evidence from archaeology, several hundred years
of travelers' tales, and contemporary witnesses. There is even less evidence about pre-Columbian Maya table manners and kitchen practices, and a paragraph or two will describe where the food was prepared and how it was eaten.

There is a lack of focus about the Maya hearth. There is no one
place where domestic preparations center; instead there are several
hearths scattered about the homestead. This was found archaeologically by Fauvet-Berthelot (1986), who describes three types of hearth
in her Classic Maya site. One was the usual Mesoamerican hearth
formed of three stones which were manipulated by the cook for her

own convenience. The second was formed of three schist slabs, so placed that they formed a U. The third was a clay hearth, a form that disappeared at the end of the Maya Classic. One can only speculate as to what dietary changes accompanied this deletion from the cultural inventory. This trio of specialized cooking areas is echoed by the modern Lacandon (Baer and Merrifield 1971: 143–144). Baer also found three kinds of hearths, the first at the edge of the house, consisting of three stones to support a *comal* or a pot. The second, he says, serves for the preparation of gruel, by which one presumes that he means *atolli*. On this hearth the pot sits directly on the fire, with no mediating stones. Finally, there is a hearth outdoors, where stewing and barbecuing take place. Other modern visitors to the Lacandon say that in certain villages extended families will cook their *nixtamal* jointly in a huge vessel on a common fire and then take portions of the softened maize and further prepare it and cook it on their own smaller hearth. Maize preparation takes up so much time and space that multiple hearths may be a way of avoiding culinary congestion.

This is borne out by the vague description of the palace of the Quiché in Utatlán, in the Guatemala highlands. The structure seems to have been on several levels, with the first for the soldiers, who had great kitchens, as well as large and well-equipped bakeries, meaning places where the carbohydrate staple was prepared, not necessarily in the form of a crusty loaf. The second level, where the princes and lords had their kitchens and bakeries, repeated this dual arrangement, as did the third, which housed the royal apartments. These last kitchens and bakeries also fed the royal women, who lived on the fourth, fifth, and sixth levels.

As far as we can tell, domestic cooking was done by women, but the cooking of large quantities, and especially outdoor cooking, was done by men. The men dug the *pib* and probably loaded it, although the women may have arranged the ingredients in the individual vessels. We have seen the men giving their game a preliminary roasting at the site of capture, and the *hmen* shaping the maize dough and ground bean or squash seed simulacrum of the heavens with dough that was made by the women, all of which seems to point to a pattern of private cooking being female and public cooking being male.

If our scanty evidence is any indication, the women probably ate separately. That is the way Landa described them, seated either on the ground or on mats. When Tomás López (in Landa 1973: 211) published ordinances for the way that the Maya should conduct their lives, he commanded that their dinners and suppers should be taken at tables, covered with tablecloths, with their wives and children eating with them, and in all cleanliness. It is probably a pretty good indication of how things were not done in sixteenth-century Yucatan. Women were allowed to drink during the ritual drinking, but they did it separately. If, at a banquet, women served the men, they had to turn their backs while the proffered drink was being downed.

In the same book where Landa fulminated against the evils of drink among the Maya, he has a Maya figure appear whose temperance he might have found admirable. It is ironic that this figure is the chosen war chief of the Maya, and it is entirely possible that while Landa was writing, some Maya warrior was undergoing the austerities he describes in hope of accumulating enough spiritual power to oust the Europeans from Maya territory. This war chief was elected and served in tandem with a hereditary war chief. The elected chief, during his three-year term, was allowed no sexual relations with women; indeed a serving maid could not even approach him. Neither was he allowed meat. Instead, he was given fish, which we may remember was particularly high-status food, as well as iguana. The latter implies that the Maya, like the Europeans, considered the iguana a fish for fasting purposes and that possibly the Roman Catholic Church derived its classification of the iguana as permissible for Fridays and Lent from the Maya. Alcohol was not allowed to him, or at any rate he was not to get drunk, and all his belongings were kept apart in his house, not mixed with the possessions of others. There is no indication that the hereditary war chief had to follow this regimen, or what his position entailed. Nor is there anything telling us whether or not the elected chief had to observe the basic Maya, Aztec, and Inca fast, which was abstinence from salt and chile.

With the figures of Bishop Landa and the Maya war chief at the time of the Spanish conquest we can bring our sketch of Maya foodways to a close. They make a good contrasting pair; Landa, who had vowed adherence to the practice of chastity, monastic discipline, and austerity, and the Nacom, the Maya war chief, practicing the exact same things for diametrically opposed ends.

TWELVE

The Inca: Animal and Mineral

Peru is different. The deserts are drier, the mountains are higher, the chile peppers on your plate are a different species. Today the desert Pacific coast of Peru exceeds the usual definition of a desert as a place where, for reasons of climatic stringency, usually drought, every plant is separated from every other plant by bare soil. In many places there is absolutely no vegetation whatsoever, but this moon landscape is in part caused by European deforestation. Even in pre-Columbian times, however, the vegetation was sparse, because for all practical purposes it does not rain on the Pacific coast of Peru. The ocean, however, is brimming over with life, because the cold Humboldt current carries immense quantities of nutrients which feed great populations of mollusks, fish, birds, and sea mammals.

A trifle inland, in the foothills of the Andes, you get the first consistent vegetation. It is watered by the mist, the *garúa,* that blows in off the sea, and therefore varies with the season. In a good year it can provide pasture and edibles like snails. Above this region, known as the *lomas,* the mountains rise rapidly, going through a series of climatic zones which end with permanent snow. The Andes as a whole are a tangled skein of north-south mountain ranges, but where our interest centers, in north-central Peru, there are only two. The Black Cordillera overlooks the Pacific, and the higher White Cordillera parallels it to the east. The two ranges are sometimes close together and at other times draw apart, leaving a high plain between them. Despite the altitude this was the most prosperous part of the Inca empire.

Beyond the city of Cuzco, which was in ancient times the seat of the court of the lords of these kingdoms, the two mountain ranges of which I speak separate, leaving between them a great plain, which is called the province of Collao. Here there are many rivers, and Titicaca the great lake, wide spaces and copious fodder, because while the land is flat it has the same altitude and climate as the mountains. No trees grow there, and there is no firewood, but they replace bread by some roots they plant which they call *papas* which grow underground, and these are the food of the Indians, who by drying them and curing them make what they call *chuño*, which is the bread and sustenance of the country. There are also other roots and herbs which they eat. It is a healthy place and the most populated of the Indies, and the richest because of the abundance of cattle which are easily raised there . . . the native ones which are called guanacos and pacos, there are also partridges to hunt to your heart's content. (Acosta in Porras Barrenechea 1986: 387)

To the east of the White Cordillera the slopes descend into the Amazon forests, and the rivers, no longer mountain torrents, begin a more sluggish stage of their journey toward the Atlantic.

Even though this description of the Inca area is of the sketchiest it should be evident that there are enormous quantities of ecological niches available. Given that for every thousand feet one ascends the temperature drops three or four degrees Fahrenheit, and adding to this all the possible differences in soils, sunny slopes or shady ones, good or poor drainage of water and frost, and protection from or exposure to damaging winds and hail, the number of available microclimates is astronomical. It makes plausible the Peruvian claim that their inventory of domesticated plants is the world's largest.

The Inca who inhabited this remarkable country when the Europeans appeared were even newer at empire building than the Aztecs. Most of their territorial expansion took place in the highlands in the second half of the fifteenth century, although, again like the Aztecs, they were surrounded by the ruins of the empires that had preceded them. The Inca, a term now used for both the people and their ruler, were more systematic than the Aztecs in their conquests. They demanded that the conquered learn Quechua, accept Inca gods and laws in addition to their own, and send their local gods to Cuzco, the Inca capital. Rebellions were crushed by exchanging populations over huge distances. Habits that the Inca disapproved of, like eating dogs and people, were eliminated.

From the culinary point of view one major difference between the Inca and the Maya and Aztecs to the north is instantly obvious. The Inca had not one but two species of domesticated large mammals: the llama (*Lama glama*) and the alpaca (*Lama pacos*). Along with the two wild species, the vicuña (*Vicugna vicugna*) and the guanaco (*Lama guanicoe*), they are known as the American camelids, which gives us a clue to their Old World relatives. The llama seems to have been domesticated in the highlands between 4550 and 3100 B.C. The Spaniards usually called llamas and alpacas *ovejas de la tierra* and *carneros de la tierra*, or native sheep and native lambs, but sometimes they switched the names.

There is nothing in Peru that is more profitable and useful than the cattle of the country, which our people call the sheep of the Indies, and the Indians in their language call llamas. Looking at them carefully one can see that of all animals known it produces the most for the least expense. From this cattle they get food and clothing, as in Europe they do from sheep, but they also get transportation . . . for they use them to bring cargo and take it away. And they do not have to waste sustenance in shoeing or saddles or packsaddles or feed, as they serve their masters for free, contenting themselves with the forage they find in the fields . . . From the meat of this cattle they make *cusharqui* or cured meat, which lasts for a long time and is highly valued. They send troops of these animals as pack animals, and a string of them, three hundred or five hundred or even a thousand, will carry wine, coca, maize, *chuño*, quicksilver, and other merchandise. (Acosta in Porras Barrenechea 1986: 383)

The Spaniards praised the animals but did nothing to encourage their increase and well-being. Thousands were slaughtered for their bezoar stones, which are intestinal accumulations of insoluble salts that were believed to have medicinal value, as Monardes tells us.

It is the moste principall remedie that we knowe nowe, and that whiche hath doone best effect, in many that have been poysoned, whiche have taken it as well by Venome taken at the mouthe as by bitinges of venomos wormes, whiche are full of poyson. It doth

Llamas used to transport maize and potatoes to the state warehouses.
From Guaman Poma de Ayala 1936: 1050.

truely a marveilous and a manifest worke, unto them that have
dronke water standying in a stinkyng lake, beyng infected with
beastes or varmentes whiche are full of poyson, and beyng swollen
imediatly after that they had dronke it: by takyng of this stone twoo
or three tymes, they were remedied, as I have seen them after this did
happe, whole and well. (Monardes 1925, 2: 27)

The chaos of a downed empire took its toll of the llama population
as well as of the human one. During Inca rule llamas infected with *ca-
racha* were slaughtered by the state shepherds and buried in an out-of-
the-way place. When this was no longer done, the infection could
spread unchecked, and by 1544 it reached the magnitude of a great ep-
idemic. An estimated two-thirds of the llama flocks died.

Llamas had a major role in Inca ideology as well as gastronomy. A
perfect white llama, decked out with red clothing and gold earrings,
was a symbol of royalty and sometimes preceded the Inca on his prog-
resses. A llama figures in at least one version of the origin myth. Llamas were sacrificed in great numbers, with llamas of specific colors being reserved for specific gods, and llama blood was used for ritual
anointing. Llama bones appear in graves, especially skulls and trotters.
Archaeologists have suggested that the meatier portions were used to
make dried meat, *charqui* (a word derived from the Quechua *cusharqui* and the source of the English word "jerky"), while the less-enticing
bony portions were left for the dead. This tells us more about the modern prejudice in favor of muscle meat than it does about ancient Peruvian eating habits. The Europeans found llama tongues and brains
great delicacies. Perhaps they were delicacies for the Inca as well, not
just useless scraps to be disposed of by pitching them into the nearest
grave.

Because the llamas were so important in Inca culture, their use was
very strictly controlled, at least in theory.

And one should know that, even though there was such a great
quantity [of camelids], it was commanded by the kings that nobody
should dare kill or eat any of them under pain of great punishment.
And if they did break this command they were punished, and with
this fear they did not dare to eat them. (Cieza de León, 1967: 49)

Every five hundred llamas in the state flocks were assigned a shepherd,
and he was accountable for every bit of every one of his charges.

If an animal died, he [the shepherd] was obliged to put the skin in one place and the wool in another, which he had to account for, and all the meat, piece by piece, insides and outsides, he had to salt with the bones; so that when they asked his accounting he could almost reconstruct the llama, taking and showing piece by piece. Thus not a piece of meat or anything else could be eaten by the shepherd or used by him for anything else without it being obvious. (Las Casas, quoted in Antuñez de Mayolo 1981: 63)

The rulers in Cuzco may have had slaughterhouses to provide them with meat, but the plebeians probably had to wait for one of the communal feasts to get a bite. What did it taste like? Antuñez de Mayolo says that the flesh of llamas more than two years old is resinous because of their diet, but the resinous taste disappears if the meat is made into *charqui*. Acosta agrees:

Their meat is good, although resinous, that of the young ones is one of the best and most delicate things you can eat, but they use little for eating, as their main uses are for wool to make clothing and as pack animals. (Acosta 1954: 136)

E. G. Squier, who traveled in Peru in the 1870s, said that the best llama meat was inferior to the worst mule meat.

If llamas were more useful when alive as transport and sources of fiber, and when dead their meat was controlled and distributed by the state, what was available to the humble householder? The answer was guinea pigs (*Cavia porcellus*), known in Peru as *cuy*. Domesticated and widespread by 2000 B.C. in the highlands, their squeaking and rustling still enliven Indian dwellings today. They are fed specially collected wild plants and, because they cannot climb, a simple sill is enough to keep them inside the house. Notorious for quick multiplication, two males and twenty females are said to be able to provide a family with a *cuy* a day.

The Indians eat this little animal with the skin on, only removing the hair as if it were a suckling pig. For them it is a great delicacy, and they cook it whole, gutted, with much chile and smooth pebbles from the river. The stones they call *calapurca,* which in Aymara means "stomach stones," because in this dish they put the stones in the belly of the *cuy*. This dish the Indians consider a greater delicacy than anything the Spaniards can make. (Cobo 1890–1893, 2: 306)

The stones Cobo describes were heated before they were put into the belly of the *cuy*. Roasting and boiling, using heated stones, were important in Andean culinary technology and had other uses as well. During the siege of Cuzco, when the rebelling Inca had a force of Europeans bottled up in the town, the thatched roofs were set on fire by hot stones hurled by the Inca. Putting a few heated pebbles in the body cavity of a *cuy* would have posed no problem. Other recipes for cooking *cuy* suggest stuffing it with mint and *Tagetes minuta*, a Mexican species of New World marigold. In aboriginal times the mint was probably replaced by *muña* (*Minthostachys setosa*) and the Mexican *Tagetes* by any of several Peruvian ones. The entrails of the *cuy* could be cooked in a soup with potatoes or made into a sauce. But even this inoffensive animal aroused the wrath of the Church.

> The usual sacrifice is of *cuys*, which they use to no good end, not only for sacrifices, but also for divining and curing. And if it were possible to get rid of them it would be a good thing, but everybody raises them in their houses, and they even have them in Rome, where I saw them being sold in public, and asking as if I did not know what they were, they told me they were "rabbits of the Indies." (Arriaga 1968: 210)

Fortunately for the hungry inhabitants of Peru, the attempt to get rid of *cuys* altogether was quashed by an early Spanish administrator.

Unfortunately for us there were also other creatures from the New World being raised and eaten in sixteenth-century Rome as "rabbits of the Indies," or *conigli d'India*. Bartolommeo Scappi, who described himself as the "secret cook" of Pope Pius V on the title page of his cookbook, which was published in 1570, gives several recipes for "rabbits of the Indies," mentioning that they are in season from November to March. But as one begins to read his description of the animal doubts begin to gather, and then they become overwhelming. Whatever the creature was (and it may have been an agouti, *Dasyprocta mexicana*, an animal from Mesoamerica which makes such delicious eating that it is reputed to have been served Queen Elizabeth II when she visited Belize), it certainly was not a guinea pig. Scappi says that it had a pointed muzzle, and there is a contemporary drawing by the natural history artist Jacopo Ligozzi labeled *coniglio d'India* and identified as an agouti picturing this eminently non–guinea pig characteristic. Another warning to culinary historians not to jump blithely to conclusions.

Other early sources describe ducks being eaten in Peru, but archaeologists have found no domesticated duck bones in the rubbish they have dug up. Bones of the muscovy duck (*Cairina moschata*) have been found in Ecuador associated with bones of domesticated *cuys* in an archaeological phase that lasted from 100 B.C. to A.D. 800 (Stahl and Norton 1987). It may have been these ducks that figure in one of the very few eyewitness descriptions of actual food by the conquistadors. The gift one of the claimants to the Inca throne sent to the advancing Francisco Pizarro was some dried ducks stuffed with wool. Whether this was elite food, incense, or an implied insult will be discussed later.

There were other edible wild animals and birds. The wild camelids have been discussed, but there were also two species of deer, the whitetail deer (*Odocoileus virginianus*) and the huemul deer (*Hippocamelus antesensis*), as well as an indigenous creature called the *vizcacha* (*Lagidium peruanum*).

> There is another kind of animal called a *vizcacha*, of the size and shape of a hare, except that it has a long tail like a fox, it lives on rock slides and stony places . . . the Indians kill it with lassos; they are good to eat when well hung; and of the skin or fur of these *vizcachas* the Indians make great mantles, as smooth as if they were of silk, and they are very highly prized. (Cieza de León n.d.: 475)

The exploitation of wild animals seems to have been as tightly controlled by the state as the utilization of the domesticated ones. Cieza de León does not mention in the following quotation what happened to the meat of the animals that were culled during these great hunts, but other sources tell us that it went into the ever-ready state warehouses.

> I have been told that the Inca had in this province a royal preserve, where under pain of death no one of the aborigines could enter to kill wild camelids, of which there was a great number, as well as some lions [pumas presumably], bears, foxes, and deer. And when the Inca wished to have a royal hunt, he ordered three or four or ten

or twenty, or however many Indians were needed to be brought together, and they encircled a large portion of that country in such a manner, that little by little they came together so that they could join hands, and in the enclosure they had made there was all the game collected. There it was greatly diverting to see the jumps the guanacos made, and the fearful foxes going from one place to another looking for a way to get out; and a certain number of Indians would go into the enclosure with their slings and sticks and kill and capture as many as the lord desired, because in these hunts they could take ten to fifteen thousand head of camelids, or as many as they wished, because there were so many of them. From the wool of these animals they made the most esteemed fabric, to ornament the temples, and for the service of the Inca and his wives and children. (Cieza de León n.d.: 400)

The sea also provided food, especially dried fish, the mainstay of the Inca army. A glimpse of the variety available is given to us by the excavations of Marcus (1987), though the site is actually slightly earlier than the Inca period. There were three areas to be exploited: the rocky cliffs, the cobble and gravel beach, and the sandy beach with mudflats at the rivermouth. From the first came limpets (genus *Fissurella*), mussels (*Perumytilus, Semimytilus*), chitons (*Acanthopleura, Enoplochiton*), and *chanque* (*Concholepas*), an abalonelike creature. Fish fed on the mollusks, and there were also bird rookeries, penguin nurseries, and sea lions (*Otaria flavescens*). The cobble beach had *robalo* (*Sciaena starksi*), bonito (*Sarda sarda*), dolphins, and more sea lions. The sandy beach provided crustaceans, skates, rays, and small sharks (*Mustelus*), and the mudflats produced mullets (*Mugil*) and sea-catfish (*Galeichthys peruvianus*). The buildings excavated provided a rare glimpse of culinary activity. There were two long hearth trenches for heating rows of pots. There were great storage jars set in the floor, with capacities of 700 to 2,000 liters. The major role of *chicha*, beer made from maize or other things, in Inca social structure will be described later, but this substantiates the chroniclers' tales. There was a room with *cuy* droppings and soiled grass, and another room with bedding for the *cuys*. Finally, there were rooms filled with fine sand, apparently to store the small dried fish the establishment prepared, the sand keeping them dry by hygroscopic action.

Frogs, including the *rana de Junín* (*Batrachophyrynus macro-*

stomus), provided meat in other places. These may be the creatures to which Monardes is referring in his picturesque Elizabethan translation:

> It raineth Todes as great as those of Spaine, the whiche the Indians dooe eate rosted, for thei are a kind of people whiche eate all kinde of venomous beastes. (Monardes 1925, 1: 143)

Mayfly larvae, which develop on the highland lakes during Lent, were also consumed, either raw and alive in great fistfuls or else prepared for storage.

> They also store them to make sauces, prepared in this manner: after being toasted and ground they make them into little loaves . . . which can be stored for a long time. With much chile added these make a sauce which the Indians find a delicacy and very appetizing. It is not badly received by the Spaniards, especially those born in this country, who are called creoles. This sauce is eaten with fish and any other thing, both on ordinary days and Lenten ones. (Cobo 1890–1893, 2: 138–139)

Caterpillars, beetles, and ants were also eaten, but we have no accounts of precisely how.

The preservation of meat, fish, and insects immediately suggests salt. There was plenty of salt available in Peru, both from the sea and from salt springs in the highlands. We know that salt was a highly valued condiment because the simpler stages of fasting and penance consisted of eating without salt or chile. Yet Cobo, considered one of the best sources, even though he was in Peru in the early seventeenth century and did not write his books until the 1650s, denies that it was ever used to preserve meat or fish.

> Even though the Indians thought so highly of salt that the most rigorous fast in the time of their paganism was to abstain from it, however, they used very little in comparison with what we use. There was little enough to put salt in, because even the meat and the fish they dried, to preserve it and take it from one place to another, was without a grain of salt, which they did in this manner: if the meat or fish was to be kept for a short time they roasted it on a *barbacoa*, and this was done by the Yunca Indians of the hot country [Ama-

zonia], but those of Peru, to store things for short or long time alike, dried their meat and fish in the sun on the sea coast and by freezing it in the highlands. Even the stews and pottages they ate were not always seasoned with salt. Instead, when they ate, they would put a lump of salt next to the dish, and that was the salt cellar, and when they ate they would lick it, giving the palate a taste of salt rather than the pottage. Sometimes, when many were eating together, and there was only one lump of salt, they would pass it from hand to hand, licking it one after another. (Cobo 1890–1893, 1: 238–239)

Although this sounds very convincing and has been accepted by many modern scholars, there are many other sources which speak of fish dried and fish salted, as if both things existed. One of them is Bartolomé de las Casas, who compiled his material in the first half of the sixteenth century but worked in Mexico and never went to Peru himself.

They ordered built on high mountains and suitable places . . . many large attached houses in rows, and they were warehouses for all the goods of the empire, excluding nothing. Some were full of maize . . . beans, lima beans, potatoes, sweet potatoes, jicamas, all good edible roots, as well as others. There were warehouses for salt, dried meat cured in the sun without salt, salt meat, salt fish, sun-dried fish without salt, and other dried meats; the greatest provision and abundance of food that could be had in the empire, and this was found all over the empire. (Las Casas 1958: 228)

The Tibetans, who live in a very similar high mountain environment, use the same technique of freeze-drying meat and then eat it without further cooking, exactly as the Europeans saw the Inca doing. Whether or not salt was used for preservation as well as a condiment, it was not the only inorganic substance eaten. There were also two edible clays.

Pasa is what the Indians of Peru call a certain clay, which is white with a few brown spots like soap . . . it is used by them as a highly prized sauce, with which, dissolved and with salt, they eat their *papas* and other roots, moistening them in this mud as if it were mustard, and for this reason it is sold in the plazas of all the towns. (Cobo 1890–1893, 1: 243)

An Indian girl, young and pretty, was going from Cuzco to Copa-
cabana, for religious purposes, in the company of others. She was so
devout, and so poor, that she was going barefoot, and eating a kind
of white earth called *chaco*. (Calancha 1972, 1: 599)

So much for the animals and the minerals. The third kingdom, the vegetables, merits separate treatment.

The Inca: Vegetable

Turning from the animals and minerals, we come to the vegetable kingdom and deal first with the goosefoot or pigweed family, Chenopodiaceae, which has several domesticated members in the New World.

Chenopodium ambrosioides was called *epazote* in Mexico and *paiko* in Peru. It appears to have been used for flavoring in both places.

Thei sente me an Hearbe that in Peru thei call Payco, thei be certaine leaves . . . and as thei come drie thei are verie thinne: and beyng tasted, thei have a notable bightyng, that thereby thei seeme to bee very hotte. (Monardes 1925, 2: 13)

Several species of *Chenopodium* were grown for their seeds in Peru and provided edible leaves for greens as well. *Chenopodium pallidicaule* (*cañihua*) is an extremely-high-altitude semidomesticated plant in Peru, where it grows at an altitude of up to 3,600 meters in the Andes. More important is *Chenopodium quinoa*, or *quinoa*, also a plant of high altitudes, although it cannot survive at the heights reached by *cañihua*. The seeds of the cultivated *quinoa* may be whitish, red, bicolor, or yellow; the seeds of the wild varieties are always dark. The seeds are covered with varying amounts of bitter saponins, which must be washed off before preparation.

Second place [after maize] among the crops which grow above the earth goes to that which is called *quinoa*, and in Spanish "millet" or "small rice," because the seeds and the color are somewhat similar. The plant which bears the seeds resembles pigweed, both in its growth and the leaf and the flowering spike, which is where the seeds are borne. The tender leaves are eaten by the Indians and the Spaniards in their stews, because they taste good and they are very healthful. The seeds are eaten in soups, cooked in many different ways. The Indians make a drink from *quinoa* as they do from maize, but that is only in regions where they lack maize. (Garcilaso de la Vega 1945, 2: 178)

Besides entering into gruels and soups and stews, *quinoa* seeds were also toasted and ground and made into various forms of bread or mixed with condiments, fat, and salt and the resulting balls steamed. The seeds of *cañihua* were treated in the same way.

Another high-altitude plant used for seeds and leaves was a lupine (*Lupinus mutabilis*), *tarwi* or *chocho*. It is a totally different plant from the *chocho* of the Caribbean (which is *Sechium edule*), thus proving once again the treachery of common names. The seeds of other species of lupines were eaten in the Old World, but the eating of lupine leaves seems to have been confined to cattle in the Old World. The seeds are beanlike and high in protein, which is not surprising because lupines, peas, and beans all belong to the family Leguminosae. Peruvian lupine seeds have to be boiled and then soaked for several days to get rid of their bitterness. Improperly treated they are poisonous. The water they are boiled in is a useful insecticide. Once processed, the seeds are recorded as having been eaten with chile and onions. There are no *Allium* species in South America, but there is another bulbous plant, *Nothoscordium andicola*, now classed as belonging to the family Alliaceae if not the genus *Allium*, which is described as tasting like an insipid garlic and possibly was used in ancient times.

A mountain climate means frost and hail and storms, against which desirable domesticated plants should be able to protect themselves and the investment of time and effort made by their growers. Root crops provide the remedy to these conditions, and among them the potato is preeminent.

The potato (*Solanum tuberosum*) was domesticated in the highlands of Peru between 3700 and 3000 B.C. Travelers visiting Peruvian markets today see a range of potato varieties undreamed of in their homelands. The tastes and textures vary as much as the looks, and Peruvians consider our commercial potatoes watery, insipid, and boring.

Although always a major foodstuff, the potato seems to have suffered ideological downgrading in Peru. We have archaeological evidence for the Inca resettling conquered tribes off their potato-growing heights into the maize-growing valleys. Despite the fact that the Inca were of highland origin themselves, they consistently exalted maize and ignored what must have been their ancestral staple, the potato. The fact that maize was the principal ingredient in *chicha,* the beer which was a vital ingredient in Inca social exchanges, may well explain their emphasis.

The most important highland root crop, after the many varieties of potato, is *oca* (*Oxalis tuberosa*). It is a member of a family, found in both the Old World and the New, which provides us with many weeds and some houseplants. The leaves and young shoots of *oca* are edible but sour, from the acid that gives it its generic name. The tubers are the most important part of the crop, and they may be white, yellow, or reddish. Like many other Peruvian roots they come in two classes: the sweet, which may be eaten raw, cooked, or sun-dried and made into *caui,* which is described as tasting like dried figs and was used as a sweetener before cane sugar was available; and the bitter, which is freeze-dried and made into a storable product called *ckaya. Ckaya* contains more protein, niacin, and minerals than *chuño,* which is made of bitter potatoes treated in the same fashion. *Oca,* any other root crop, and even maize can be fermented into a product called *tokush,* which is said to smell like vomit and not taste very good either.

Another tuber is provided by a familiar family of decorative plants that usually goes unmentioned when New World domesticates are listed. Perhaps the terminological tangle is the reason for this silence. The edible watercress, a plant of European origin, now carries the Latin name of *Rorippa nasturtium-aquaticum.* An obsolete name is *Nasturtium officinale.* What are popularly called nasturtiums belong to the genus *Tropaeolum,* which is of South American origin. The flowers and leaves of some species were eaten, and Cobo describes using the flowers in salads, as is done today (Cobo 1890–1893, 1: 398). He does not mention the dodge of making imitation capers by pickling the buds. Linnaeus named the genus *Tropaeolum* from the Greek word for a trophy, the victors' display of the weapons of the vanquished. To Linnaeus the round leaves of the nasturtium, with their central stem, looked like shields, and the red-streaked yellow flowers resembled blood-stained golden helmets. It is not the leaves or the flowers of *Tropaeolum tuberosum, mashua* or *añu* in Quechua and *is-*

año in Aymara, the other major highland language, that are eaten, but the tubers. The plant is said to be very drought resistant, and according to Vilmorin, the prominent French seed firm which attempted to introduce many exotic crops, including *oca, mashua,* and *ullucu,* into nineteenth-century France, the tubers are not affected by frost as long as they stay in the ground (Vilmorin-Andrieux 1885).

> Chewed raw, *isaño,* which is the root of the plant, is somewhat bitter. It is very sharp, and so bites the tongue that it is impossible to eat it, however, cooked, it becomes sweet. (Cobo 1890–1893, 1: 367)

> When boiled like carrots or potatoes, the tubers are watery and have a rather unpleasant taste, although the perfume is agreeable. In Bolivia, where the plant is extensively cultivated in high mountain districts, the people freeze the tubers after boiling them, and they are then considered a delicacy and are largely consumed. In other places they are eaten in a half-dried state, after having been hung up in nets and exposed to the air for some time. It is, therefore, not surprising that the quality of the fresh tuber appears to us to be very indifferent, since, even in its native country, it is not eaten until it has undergone special preparation. (Vilmorin-Andrieux 1885: 354)

The tubers had a reputation for being anaphrodisiac, while the *oca* was believed to be an aphrodisiac. After the conquest this became rather a joke, but the Inca apparently took these qualities of *isaño* or *añu* seriously:

> This root has the quality of suppressing the venereal appetite according to the Indians. They claim that the Inca kings of Peru carried loads of this food as supplies for their army, so that when the soldiers ate it, they would forget their wives. (Cobo 1890–1893, 1: 367)

The last of the three high mountain tubers which Vilmorin-Andrieux tried unsuccessfully to introduce into Europe was the *ullucu* (*Ullucus tuberosus*). This is related to New Zealand spinach, both plants being members of the Basellaceae. It is described as an insipid starchy root and apparently never did well in Europe. Cobo (1890–1893, 1: 368) says it comes in the same colors as *oca* and resembles it, and he calls it gluey. In its native country it was freeze-dried or fermented and could be cooked with dried meat or made into a soup with potatoes.

Vilmorin-Andrieux (1885) missed two other high-altitude roots, *maka (Lepidium mayenii)* and *llakhum (Polymnia sonchifolia)*. The former belongs to the same genus as the common European cress (*Lepidium sativum*), which is not to be confused with the watercress which we have just discussed. It was capable of producing a crop of roots in the highest and coldest parts of the Andes, but today it is only cultivated in the Junín highlands. The *llakhum* or *yacon* Cobo describes as follows:

> Each plant gives three to six, and sometimes more, roots, which are the size of middling turnips, although they do not come to a point like turnips. They are sweet and watery, earth-color outside and white inside, and tender like a turnip. They are eaten raw like a fruit and taste very good. They are even better if they are dried in the sun . . . They are a marvelous thing for sea voyages, because they keep a long time. I have seen them taken on the sea and lasting more than twenty days, and because they are so juicy they get sweeter and are very refreshing when it is hot. (Cobo 1890–1893, 1: 365–366)

This catalog of roots should not be taken to mean that greens were neglected. Indeed, there were so many that earlier writers despaired of ever being able to catalog them all.

> It is difficult to list all the greens, because there are so many of them and they are so small. It is enough to say that the Indians eat all of them, the sweet and the bitter alike. Some of them are eaten raw, as we eat lettuces and radishes, some of them cooked in soups and stews. They are the food of the common people who did not have an abundance of meat as the rulers did. The bitter greens . . . are cooked in two or three waters and dried in the sun and stored for the winter time when greens are not available. Such is the diligence that they apply to finding and preserving greens to eat that they do not overlook anything, even the algae and water worms that live in the rivers and gullies are gathered and prepared for their food. (Garcilaso de la Vega 1945, 2: 189)

There were also starchy roots on the coast. One, *raqacha* or *arracacha (Arracacia xanthorrhiza)*, was described by the Europeans as a purplish carrot, reasonably enough, as they are kin, both being Umbellifers. The Royal Horticultural Society *Dictionary of Gardening* (Chittenden 1974, 1: 181) says that they are to be used in the same way as potatoes and that they are "very palatable and easily digested." Another is the fleshy rhizome of *Canna edulis* and therefore a close relative of the cannas which used to be planted in flower beds in front of railroad stations, in the days when we had flower beds and railroad stations.

> The tuberous rhizomes contain starch, and when they are roasted in an earth oven . . . produce an edible substance with a sweet taste. In Cuzco, during the religious festival called Corpus, which by order of the viceroy Toledo replaced the ancient festival of *R'aimi,* according to a traditional custom they consume a lot of this rhizome cooked, as it is a specialty of the season. (Yacovleff and Herrera 1934–1935: 312)

The fact that *achira,* which is the native name, does not grow above 2,000 meters and had therefore to be carted up to Cuzco to be a major part of a festival that replaced one of the most important pre-Columbian ones suggests that it enjoyed some special importance in earlier times.

The mention of edible algae a few paragraphs back leads us to another resource that was fully exploited. Seaweeds were harvested and eaten fresh on the coast or dried into sheets or blocks and traded into the highlands. This *cochayuyo* consisted of many different genera: *Porphyra* in the south of Peru, *Gigartina, Ulva lactuca, Durvillea antarctica,* and others in the north. Fresh-water algae were also consumed, blue-green algae of the genus *Nostoc* being eaten raw or processed for storage. In postconquest times *Nostoc* was made into a dessert by being boiled with sugar.

Among the fruit trees which were used in Peru was the pepper tree (*Schinus molle*), a common street tree with drooping branches and small leaves which is planted in southern California. This pungent-smelling tree produces the pink peppercorns that were recently in vogue but were subsequently found to be carcinogenic, or at least potentially harmful.

> Among these fruits we may include that of the tree called *mulli,* which grows wild in the countryside. It produces long narrow

bunches of fruit in the form of red berries the size of dry coriander seeds. The leaves are small and evergreen. When ripe the outside of the berry is sweet and soft and very tasty, but the rest is very bitter. A beverage is prepared from these berries by gently rubbing them with the hands in hot water until all the sweetness has been extracted: care must be taken not to get the bitter part or the drink is spoiled. The liquid is strained and kept for three or four days until it is ready. It makes a delightful drink, being full of flavor and very wholesome . . . If mixed with the maize beverage the latter is improved and made more appetizing. If the water is boiled until it thickens a very pleasant syrup is left. The liquid, if placed in the sun with the addition of something or other, becomes sour and provides a splendid vinegar . . . The tender branches make excellent toothpicks. (Garcilaso de la Vega 1945, 2: 182)

The author of this description does not tell us whether the beverages had time to become lightly fermented or not, but a superior *chicha,* a beerlike fermented drink, was among the products made from the *molle,* as the pepper tree is now known in its native country.

It produces a little red fruit in racemes like the willow of which the Indians make *chicha,* and it is so strong that it makes one drunk more than that which is made of maize and other seeds, and the Indians consider it more valuable and a delicacy. (Cobo 1890–1893, 2: 84–85)

Passion fruit (*Passiflora* spp.) are another New World domesticate, although there are also a few species native to the Pacific area. Most of them are vines that are cultivated for their aromatic fruit, which vary in size from that of peas to that of medium melons. The name does not come from any property of the fruit but because the complex flowers seemed to the early explorers to contain the symbols of the passion of Christ. Cobo (1890–1893, 1: 457) says that in the flower we can find the lashes Christ received, the crown of thorns, the column, the five wounds, and the three nails. He found the fruits of some species sour, others delicate, and one that could be eaten skin and all. He poked fun at the Spanish name *granadilla,* "little pomegranate," saying the similarity was very slight indeed. Actually the resemblance is not as far-fetched as he seems to think, because both fruit contain a mass of crunchy seeds surrounded by a more or less juicy covering.

The *paqay* (*Inga feuillei*) figures in the eyewitness description of the conquest of Peru by Pedro Pizarro, a much younger half-brother of the leader of the enterprise, Francisco Pizarro. It is a confusing fruit because it is also called *guaba,* but it is not the same as the guava (*Psidium guajava*). Nor is it the same thing as the Mexican *pacaya* (*Chamaedorea* spp.), the bitter but edible flowerbuds of a palm. Pedro Pizarro, writing long after the event, tells us how an Indian, who they thought was named Apoo, though that was actually his title rather than his name, showed up with a basket of these fruit to offer the Europeans while they were marching toward the place that later became Cajamarca. He presented the fruit to Hernando Pizarro, another of the brothers, and was knocked down and kicked for his pains. Understandably, when he returned to Atahualpa, one of the two claimants to supreme power in the civil war then going on, he described the invaders as "a pack of bearded thieves who had come out of the sea" (Pizarro 1978: 28). The fruit itself is portrayed by Cobo:

> These pods are two or three fingers wide and one finger thick, the skin is tough and leathery, it is green outside. Inside there is a row of seeds as big as broad beans [European *Vicia faba*], each covered with a white spongy, sweet substance, which is rather similar to cotton dipped in syrup . . . This fruit is more of a snack than a thing of substance, because even if a man eats a basketful of *pacaes,* he is neither satisfied nor surfeited. (Cobo 1890–1893, 2: 45)

Another fruit, the *rukma* or *lucuma* (*Lucuma bifera*), seems to have been cultivated enough to have developed superior varieties. However, once a superior tree was identified, there was no way that it could have been propagated, because the sources are unanimous in saying that the practice of grafting was unknown in the New World. The seeds of a selected tree, if cross-fertilized, would give an assortment of progeny, none of them genetically identical with their desirable parent.

> The fruit is the size of a medium pomegranate, round with a point on the upper part; it has a thin and tender skin so that it can be eaten without peeling, and even when it is ripe the skin is between green and yellow in color. The pit is very similar in smoothness, size, and aspect to a chestnut, even though the shell is harder than that of a chestnut. The meat inside is similar to a chestnut also, and may be eaten roasted, but it is not usually eaten because it is insipid. The

flesh of the *lucuma* is very yellow, hard, and not juicy, and some-what hard to swallow, and not of a very good taste, which is why the fruit is not highly thought of. There are some large *lucumas,* larger than quinces, somewhat tapered, somewhat darker outside and juicier inside. (Cobo 1890–1893, 2: 23–24)

The fruit which obtained the highest praise were the almonds of Chachapoyas (*Caryocar amygdaliferum*). They were luxury goods long before the arrival of the Europeans, appearing in early tombs on the coast.

Inside the spiny husk there is a seed three times larger than common almonds, very white, tender, juicy, and smooth. These fruit are the most delicate, tasty, and healthy which I have eaten in the Indies. They are sent, as a very valuable thing, from the province of Cha-chapoyas to the city of Lima, and candied there is not a delicacy that can compare with them.

Where this fruit, so worthy of appreciation, grows, there are many bats which destroy it, because before the husks get hard they eat the heart without detaching the fruit from the tree, so that many times when it is time to harvest them one can find only the empty husks. It is a great shame to think of such soft and delicate fruit, worthy of being enjoyed in the courts of the greatest princes, re-maining hidden in deserted mountains, sustenance for such vile ani-mals as bats. (Cobo 1890–1893, 2: 61–62)

The last fruit we will have the sources describe, although there are many more, is the *pepino, kachun* in Quechua and *Solanum murica-tum* in Latin. It has recently appeared in the exotic fruit sections of the supermarkets.

This is a very well known fruit in Peru, which the Spaniards call *pe-pino de la tierra* [native cucumber]; the plant is similar in size and character to that of the eggplant . . . The fruit does not resemble a cucumber in the slightest, unless it be a little bit in size and structure, and therefore I do not know what led the Spaniards to call it *pepino de las Indias,* except that perhaps they could not find another fruit in Spain that resembled it more closely . . . Truly there is a great variety among *pepinos,* they differ in size, shape, and color, some are bigger than others, some egg-shaped, some round, and some elongated;

some are reddish, others white, yellow, and other colors; but the
most common are reddish with stripes of another color, or the same
color but darker, along their sides. The skin is a very thin but tough
membrane, leathery and peppery, so that it is not usually eaten without peeling, although the fruit may be eaten with the skin as one eats
an apple. The flesh is yellow, very watery and sweet . . . It is a very
tasty and fragrant fruit, and suitable to refresh oneself during the
hot weather, in place of a drink of water; but it is not a delicate fruit
that would be esteemed by pampered folk, because it is considered
indigestible, for which reason it is not recommended for those with
weak stomachs.

The best *pepinos* grow in the valleys on the coast of Peru. The valleys of Trujillo, Ica, and Chincha are especially famous for them, because they like heat and sandy soil. They have been taken to Mexico, but they do not do well there, because the climate does not suit
them. I saw them in the convent of Carmen in the Atrisco valley, and
proved to myself that they were tasteless, and without the sweetness
which they have in this kingdom. (Cobo 1890–1893, 1: 381–383)

Cobo was not the only person to properly appreciate the *pepinos*
that grew in the coastal valleys. The last undisputed Inca emperor,
Huaina Capac, traveling along that coast shortly before his death from
a pestilence, probably smallpox introduced by the Spaniards but out-
running them, also savored their sweetness.

And they say of him, that traveling in the beautiful valley of the
Chayanta, near Chimu, where the city of Trujillo now stands, there
was an old Indian in a field, who having heard that the emperor was
passing near by, picked three or four *pepinos* from his field, and
took them, and told the emperor "Ancha atunapu micucampa,"
which means "Great lord, eat these." And before the lords and other
people he took the *pepinos,* and eating one of them, said, in front of
everybody, to please the old man, "Xuylluy, mizqui cay," which in
our tongue means "They really are very sweet, aren't they," which
pleased everybody very much. (Cieza de León 1967: 222)

EL OИ3EИOÍИGA GVAIИACAPAC

Reyno chacha ciccho guanca   poya qui bilca cayan   to. Cataconga bi canari- guayna

Huaina Capac.
From Guaman Poma de Ayala 1936: 112.

The Inca

Who was Huaina Capac? He was the ruler of a kingdom which stretched from northern Chile, Argentina, and Bolivia, through Peru, and north into Ecuador. He was at the apex of a hierarchy that was supported by a complex system of tributes and warehouses, all meticulously recorded on *quipus,* great clusters of knotted cords. Much ink has been expended on discussions of whether the Inca state was or was not "socialist." If a New World civilization can be forced into European categories, it would seem to be more like an empire of accountants. Among the first things that Atahualpa, one of the sons of Huaina Capac who was fighting for the right to wear the royal insignia, said to the Europeans was "We know what you have taken, and where you took it from, and you had better give it all back immediately." Thirty years after the conquest it was said that it was still possible to account for every grain of maize consumed by the armies of Huaina Capac during his campaigns.

Huaina Capac was a descendant of the sun and of the first Inca, Manco Capac, who emerged from a cave, or perhaps on an island in Lake Titicaca, depending on the version of the Inca origin myth you read.

> The first brother was called Manco Capac, and his wife was called Mama Ocllo. They say that he founded the city and called it Cuzco, which in their language means navel, and conquered those nations and taught them to be human, and all the Inca descend from him. The second brother was called Ayar Cachi, the third was called Ayar

Uchu, and the fourth was called Ayar Sauca. The word *ayar* has no meaning in the common language of Peru, it must have had a meaning in the special language of the Inca. The other words are from the common language, *cachi* means salt, that which we eat, *uchu* is the condiment which they put in their stews, which the Spaniards call *pimiento*, the Indians of Peru had no other spices. The other word, *sauca*, means joy, content, and happiness. (Garcilaso de la Vega 1945, 1: 46–47)

This passage is further explained as the salt standing for the teaching of the Inca, the *pimiento* (chile) as the taste they got from it, and the happiness as how they lived ever after.

Although these accounts should be read more as fairy tales than as narratives of historical fact, we do have a passage about the food of the first *coya*, the sister and wife of Manco Capac, and her successors.

Her daily food was usually maize either as *locros anca* [stew], or *mote* [boiled maize grains], mixed in various manners with other foods, cooked or otherwise prepared. For us these are coarse and uncouth foods, but for them they were as excellent and savory as the softest and most delicate dishes put on the tables of the rulers and monarchs of our Europe. Her drink was a very delicate *chicha*, which among them was as highly esteemed as the fine vintage wines of Spain. There were a thousand ways of making this *chicha* . . . and the maidens of her household took great pains with it. (Murua 1962: 29)

The third *coya* is said by Guaman Poma de Ayala to have eaten raw maize and *ciclla yuyo*, an edible herb. However, Murua gives her credit for a more expansive way of life:

She was very fond of banquets and fiestas, and often invited the principal lords of Cuzco . . . giving them splendid food and abundant drink, and they could take home everything they had not eaten. (Murua 1962: 33)

The wife of the fourth Inca had a particular interest in horticulture:

And to sow her fields she chose many special women who took the greatest care of the fields of the finest maize and all sorts of chile, of which the most esteemed and the best was called *asnac uchu,* meaning fragrant chile. She had a great number of fruit trees, such as *tunas* [cactus fruit], *guabas, plátanos* [plantains], *pacayes,* and all the other kinds and varieties that grow in these provinces. (Murua 1962: 36)

The author is mistaken when he includes plantains in the inventory of this garden. Many early European chroniclers thought that bananas and plantains (*Musa* spp.) were native to the New World. This has been endlessly repeated by later authors, but although *Musa* species spread far and fast in the New World, they came to the Americas with the Europeans from the Canary Islands and ultimately from New Guinea.

The fifth *coya:*
She bathed twice each day, and always ate alone. The table was carved, and three or four feet long, the tablecloth and napkins were colored. (Murua 1962: 38)

The wife of the sixth Inca had a thousand Indians as attendants, all of whom ate from the royal storehouse. She also had a thousand, or some say three thousand, waiting women, who presumably also ate from the inexhaustible granaries. It was either her son or the son of the sixth Inca by some other wife who conquered the eastern slope of the Andes and brought back *coca* (*Erythroxylum coca*). While not a foodstuff strictly speaking, *coca* was of such importance in Inca culture that it is worth a few words. Originally its use was restricted to the nobility for religious purposes, including funerary offerings. The leaf is described by Cobo as like a lemon leaf, and after a complicated curing process, a wad of it was put in the mouth, with a bit of lime from burned limestone or seashells. The leaves were not chewed, but the juice was swallowed. Oddly, Pedro Pizarro was told by two high-ranking Inca that it did not have the effect it was claimed to have:

. . . while they made others gather *coca,* which is an herb they carry in their mouths, which they prize highly, and use for their sacrifices and idolatries, and this *coca* does not keep them from thirst, or hunger, or exhaustion, even though they say it does. So I was told by Atahualpa and Manco Inca. (Pedro Pizarro 1978: 96)

Dr. Abraham Cowley, a seventeenth-century English poet engaged in the integration of New World plants into Old World mythology, was convinced of its invigorating qualities, whether or not he ever used the plant or even laid eyes on it.

> Mov'd with his Country's coming Fate (whose Soil
> Must for her Treasures be exposed to spoil)
> Our Varicocha first this Coca sent,
> Endow'd with leaves of wond'rous Nourishment,
> Whose Juice Succ'd in, and to the Stomach tak'n
> Long Hunger and long Labour can sustain;
> From which our faint and weary bodies find
> More Succor, more they cheer the drooping Mind,
> Than can your Bacchus and your Ceres join'd.
>
>   * * *
>
> Nor Coca only useful art at Home,
> A famous Merchandize thou art become;
> A thousand Paci and Vicugni groan
> Yearly beneath thy Loads, and for thy sake alone
> The spacious World's to us by Commerce Known. (Cowley in Mortimer 1901: 26–27)

Today *coca* is still involved in commerce throughout the "spacious world," but it is in the unfortunate form of cocaine. That *coca* was not altogether benevolent even as used aboriginally is substantiated by the description of the eighth *coya:*

> She ate many dishes, and was also addicted to *coca, coca* was a vice with her, while she slept she had it in her mouth. (Guaman Poma de Ayala 1980, 1: 113)

One of the several Inca Yupanquis, presumably her father and father-in-law, is said to have founded the system of warehouses and established the redistribution network of the Inca state.

> He ordered that all the lords and chiefs who were there would meet in his house on a certain day, and when they had come together as he had ordered, and being in his house, he told them that it was necessary that there be in the city of Cuzco warehouses of all the foodstuffs: maize, chile, beans, *tarwi, chichas, quinoa,* and dried meat,

and all the other provisions and preserved foods that they have, and
therefore it was necessary that he order them to bring them from
their lands. And then Inca Yupanqui showed them certain slopes
and mountainsides around the city of Cuzco and visible from it and
ordered them to build granaries there, so that when the food was
brought there would be somewhere to put it. And the lords went to
the sites that the Inca showed them, and got to work, and built the
granaries. And it took them five years to build them and divide the
lands, because there were so many granaries to build, as was ordered by Inca Yupanqui, so that they would hold much food, and
there would be no lack of them. And with that supply of food he
wanted to build the city of Cuzco of masonry and shore up the gul-
lies surrounding it, and he thought that having supplies in such
quantity that they would never lack, he could put as many men as he
wished to building and rebuilding the public buildings and the
houses. (Betanzos 1968: 35)

Once the granaries were built and stocked the distributions could
begin.

And he had divided among them maize, and dry meat, and dry fish,
and llamas . . . and dishes to use, and everything else he thought necessary for their housekeeping. And he commanded that every four
days they give and share out among everybody in Cuzco what each
one needed of food and provisions . . . ordering that the food and
provisions be taken out of the granaries and put on the plaza of the
city in great heaps . . . and that from there they be divided by measure and number and reason, giving each what he needed . . . and
thus from the time of Inca Yupanqui this foresight and beneficence
continued until the Indians were subjugated by the Spaniards, with
whose arrival all this ceased and was lost. (Betanzos 1968: 40)

Inca laws commanded not only storage and distribution but what
should be grown, what should be eaten, and how it should be treated.

We command that there be an abundance of food throughout the
kingdom, and that they plant very much maize, potatoes, and *ocas;*
and make *caui, kaya, chuño,* and *tamos* [different preserved roots],
and *chochoca* [maize lightly boiled and sun-dried]; and *quinoa, ulluco,* and *masua* [*Chenopodium quinoa, Ullucus tuberosus,* and

Auditing the accounts at the state warehouses.
From Guaman Poma de Ayala 1936: 335.

Tropaeolum tuberosum, respectively]. That they dry all the foods including *yuyos* [greens] so that there will be food to eat all year round, and that they plant communally . . . maize, potatoes, chile, *magno* [greens to dry] . . . Let them make up the accounts each year, if this is not done the *tocricoc* [royal official] will be cruelly punished in this kingdom.

We command that nobody spill maize, or other foods, or potatoes, nor peel them, because if they had understanding they would weep while being peeled, therefore do not peel them, on pain of punishment. (Guaman Poma de Ayala 1980, 1: 164)

That they observe the fields to see which plant or seed does the best, and plant nothing but the best seed there, without mixing it with others; here grains, there beans, here cotton, there chiles, here roots, and there fruits, and this way for all the rest. (Anon. 1968: 178)

They did not have the right to eat whatever they wanted but what the Inca felt they should eat. (Cobo 1979: 240)

This system of collection and distribution greatly impressed at least some of the Europeans.

No thinking man there can be that does not admire such an admirable and provident government, because being neither religious, nor Christian, the Indians in their own manner reached this high perfection, having nothing of their own, yet providing everything necessary to everybody, and sustaining so generously the things of religion, and those of their lord and master. (Acosta 1954: 196)

Mythological history credits the ninth Inca, Pachacuti, with instituting banquets as part of the redistribution system. The archaeological evidence for them exists, although the process was probably not simple and straightforward. When Thompson and Morris (1985) investigated the ruins of Huánuco Pampa, they found that the large structures around the main square were not, as they had thought, to house Inca bureaucrats. They were full of cooking debris because they were places to prepare, serve, and in case of bad weather consume the redistribution banquets Pachacuti is supposed to have started.

This lord introduced another laudable custom, which resembles the simplicity of the ancients. This was that everybody should eat in the plazas, and as the originator of the custom he was the one that most used it. As the sun rose he emerged from his palace and went to the plaza: if it was cold they made a great fire, and if it rained there was a great house suitable to the settlement that they were in. After a brief time for chatting, and as the usual meal hour approached, the wives of all who were there came with their food in their little jars, already cooked, and a little container of wine on their backs, and if the lord was there they began with serving him, and then they served the rest. Each one was served and given to eat by his wife, and the lord the same, even if he was the Inca himself, who was served by the queen, his principal wife, with the first dishes and the first drinks, the rest of the serving was done by the male and female servants. Each woman sat back to back with her husband, she served him all the rest, and then starting with the first dish she ate of what she had brought in her separate place, being, as I have said, back to back.

One invited the other to share what he had, and got up to serve him with it, drink as well as food. They never drank until they had finished eating. They invited each other to drink, each inviting his friend, and if someone invited the lord to drink, the lord took it from his hand and drank with good will.

With the meal finished, if it was a fiesta day they sang and danced and spent the whole day amusing themselves, but if it was a working day they all went off to their place of work.

They did this every day for their morning meal, which was the main meal. At night each dined in his house on what he had, and they never ate more than twice a day, and the morning meal was the main one.

They all ate on the ground seated on some mats, and they ate a diversity of dishes, all with chile, green or red; and just a bit of everything, because all of what they prepared for their meals was almost nothing. Nobody had to watch other people eating who had nothing himself, because as I have said, nowhere in the world do they share so with those who have not, and they say that we Christians are bad people because we eat alone and invite nobody, and they laugh at us when we offer to invite someone, saying that they invite in truth and in deed, not just words. They, even if they have nothing but a grain of maize, must share willingly, sometimes forcing those who refuse, when they see that they have little, to take it. (Las Casas 1958: 667–668)

There are other accounts which give slightly different pictures of these meals, but they remain a means of redistributing the contents of the warehouses.

They had sumptuary laws, which forbade luxury in everyday dress, and expensive things like gold, silver, and precious stones, and completely did away with excess in banquets and meals. And it was ordered that two or three times a month the inhabitants of each settlement should eat in the presence of their chiefs, and perform military or secular games, to reconcile enmities and keep the peace, and so that herdsmen and other workers in the fields would be encouraged and supported. The law on what they called the poor ordered that the blind, mute, crippled, maimed, decrepit old men and women, the chronically ill, and all others who could not work the soil for their food and clothing be fed from the public storehouses. There was also a law that commanded that the same public storehouses provide for guests. The foreigners, the pilgrims, and the travelers, for all these there were public accommodations which we call *corpahuaci,* which means inn, where they were given all that was necessary and did not have to pay anything. (Blas Valera in Porras Barrenechea 1986: 466)

The tenth Inca was Topa Inca:

In the morning he ate, and from midday into the afternoon he held audiences, surrounded by his guard, with those who wished to speak to him. The rest of the time, into the night, he spent drinking, and then supped by the light of wood fires, because they used neither fat nor wax [for lighting], although they had plenty of both. (Cieza de León 1967: 192)

Topa Inca is supposed to have started the system of *chasquis,* the post houses and messengers which, combined with the excellence of the Inca roads and bridges, gave them a system of communication unrivaled in the New World. Unfortunately many authors think that this system was in use all over the New World, so we get many references to runners providing Motecuhzoma with ocean-fresh fish in his capital of Tenochtitlan, whereas the ruler actually being provided with fresh fish was the Inca in Cuzco, thousands of miles and a continent away.

This kind of mail, which in Peru are called *chasquis,* are certain Indians put on the road by order of the neighboring towns, as far apart as three crossbow shots, more or less, depending on the character of the country. The chiefs were obliged, under threat of the most severe punishment, to support them in these places, changing from month to month, or as they saw fit. There were two of them in huts or shelters erected for their use, ready to go at any time, and the news they had to carry or the message they had to take went from mouth to mouth, so that when one of the *chasquis* was close enough so that the other could hear his voice, he began to repeat his message, and the other learned it so carefully that not one word or syllable or letter was forgotten, and when the runner arrived the other had learned the message, and the newly informed ran until he came to the next station and repeated the process, and so on and on, and in this manner it was admirable how quickly news traveled two and three hundred leagues, and not only news was carried in this fashion but presents and important tributes. (Cabello Valboa 1951: 424–425)

And when the Inca wished to eat fish fresh from the sea, and as it was seventy or eighty leagues from the coast to Cuzco . . . they were brought alive and twitching, which seems incredible over such a long distance over such rough and craggy roads, and they ran on foot and not on horseback, because they never had horses until the Spaniards came to this country. (Murua 1962, 2: 47)

The runners were specially selected and trained, and Murua claims that in training they were fed only *hamca,* toasted maize, once a day and allowed to drink once a day. On the job, however, their supplies included water, maize, chile, *charqui,* "partridges," *cuys,* and *chicha,* with fruit if available from nearby valleys—*guabas,* avocados, *pacayes,* and passion fruit.

The eleventh *coya* "believed in working every day, daily she fed two hundred poor people . . . and she also fed the lords and princes, five hundred men of this kingdom" (Guaman Poma de Ayala 1980, 1: 119). She was the wife of Huaina Capac, the Inca in the episode of the old man and the *pepino.* The fact of her working is not unusual. It is said that even the Inca hoed his own garden, in order to set a good example and to show that nobody was so rich that he could afford to insult the poor.

Huaina Capac is on the border of Western recorded history. Toward the end of his reign the Europeans were probing the northern coasts of his dominions. Guaman Poma de Ayala says that one of the two Europeans left behind on the coast during a reconnaissance expedition was brought to Huaina Capac in Quito, and Huaina Capac asked him, presumably in some sort of sign language, what he ate. The European answered, presumably also using signs, that he ate gold and silver. The Huaina Capac of the story should have locked him up for a few weeks with lots of gold and silver but no food or water. Instead he loaded him down with riches, and the European returned to his own country a rich man. Another version of this tale is that while Huaina Capac did indeed wish to see a specimen of the curious beings who had landed on his coast, they were killed before they got to him, to his great displeasure.

The only information we have about his food habits concerns his *chicha* drinking. The word for *chicha* that he would have recognized would have been something like *asua*. The Europeans replaced the Quechua word with the Taino *chicha,* which they had learned in the Antilles.

> The Indians say that he was a great friend of the poor, and ordered that especial care be taken of them in all his dominions. They say he was very affable with his people, yet grave. They say that he drank more than three Indians put together, but nobody ever saw him drunk; and when his captains and great lords asked him how he could drink so much and not get drunk, he said he was drinking for the poor, because he was much concerned with their sustenance. (Pizarro 1978: 49)

Chicha was a major part of Inca life, important in ritual and religion as well as a source of nourishment. However, European writings on the subject must be read with the same sort of caution that one uses with the European sources on Mexican cannibalism. What was the writer trying to prove? Was he justifying the enslavement of the Indians by making them less than human and dwelling on their disgusting and depraved habits? Is the subject under discussion linked to idolatry and therefore to be painted in the darkest colors, because it stands in the way of the triumph of Christianity? Or was the author convinced

"We eat gold."
From Guaman Poma de Ayala 1936: 369.

that the American Indian was the repository of virtues and customs that had abandoned Europe with the end of the golden age? Most of the colonial sources should be treated as advocates of one of these points of view or another, and we must never forget the silent, shadowy figures of the Indians, whose evidence survives filtered through their conquerors and descendants, if at all.

Firstly, drunkenness and intemperance in drinking was a passion with this people, the source of all their ills, and even their idolatry. This vice exempted neither dignity nor status. At the beginning, when they settled in the country, for a long time they had no wine, only cold water, and they say that at that time they had no vices, and were not given to idolatry. Then they tried to find something that was better for them to drink than the water of that country, because, if you look into it, you will see that certain provinces have water so thin that it corrupts, and in others it is so thick that it makes for *vascosidades* and stones. On the coast most of the water you drink is brackish, more or less, and it is usually warm, as the Spaniards there know . . . So to remedy this, and to free themselves from sickness, they invented wine made from maize, which if it is pure refreshes the digestive system and the liver . . . The doctors ordered that for the wine to have the desirable effect of flushing the bladder and dissolving stones, the maize should be mixed with human saliva, which is very medicinal. From this came the chewing of maize by children and young maidens, and once chewed it was put into cups, so that afterwards it could be cooked, and strained through various strainers of cotton cloth, with clean water, and the liquid that comes through all this is the wine, and it has been used for a long time. As it is medicinal there is no reason to be disgusted about the maize being chewed, because for reasons of health today people take all sorts of horrible things, like dog feces, urine, and other disgusting things, and in comparison to them human saliva is very clean. And when our wine is put on the table we do not remember that it has been trodden out and pressed by people's dirty and dusty feet.

  This wine, which had been made in Peru from the most ancient times as a medicine, then became a delicacy and a drink to celebrate festivals with . . . Thus the days of triumph for victories won, the days of plowing the earth, the days of planting the maize, of reaping and harvest, those of *Aymoray*, which is taking the grain to the *troxe* and storehouse, it was open to everybody to drink as much as they wanted. The exceptions were the boys and girls, the temple priests, the vestal virgins, the king's guard, the soldiers of the fortress, the judges, the weekly workers, the women who had to attend to the services of the house, the plebeians, and the craftsmen. They spent the whole day drinking, and having digested the wine they gave permission for the next day for all who had not drunk on the first day, except for the vestal virgins, and the priests of the idols, to whom it was never permitted. For the guards and the garrison of the fortresses they substituted other soldiers who had drunk the day before. This was common usage for their festivals, at the time of plowing and planting and reaping and taking the maize to the *troxe*, because first they did the work they had to do, finishing it in every respect, and then began the invitations and the banquets. At the banquets the food was very scanty, one of us could barely live on what five of them ate. But the drinking made up for it, because *chicha* is a true potation, providing as much nourishment as solid food, almost in the same fashion as chocolate in Mexico. (Anon. 1968: 174)

The idea of *chicha* as more than just a drink is also brought out by Fernando de Santillan in his description of the situation after the conquest.

Their food is maize and chile and greens, they never eat meat or anything of substance, except for some fish for those who are near the coast, and for this reason they are so fond of drinking *chicha*, because it fills their bellies and nourishes them, and if it does not befuddle them it is very nourishing, which is not true of the one called *sora*, which is very strong and takes away their judgment. (Santillan 1879: 77)

The refusal of the aborigines to drink plain water was something that struck the chroniclers over and over again, coming as they did from the Mediterranean, where the connoisseurship of the taste of various springs and fountains has been a branch of knowledge at least since classical antiquity.

They are great enemies of water, and never drink plain water unless there is a lack of other drinks, and there is no greater torture for them than to make them drink it, a punishment which the Spaniards

inflict on them occasionally, and which they feel more than blows.
(Cobo 1890–1893, 3: 35)

Under the name of *chicha* we include all the drinks that the inhabitants of this New World use in place of wine, and which they frequently use to make themselves drunk. They are so inclined toward
this vice that neither their conversion to our holy faith, nor their
dealings and connections with the Spaniards, nor the punishments
inflicted on them by their priests and judges, will discourage them
from it, although in some provinces there is some improvement, and
in general the drinking bouts are nowhere as frequent as they used to
be in the time of their paganism. *Chicha* is made of many things,
each nation using the fruits and seeds that their country produces in
the greatest abundance. Some *chichas* are made of *ocas, yucas,* and
other roots, others of *quinoa,* and the fruits of the *molle.* The Indians of Tucumán make it of *algarrobas,* those of Chile of strawber-
ries, those of Tierra Firme of pineapples, the Mexicans make the
wine they call *pulque* from maguey, and thus in this fashion the different regions use different fruits and vegetables, and there seems to
be a conspiracy of the inhabitants of America against water, because
they refuse to drink it pure. The best *chicha* of all, and that most
commonly drunk in this country, that which holds the first place as a
precious wine before all the other drinks of the Indians, is that which
is made of maize. This is made in many ways, and the differences are
that some *chichas* are stronger than others, and of different colors,
because *chicha* is made red, white, yellow, gray, and other colors as
well. A very strong one is called *sora,* which is made of maize which
has been buried for a few days until it sprouts; another is made of
toasted maize; another of chewed maize; and there are other variations as well. The one most commonly drunk by the Indians of Peru
is made of chewed maize, and because of this one sees, not only in
the native villages, but in Spanish towns where there are many Indians, such as Potosí, Oruro, and others, little groups of old women
and boys sitting and chewing maize. It disgusts the Spaniards not a
little even to see this, but it does not bother the Indians to drink
something made so filthily. They do not chew all the maize of which
the *chicha* is made, but only part of it, which, mixed with the rest,
acts as yeast. The Indians think this so necessary to give the right finish to the *chicha,* that when the maize is ground in our watermills
they chew the flour in their mouths until it is dampened and made

into dough, and those who make it their business to chew maize or flour take their pay by swallowing as much as they need to assuage their hunger. (Cobo 1890–1893, 1: 347–348)

Cobo is of course mistaken that the chewed maize acts as yeast. It is the action of the enzymes in human saliva that produces the desirable effect.

One of many special *chichas* made for the Inca was supposed to be extra smooth because it was aged for a month. Certain coastal valleys were renowned for their vintages:

As soon as you leave Trujillo you enter the Guañape valley, which is seven leagues toward Lima, which was as famous among the aborigines in times past for the *chicha* which was made there, as Madrigal, or San Martín in Castile, for the good wine which they produce. (Cieza de León n.d.: 366)

An elaborate etiquette grew up around *chicha* drinking, as well as all sorts of technology having to do with the drinking itself.

Because you must know that there was a custom, and a sign of good breeding, among these lords and all others of that country, which is that when a lord or lady goes to the house of another, to visit them, or see them, they must take . . . a jar of *chicha,* and coming to the place of the lord or lady they are going to visit they pour the *chicha* into two cups, and one is drunk by the person who visits, and the other drinks the *chicha* given him, and thus they both drink. The same is done by him who is being visited, who has to get two other cups of *chicha,* and give one to the visitor, and drink the other one. This is done between lords, and it is the greatest honor they have, and if this is not done when they visit, the person visiting thinks they are insulted if not given to drink, and no longer visits the person, and in the same way the person who gives a drink to another who refuses it thinks themselves insulted also. (Betanzos 1968: 55)

This pleasant social custom could lead to melodramatic scenes.

And thus that day they celebrated the peace, all eating together, which is to say on a plaza, facing each other. Once the meal was finished, the chief arose and took two vessels of his drink to toast his

new friend, as was the common custom of the Indians. He had one
vessel poisoned to kill him, and when he came opposite the other
chief, he invited him to drink from it. The one invited had either
changed his opinion of the one who had invited him, or was not sat-
isfied enough to trust him and suspected what was going on. He said
"Give me the other vessel and you drink this one." The chief, so as
not to show himself a coward, quickly switched hands, and gave his
enemy the innocent vessel, and drank the deadly one. Within a few
hours he had died, as much from the strength of the poison as from
the rage of seeing that by wishing to kill his enemy he had killed
himself. (Garcilaso de la Vega 1945, 1: 170)

The vessels used for all this drinking were of many materials. The
Europeans found the gold and silver ones most interesting, but there
were also elaborately painted wooden ones called *keros,* and trick vessels that made strange sounds and led the *chicha* on a circuitous path
before it got to its destination.

And I saw the head with the skin, the dry flesh with the hair, and it
had the teeth clenched, and there was a silver tube there, and there
was a big gold cup attached to the top of the head, which Atahualpa
drank from when he remembered the wars his brother had made
against him. He put *chicha* in the big cup, and it came out of the
mouth and the tube, from which he drank. (Cristóbal de Mena in
Biblioteca Peruana 1968: 152)

Making *chicha* cups out of the skulls of defeated rivals must have
been a regular and expected practice if one is to take this story of Atahualpa during his captivity seriously.

He was laughing one day, and looking at him the Governor Pizarro
asked him what he was laughing about, and he said, "I will tell you,
sir, that my brother Huascar said he was going to drink out of my
skull. They have brought me his skull to drink out of and I have
done so, you will drink out of his skull and out of mine. I thought
there were not enough people in the whole world to conquer me, but
you with one hundred Spaniards have captured me, and put to death
a large part of my people." (Molina 1943: 46)

A self-righteous shudder by Europe-centered readers is out of place here.

> Nicephorus [Emperor of Byzantium] set out for Bulgaria [in A.D.
> 811] with a formidable array of troops . . . As soon as he saw them
> Krum [the Bulgarian Khan] sued for peace, but Nicephorus ignored
> Krum's offer, easily took possession of Pliska and the Bulgarian pal-
> ace, and again refused to discuss terms. This time, however, the Bul-
> garians sealed off the passes leading out of the mountain defile in
> which the Byzantine army had carelessly encamped . . . They then
> swooped down upon the trapped Byzantines and butchered the en-
> tire force, including the Emperor and many of his chief officers.
> Krum cut off the Emperor's head, and after exhibiting it on a stake
> for several days, had the skull covered with silver and used it as a
> drinking bowl. (Anastos 1966: 94)

No matter what type of container held the brew, drinking it appears to have been as tightly regulated as everything else was in the Inca empire.

> That they be moderate and temperate in their eating, and more so in
> their drinking, and if somebody gets so drunk that they lose their
> judgment, if it is the first time they are punished as the judge shall de-
> cide, for the second offense exiled, and for the third deprived of their
> offices if they are magistrates, and sent to the mines. In the beginning
> this law was rigorously observed, but later it was so relaxed that the
> ministers of justice were those who drank the most, and got drunk,
> and there was no punishment. The *amautas,* who were their schol-
> ars and wisemen, interpreted the law as making a distinction be-
> tween *cenca,* which is to become heated, and *hatun machan,* which
> is to drink until you have lost your judgment. The latter was what
> usually happened, but they ignored the follies of the madmen, and
> little or nothing happened to them. (Anon. 1968: 178)

The last word on Inca drinking should be given to Miguel de Estete, who was one of the 168 Spaniards who captured Atahualpa in 1532. His words, those of his companions Pedro Sancho and Francisco de Xerez, Pedro Pizarro and Cristóbal de Molina of Santiago (both of whom wrote many years later), letters written for the illiterate Francisco Pizarro, and a few letters from the religious on the expedition, Vincente de Valverde, are the only eyewitness reports we have.

Everybody placed according to their rank, from eight in the morning until nightfall, they were there without leaving the feast, there they ate and drank . . . because even though what they drank was of roots and maize and like beer, it was enough to make them drunk, because they were people of small capacity. There were so many people, and such good drinkers, both men and women, and they poured so much into their skins, because they are good at drinking rather than eating, that it is certain, without any doubt, that two broad channels, more than half a vara [vara = .84 m] wide, which went under the paving to the river, which must have been made for cleanliness and to drain the rain which fell in the plaza; or possibly for this same purpose, ran all day with urine, from those who urinated in it; in such abundance as if there were fountains playing there; certainly matching the quantity that was drunk. Considering the number of people drinking it was not to be marveled at, but to see it was a thing unique and amazing. (Estete 1924: 55)

As with his near contemporary Motecuhzoma, the death of Huaina Capac and the destruction of his empire were supposedly foretold by mysterious portents. There was a green light in the sky before Huaina Capac died, and when he saw the same light some five and a half years later, his son Atahualpa correctly predicted his own death. According to Pedro Pizarro, Huaina Capac was fasting (which meant that he was abstaining from salt, chile, *chicha,* and women) when three very small Indians, dwarves, entered the room where he was in seclusion. They said that they had come to call him, but we do not know what for. Nobody else saw them, and they vanished as mysteriously as they had come. Still more eerie, although reminiscent of Pandora's box, is the omen reported by Joan de Santacruz Pachacuti Yamqui (1968: 311), who tells of a black-cloaked messenger delivering a box to the Inca. Told to open it the messenger refused, telling the Inca that he must do it for himself. When the box was opened the contents came fluttering out, like butterflies or bits of paper. It was the smallpox. Within a few days people began to die, and soon Huaina Capac was among them. Even the fact that some of the oracles gave the wrong advice was interpreted as an evil omen. The great oracle of Pachacamac, not far from Lima, the present capital of Peru, said that the ailing Inca should be taken outside so that the rays of his deity and ancestor, the sun, could shine on him and cure him. The oracle's prescription was followed, but the sun's rays killed rather than cured. The oracles in Purima, twelve leagues outside of Cuzco, are said to have told the people that bearded men were coming to conquer them and they had better eat, drink, and spend all they had so that there would be nothing left for the conquerors. As in Mexico there was supposed to have been a myth about gods, Viracochas in the Peruvian case, who had sailed away across the seas. When the Europeans arrived from the sea they were considered to be the Viracochas returning. Calancha says that this identification became even more certain when the Europeans showed their true character, their ferocity and inhumanity making it obvious that they were gods and not men (Calancha 1974, 1: 245). As usual, such "predictions" smell more of Spanish policy than aboriginal prescience.

> Before his death, Huaina Capac called . . . his vassals, captains, chiefs, and nobles, and told them that he knew from his oracles that the twelfth king of this country would be the last, and that he was the twelfth king of this country, and that after his death they must expect other lords who were going to subjugate that country, who would be unknown people, soon to appear, who would destroy the inhabitants, and put a stop to their religion and cult of idols, and he told them, "Pay attention that I command you to serve and obey those people, because their rule will be better than ours, nobody should take up arms against those people, but give them help, tribute, and gifts." (Calancha 1974, 1: 234)

Huaina Capac, whether or not he actually believed that he was fated to be the twelfth and last Inca, did lay the foundation for the civil war that was raging in his empire when the Europeans arrived. The son he had named as his successor at his death in 1527 had died before he could ascend the throne, and there was no order of succession beyond the named heir. The claimants to the imperial fringe were two other sons: Huascar, a son by the principal wife, and Atahualpa, a son by a lady of Quito. The five years between the death of Huaina Capac and the arrival of the Europeans were ones of continuous warfare. How the Inca empire might have developed had things run their course without foreign intervention will forever remain unknown, just as we will never know what might have happened had the Europeans chanced upon an Inca empire united.

FIFTEEN

The Inca and the Europeans

Francisco Pizarro's first scouting trip to Peru was in 1525. He got as far as present-day Tumbes in northern Peru, saw and appropriated some llamas and some gold, and took or was given as food two young boys, one later named Martinillo and the other Felipillo or Francisquillo. They became interpreters, even though they were not native speakers of Quechua but had learned it as a second language, as all the inhabitants of the Inca empire were required to do. The death of Atahualpa is sometimes attributed to calculated mistranslation by Felipillo, who is said to have lusted after one of Atahualpa's wives. There are a few culinary points of interest in the reports on the villages seen on this first voyage.

> It is very flat country, they live by irrigation, it does not rain here. They raise many llamas, they raise many ducks and rabbits [*cuy?*]. The meat which they eat they do not roast or cook, and the fish they make into pieces and dry in the sun, and the same thing with the meat. They do not eat bread as we do, the maize they eat toasted and cooked, and that is their bread. They make wine in great quantities from this maize. (Ruiz de Arce in *Biblioteca Peruana* 1968: 420)

Pizarro returned to Spain in 1528 to seek official appointments for himself and for his companion in arms, Diego de Almagro. He returned governor-designate and a knight of Santiago, but there were no such plums for Almagro. If the struggle for the throne between Atahualpa and Huascar caused destructive divisions among the Inca, the absolute power that Charles V gave Francisco Pizarro was to be equally damaging, as it led to protracted infighting among the Europeans and inflicted another dose of bloodshed on the Indians.

By the time Pizarro got back to Peru, in 1532, Huaina Capac was five years dead and the succession was being fought over. He stopped at an island off the north coast and found five extremely fat llamas, so fat that they couldn't multiply, according to his half-brother Pedro. Pedro also mentions seeing a storehouse full of dried lizards, which he was told was part of the tribute that was going to Cuzco. These lizards, and the techniques for catching, drying, and eating them, have been described with some care by a modern ethnographer (Holmberg 1957). *Dicrodon holmbergi,* the lizard, lives in holes in the ground under *guarango* trees, and the fruit of these trees is the only thing that the lizard eats. The tree is also called *algarroba, mesquite,* or *Prosopis juliflora,* and human beings eat the pods as well. From April to November the lizards hibernate, and we presume that the tree has no ripe fruit. As the fruit matures, the lizards emerge from their holes and sometimes even climb the trees to get it. The lizards are trapped, and their front legs and backs are broken to paralyze them. They are then thrown on the embers of a fire and scorched until their scaly skins may be removed by hand. Once skinned, they are buried in a shallow depression in the heated sand and covered with hot ashes. Ten minutes of cooking, followed by cooling off and gutting, makes a product that may be stored for a year or consumed immediately. Holmberg said that it could be eaten in *seviche,* the dish of fish marinated in lime juice, as well as in soups, stews, and omelets.

As the Europeans went on they were twice visited by Apoo, the Inca lord. The second time he brought another gift, but to figure out what it was gives an example of the difficulties of culinary history. Pedro Pizarro laconically records "some dried ducks" and goes on to tell how Apoo asked to see the Europeans' swords, counted the men and the horses during the banter, and returned to his leader to report 190 men, thieves and braggarts, nothing to fear.

Juan de Betanzos (1987), a European chronicler who was married to a noble Inca woman and whose narrative in its complete version was only recently discovered, tells us that Apoo brought back a great deal more than military information. Atahualpa was not only interested in weapons, he wanted to know what manner of men the strangers were. And the first questions that he asked to elicit this knowledge were about their food. Did they eat their meat raw or cooked, he asked?

Atahualpa was told that sometimes the strangers ate it cooked in their *ollas* and very well done, and sometimes they ate it roasted, and also very well done. The next question was, Did they eat human flesh? Apoo and his companions were cautious. They had not seen any human flesh consumed, but they had seen llamas, alpacas, ducks, pigeons, and deer being eaten, as well as some maize tortillas. The latter are not described more completely, and we are left wondering if they were Mexican-type tortillas, a hitherto unknown breadstuff from the north coast of Peru, or some other maize product.

Apoo's gifts are mentioned by other sources besides Pedro Pizarro, but they are all mutually inconsistent. Zarate (1968: 79) says that there were two loads of dried geese and that they were used as incense by the lords of the country. Cieza de León (Cantù 1979: 241) says that the gift consisted of some little baskets of fruit, ten or twelve ducks badly roasted with the feathers on, and three or four quarters of "sheep," so roasted that there was no goodness in them. Diego de Trujillo says, "And the present was some ducks dried and full of wool, which looked like decoys to kill birds; and asking him what this was he said—Atahualpa said that this ought to be done with your hides, if you do not return what you have taken from this country" (Trujillo 1948: 55). Francisco de Xerez (1988, 6: 732), an eyewitness, said that dried ducks were made into powder and then used as seasoning by the lords of the country. What are we to make of this? Possibly the ducks were used for all of the above. We have descriptions of llama meat being burned as incense; there is no reason why duck meat could not have been used in the same way. After reading how the dried lizards were used, crumbling dried ducks into stews and soups seems plausible. We do not know if the dried ducks could also have been a threat or an insult, telling the Europeans that they were dead ducks, as it were.

Atahualpa sent more messengers with llamas, cooked llama meat, maize bread, and vessels of *chicha*. The Europeans directed their march toward Cajamarca, where he was reported to be, and investigated some storehouses that they found along the way. They were full of footwear, loaves of salt, and a food that looked like dried meatballs, possibly the dried fruit of *cayua* (*Cyclanthera pedata*) stuffed with meat; all stored to supply the army.

The town now named Cajamarca was empty, except for the women who made the *chicha* and the guards guarding them. Atahualpa and his court were at the baths of Cajamarca, some distance away, and Francisco Pizarro sent his brother Hernando and some other men to coax him to Cajamarca. Atahualpa said that he was fasting, but on the next day, after he had drunk, he would come. The Europeans were offered food, which they refused, saying that they were also fasting. Offered drink, some of them accepted. The Inca, however, was interested in something else.

> The Inca told Unan Chullo to bring the *chicha* in vessels of fine gold, because he wanted to see if the Spaniards, as he had been told, would take the vessels because they were of gold, he had been told that they were fond of gold, and the *chicha* was soon gotten and given to the Spaniards, who took the golden vessels in their hands, and some of them fearing that some poison might be given to them in the *chicha* did not wish to drink it, and others drank it without fear, and after they drank they returned the vessels to the Indians who had given them to them. (Betanzos 1987: 270)

On the next day, the Europeans concealed themselves around the square of Cajamarca and awaited the arrival of Atahualpa. They had a long wait. Atahualpa had finished his fast, and having been told that the Europeans were wetting themselves from fear, he proceeded to have a meal with his entourage.

> These lords had the custom of eating in the mornings, as had all the natives of this kingdom; the lords, after having eaten as I have said, spent all the day until nightfall drinking, when they had a very light supper, while the poor Indians spent the time working. (Pizarro 1978: 36)

Juan de Betanzos (1987: 275–276) presents another version of Atahualpa's last repast as a free man. According to Betanzos the Inca awoke late, after a night of consultations with his military commanders. He asked for food and then for drink, and drank so much that he was drunk. He was in this condition when a messenger came from Cajamarca who told him, "Capa Inca, you must know that those people have gotten into the houses of your father and divided everything among them." The Inca set out, and he had not gone half a league when another messenger came. "Capa Inca, you must know that those people have entered the houses of the sun, and everything there they have divided between them." The procession continued, with frequent pauses for the Inca to drink, while the dancers danced and the drummers and musicians played. Halfway to Cajamarca a third messenger met them. "Capa Inca, you must know that those people have entered your house and taken everything there, and they have also taken your women and raped them." This messenger suffered the usual fate of those bringing bad news. The Inca ordered his head cut off.

Once in Cajamarca, the Inca all crowded into the square. The religious of the expedition, Vincente de Valverde, Bible or breviary in hand, went out to convert the pagan monarch. He gave a long harangue, and when Atahualpa asked through the interpreter where he had heard all that, handed him the book. The Inca had no writing, only their accounts on knotted cords, and one story has Atahualpa listening to the book and throwing it down when it said nothing to him. Vincente de Valverde considered this sacrilege and gave a signal to the concealed Europeans for the slaughter to begin. An Inca account conflates the visit and ceremonial toasting at the baths of Cajamarca with the throwing of the book in the square of Cajamarca and says that the Europeans had spilled some of the drink that they had been offered, and this angered Atahualpa so much that he threw away the book.

Whatever precipitated the attack, Atahualpa was tipped out of his golden litter and captured by Francisco Pizarro, who put his left hand on him and said "Santiago." Saint James, who had earned the epithet of *matamoros,* or killer of Moors, during the battles to expel the Moors from Spain, acquired a new role in the New World, that of Santiago *mataindios,* or Indian slayer. The rest of the story of the captivity—the room filled with silver and gold as ransom, and the death of Atahualpa, who as a convert was granted the privilege of being garroted rather than burned at the stake—is too well known to need repeating here.

Before the final act of the tragedy, however, there was a brief period of coexistence. The captive Atahualpa learned to play chess, and Pedro Pizarro observed some things of interest.

> The ladies already mentioned brought him the food, and put it before him on some little green reeds, very small and thin. This lord was sitting on a wooden stool, little more than a *palma* high. This stool was made of very fine painted wood, it was always covered with a very fine cloth, even when he was sitting on it. The reeds above mentioned were always before him when he wished to eat, and there they put all the dishes of gold and silver and clay, and that which appealed to him he signaled to be brought to him, and one of

CONQVISTA
PRESOATAGVALPAINGA

guarda

preso atagualpa enla ciudad caxamarca como
atagualpa ynga dixo adon fran pizarro q̄ leyese un escrito
dixo qno sauia y dixo q̄ ley se un sol dado y leyo dixo atagualpa

The captivity of Atahualpa.
From Guaman Poma de Ayala 1936: 387.

the ladies held it in her hand while he ate. Eating in this manner, while I was present, lifting a slice of food to his mouth, and spilling a drop on the clothes he had on, he gave his hand to the female Indian, arose, and went into his room to change his clothes. (Pizarro 1978: 67)

Pedro Pizarro later discovered that everything Atahualpa had touched or worn was stored in a special warehouse. This included the green reeds put before his feet, the bones of the birds and animals that he had eaten, and the cobs of maize that he had held in his hands. Everything thus accumulated was burned every year, and the wind blew the ashes away so that no one could touch them.

Martín de Murua (1962, 2: 30), who was not an eyewitness, said that all the food was chopped so fine when it was cooked that there was no need of carvers. This makes the presence of bones and maize cobs in Atahualpa's trash hard to explain. Murua also contradicts the story of the Spaniards being given *chicha* in golden goblets, saying that the Inca did not drink from gold and silver but from wooden vessels called *keros,* which had medicinal and poison-preventing qualities. If they did use gold and silver, it was only for pomp and show, and after use the gold and silver vessels were melted down, it being considered wretched and despicable to drink out of the same vessel twice. Murua says that the wives did not cook for their husbands, but this may have been a regional difference.

They [highlanders] ate, seated on their low stools, which they always carried with them, many foods cooked in many different ways, being served by their own wives, which the lords of the coast did not do, having their cooks and servants for that. For bread the people of the highlands ate maize kernels toasted and cooked, and they drank *chicha* with other dishes and drinks that their wives made. (Las Casas 1958: 416)

According to Murua the cooking for royalty was done in the establishments that the Spaniards called "nunneries." There were three grades of these nunneries, where girls selected from the general population could spend anything from a short period to the rest of their lives. The virgins of the sun were the most exalted. Murua says that they made excellent *chicha,* superior to that drunk by the Inca and only used for sacrifice. These ladies were so refined that when they left

their house they carried a piece of fruit with them to nourish themselves on the scent. A disagreeable odor might prove fatal. The cooks
of the Inca were earthier. They worked in the garden plots, made many
different kinds of *chicha* for the Inca to drink and to offer as sacrifice,
and cooked the other food. Murua says they themselves ate "meat
cooked with nettles" (Murua 1962, 2: 75).

It is hard to ascertain whether the Inca court was fed from the general warehouses or if there was a separate supply system. Garcilaso de
la Vega thought that the Inca, at least as far as meat was concerned,
just took his share from the communal hunts.

> The expenditure on food of the royal house was very great, espe-
> cially the expense of the meat, because the house of the Inca pro-
> vided it for all those of the blood royal who resided at the court, and
> they did the same wherever the person of the king might be. Maize,
> which was the bread they ate, was not consumed in such quantity,
> except for the servants of the royal house, because those outside
> were given enough to support their establishments. Game like deer
> . . . guanacos or vicuñas, was not killed especially for the royal
> house or any other lord, except for birds, because the animals were
> reserved for the regularly scheduled hunts . . . and then they divided
> the meat and the wool among the poor and the rich. The drink con-
> sumed in the house of the Inca was in such quantity that there was
> no keeping track of it. The main privilege of all those who came to
> serve the Inca was to be given drink, whether they be chiefs or not,
> whether they came to visit him, or bring tribute for peace or war, it
> is incredible how much was spent on it. (Garcilaso de la Vega 1945,
> 2: 14)

Pedro Pizarro claimed that the lords had a special slaughterhouse
where the cattle of the country were killed daily and their meat divided
among the nobility. Guaman Poma de Ayala, an Indian who wrote a
long illustrated book on the Inca early in the seventeenth century, also
seemed to think that the Inca got special supplies, not just a share of
the pooled goods.

> The Inca . . . ate selected maize which is *capya utco sara,* and *papas
> manay* [early potatoes], . . . and llama called white *cuyro,* and
> *chiche* [tiny fish], white *cuy,* and much fruit and ducks, and very
> smooth *chicha* which took a month to mature and was called *yamor*

aca. And he ate other things which the Indians were not to touch on pain of death. (Guaman Poma de Ayala 1980, 1: 306)

Whoever cooked for the Inca and however the food supply was organized, the household did not come to a halt with the Inca's death. Although many of the household staff accompanied their dead lord or lady to the underworld, they must have been replaced, because the important dead were mummified and continued their daily routines in this condition. They were cooked for, and the meals either were burned before the mummies or were eaten by the attendants after being shown to the mummies. *Chicha* was made for them, so that the dead could drink with the dead or with the living. The immense expense of supporting the households of an ever-increasing number of revered dead has led some modern authors to speculate that the Inca state would have shortly collapsed of its own accord because of this drain on the economy.

The sources are unsatisfactory as to what actually constituted a meal for the Inca and the nobility. A sacrifice offered, presumably daily, by the virgins of the sun might be the equivalent of the Christian bread and wine. At noon every nun took a plate of maize, a plate of meat, and a jar of *chicha* and offered it to the image in the middle of the patio. The maize and the meat were burned in a great silver brazier afterward, and the *chicha* was poured into the adjacent fountain. Maize and meat were the food of the gods, and bones and maize cobs were the remnants of Atahualpa's meal. The meals of the poor would have left little to be stored in a ceremonial warehouse.

The food of the poor was roots and greens, but the actual roots and greens eaten varied according to the residence of the eater. Guaman Poma de Ayala (1980, 1: 55) gives two lists of edibles, one for the highlands and one for the lowlands. The highland list includes six kinds of maize, three kinds of potatoes, *oca, ulluco,* and *añu,* both fresh and preserved, *quinoa* and lupines, three kinds of mushrooms, and at least nine named greens. For the occasional meat he gives all four camelids, two kinds of deer, *cuy,* ducks, "partridges," water flies, fish, shrimp, and crabs, presumably from fresh water or brought fresh or dried from the coast. For the lowlands he starts with maize of the hot country, sweet potatoes, *racacha,* pumpkins, *achira, llacon, yuca* (sweet manioc), lima beans, *cayua* (*Cyclanthera pedata*), peanuts, jícama, four kinds of chiles, *pepinos, lucumas, pacayes,* and avocados, plus a catch-all category for other herbs and small stuff. He does not mention any meat or fish. According to him the diet of the under-thirties was restricted, with fat, honey, vinegar, chile, and certain delicacies being prohibited.

There were inspectors who visited all the houses to make sure that everybody was properly provided for. Not only did they have to have a stock of dried greens and other dried plants, but they were also required to possess a battery of clay and wooden vessels for food preparation and storage.

Whatever fish and meat was available in both the highlands and the lowlands was often eaten raw or dried. Zarate recorded it on the coast: "They eat fish and flesh always raw, and maize either boiled or toasted" (Zarate 1968: 80). Fernández de Oviedo repeats this for the highlands: "The highland people often eat meat raw, especially when they find themselves in a place where they can't have a fire" (Fernández de Oviedo 1959, 5: 106).

The nobility ate more meat; the plebeians ate more green stuff. The consumption of maize seems to have taken place at all social levels. What is difficult to explain is the sparse mention of the potato and the lack of agricultural rituals connected with it. A clue to this anomalous situation might be found in some archaeological work done in the upper Mantaro valley (Earle et al. 1987). There the excavators found that in the Wanka II period, A.D. 1300 to 1470, the population lived in compact settlements high up in the mountains. Carbon pathway analysis of their bones shows that they ate mostly tubers and *Chenopodium*, that is to say *quinoa*. After the Inca conquest they were moved down into the valley, where maize would grow more successfully. The bones, especially those of the males, show that maize became a major portion of their diet, presumably in the form of *chicha*. Not even carbon pathway analysis can tell us the geopolitical considerations that led the Inca to resettle the population in this manner and presumably downplay the potato.

A large portion of the maize was consumed as *chicha*. The rest was eaten in many different ways, all of which the Spaniards called *pan*, bread in the broadest sense of the word, meaning the staple carbohydrate. Nixtamalization was unknown. Garcilaso de la Vega, the son of a Spanish soldier and an Inca princess, describes his early diet in the years immediately following the conquest:

Until I was nine or ten years old I lived on *sara*, which is maize. The bread made of it has three names, *sanco* was the bread for sacrifices,

huminta was for feasts and as a treat, *tanta* . . . was the daily bread;
the toasted maize was called *camcha* . . . and the cooked *sara* was
called *muti*. (Garcilaso de la Vega 1945, 2: 177)

Cobo gives us much more material, but it must be remembered that
he wrote later. There is some suspicion that the *huminta* is not a native
Peruvian dish but an offspring of the Mexican tamale.

After the maize is dry the Indians boil it in water, and so cooked it is
called *muti*, and is the daily bread of the plebeians. Sometimes when
it is half-cooked they dry it in the sun to keep as we do biscuits, and
they call that *cocopa*, and put it in their stews. They also eat it
toasted [which is called in Quechua *camcha* and *hancca*], and the Indians who go traveling take no other supplies than a little bag of it,
or flour made from it, which they eat dissolved in cold water, and it
serves them as food and drink. This flour of toasted maize is called
pito. (Cobo 1890–1893, 1: 343)

There is a certain kind of maize that they toast until it bursts, and
they call it *pisancalla*, and they use it as a snack and a confection.
Aside from the tortillas and cakes, which they make of maize flour,
and which they call *tanta*, as a delicacy they make some dumplings
of this flour which they put in the pot and call *huminta* . . . In ancient times their soups and stews were very few: of whole maize with
some greens and chile they make a dish called *motepatasca*, cooking
the maize until it bursts. (Cobo 1890–1893, 4: 173)

Cobo gives us the best description of the Inca kitchen. The maize
was ground by putting it on a flat stone slab and then rocking another
stone shaped like a half-moon over it. A mortar and pestle took care of
grinding lesser quantities of smaller things. Every house had a tiny clay
stove with a little opening for stoking the fire and two or three holes
where the pots could be put to heat. It was extremely economical of
fuel, which made it suitable for this fuel-poor region, and Cobo said
that one Spanish kitchen used more fuel than twenty Indian ones.
    The grinding system seems highly inefficient, but very little maize
dough was made. Garcilaso de la Vega implies that it was only for ceremonial use.

The women of the sun spent that night making a great quantity of
maize dough called *sanco*. They made round loaves of it, the size of

a common apple, and one must remember that these Indians never ate their grain as dough made into bread except on this feast [Raimi] and another called Citua, and they did not eat this bread during the whole meal, but only two or three mouthfuls at the beginning. Their ordinary food, in the place of bread, is *sara* [maize], toasted or cooked in the grain. (Garcilaso de la Vega 1945, 2: 48)

To search for what was actually in the pots and pans we must turn to the early dictionaries.

The Quechua dictionary of Diego González Holguín (1952), first published in Lima in 1606, starts out with a long list of words having to do with *aka* or *asua,* the Quechua word for what we have been calling *chicha.* The words go from "he who makes or sells *chicha,*" to "he who is very given to drinking *chicha,*" to the final step, "he who is so very given to drinking *chicha* that he dies crazy from it."

Tupa cocau was the "royal food that the Inca gave to the people that he sent abroad; it was a small bag of maize, and because it was a gift from the Inca it was most sustaining, and eating just one grain a day was enough to assuage one's hunger" (González Holguín 1952: 369). Could this have been grain from the very sacred, and very limited, crop of maize that was grown on an island in Lake Titicaca?

There was a drink seasoned and sweetened by adding maize dough that had been boiled and rested, and there was also a fermented maize dough, but we are not told how it was used. *Mutti,* an alternative spelling for *muti,* was cooked maize or cooked grain of any sort, and the impoverished eater said, "Muttillacta micupayani" (I always eat *mutti,* it's all I have). *Motepatasca* was grain cooked so long that it burst open, with greens, chile, and dried meat added. Maize could also be partially cooked, dried, and then added to stews. According to González Holguín *rokro* or *locro* was a stew of chile and potatoes, meat, maize, and beans. For Cobo it contained both meat and potatoes in their fresh and dried forms, and no maize.

There were also many stewlike dishes containing *quinoa.* It could be cooked with fresh and dried potatoes and chile. *Kispino* seems to have been both a "rustic bread" made of *quinoa* and steamed balls of ground *quinoa* with condiments, fat, and salt. *Quinoa* leaves could be made into a soup with other leaves and chile. Cakes could be made of cooked potato or ground *quinoa* and then dried for storage, or *quinoa* could be an ingredient of a sweet gruel, along with dried potatoes, toasted flour, and sweet dried *oca* roots. The Aymara dictionary of Ludovico Bertonio (1879), originally published in 1612, gives many words for *quinoa* gruels and also a name for a cake made of *quinoa* flour mixed with snow as a leavening. Snow has a lot of air in it and has been used as leavening in other snowy parts of the world, including New England, where there are recipes for snow-leavened pancakes.

The Aymara dictionary contains more on potato usage because Aymara speakers lived in the highland province of Collao and were only conquered by the potato-suppressing Inca in the fifteenth century. *Tunta* were potatoes aged in water, which were either used to make gruel or cooked whole like the freeze-dried potatoes, *chuño*. The right varieties of potatoes could also be roasted in the little ovens or out in the fields during the harvest, using dried potato stalks as fuel. There are endless stews and gruels combining potatoes, sometimes in many different forms, with meat and greens. Even periods of time were defined with reference to the potato. *Luki huaycu* was one hour, the time necessary to cook potatoes.

The Aymara also ate *locro*, a thick stew, and they ate it out of a vessel called a *chua*, made of reeds. It was apparently the most common eating vessel, which gives us a hint as to what the most common food was. "Are you a great lady, that you are always seated with your *chua*, and never doing any work?" Bertonio asks.

What we have been told about the consumption of meat raw in Peru is borne out by the Aymara dictionary, which gives us the name for a dish of raw liver with chiles, as well as raw llama entrails with the same. But then everything was eaten with chile, and there was a saying to prove it. "Am I your salt or chile that you always have me in your mouth and speak ill of me?"

Llama blood was important as food, as well as having ritual uses. There are hints that sophisticated means were used to keep the blood from clotting, including the use of the fruit of various species of papaya (*Carica papaya* and *Carica candicans*), today known for their tenderizing enzymes. The blood could be cooked to eat, or a gruel could be made with it. The sacred bread mixed with blood was a form of communion, not nourishment. Blood dishes appear in the Quechua word lists as well. Blood could be eaten with pressed potatoes and in a stew with viscera, potatoes, and fresh and dried meat.

The definition of eating splendidly was to have many dishes together. One who had five dishes at one meal was a high-status person indeed. Quechua speakers differentiated between *chupe* and *locro*, both being stews, but the former containing more liquid than the latter. They also used more seafood than the Aymara because of their conquest of the coast and their system of *chasqui* runners. The *cuy*, the guinea pig, could be cooked with dried seaweed, as well as with fresh and dried potatoes or chopped dried potatoes and vegetables. Fish could also be cooked with dried potatoes or made into a stew with small peeled potatoes, greens, and chile.

The Quechua ate their meat grilled, as well as stewed and raw. It was cooked over the coals with the omnipresent salt and chile, and the virgins of the sun ate grilled meat called *hanchasca,* but we are not told what distinguished it from the ordinary form. If the meat was not grilled it could be cooked in a *pachamanca,* an oven dug in the earth and lined with leaves that produced a fragrant steam. Pots of stew, and tubercules, could be included in the earth oven along with the meat. A meat dish which sounds vaguely familiar was *lagua,* consisting of cooked, sun-dried, unskinned guano birds. Perhaps the birds Apoo brought Pizarro were the makings for *lagua.*

The statement is often made that the American Indians knew no other spices besides chile. This is true only if you define spices as products of the East Indies: black pepper, cloves, cinnamon, ginger, nutmeg, mace, and the rest. We have already mentioned *muña* (*Minthostachys setosa*), which was used as a flavoring as well as a means of keeping the stored potatoes free of insect infestation; *paiko* (*Chenopodium ambrosioides*); a species of *Tagetes,* or New World marigold; and something like an onion. There were many others, including what the Europeans used as a replacement for saffron, possibly *Buddleja utilis.*

One Inca spice really unleashed the cupidity of the Europeans. From our viewpoint, it seems absurd that Europeans, awash in the silver and gold from the Peruvian mines, should have wasted their time pursuing a rumor of cinnamon. But spices were the original cause of the discovery of the New World and enormously valuable commodities. In a letter of July 28, 1533, to Charles V, one Licenciado de la Gama runs on in his excitement:

They say that there is cinnamon, and the chief Atabalica [Atahualpa] that they hold prisoner says that they bring it from beyond, and he says that he has eaten it, and held it in his hands. (De la Gama in Porras Barrenechea 1959: 63)

Other reports were glowing:

The fruit, leaves, bark, and root of the tree all taste and smell and have the substance of cinnamon, but the fruit are the best. In shape they are like the acorns of the cork tree, but bigger. Although there are many of these woodland trees throughout the land, which seed themselves, and bear fruit without cultivation, the Indians also have many on their plantations, which they cultivate, and which yield far finer cinnamon than the others. They value it highly, and barter it with the neighboring countries for provisions and clothes and everything else that they require for their subsistence. (Zarate 1968: 192)

Gonzalo Pizarro, another brother, set off with his men to find this treasure, leaving Quito in 1541 with 6,000 pigs, 300 horses, 900 dogs, and many llamas and alpacas. All this livestock had gone astray, died, or been eaten by the time the starving expedition staggered back to Quito. Spurred by the rumors of El Dorado, the man gilded with gold dust, some of them had deserted earlier and made their way down the Amazon and into the Atlantic. It was a disillusioned Gonzalo Pizarro (in Porras Barrenechea 1959: 460–461) who wrote Charles V on September 3, 1542. There were very few trees, and they were far apart, he reported. The buds and the leaves tasted like cinnamon, but the rest of the tree had no taste whatsoever. There was no profit to be found among the "cinnamon" trees of the eastern slopes of the Andes.

Little remains to be said about the Inca after the European conquest. Despite the bloody internecine feuding of the Europeans, disease and demoralization had taken such a toll of the Inca that their resistance collapsed. The warehouses which might have supplied an Inca resistance were looted by the Europeans, who sold the contents for their own profit.

... someone in Cuzco had gathered from the Indians 200,000 *hanegas* of maize and was selling it on the market, and that in this way the soldiers and inhabitants bring all the clothing and food of the Indians and sell it in the square for prices so low that they give a llama for half a peso, and kill all they wish for no other reason than to make candles, and as if this was not bad enough there is worse to come, because the Indians have nothing to plant, and no cattle, or any way of getting some, and they have no alternative but to die of hunger, because there is only one maize crop a year here. (Pascual de Andagoya in Porras Barrenechea 1959: 371)

That was in July 1539. By September of that year things had gotten worse. People were dying of hunger in Cuzco; tens of thousands of Indians were marching in the streets with crosses, begging for food. It made a striking contrast to the orderly and equitable distribution of food under the Inca.

This was not lost on some of the conquerors. Years later, their last survivor, his great age perhaps inclining him toward an Edenic fallacy that what he had participated in was the destruction of a perfect paradise, wrote his will and prefaced it with an anguished appeal to Philip II. The writer was Captain Mancio Sierra de Leguizamo, who won fame during the conquest and place in a proverb because the great golden sun from the main temple in Cuzco had been his share in the division of the spoils, and he had gambled it away before sunrise. The will was written in Cuzco on September 18, 1589 (Calancha 1974: 221–222). The Inca, he said, governed his country so that everything was divided by lot. War did not impede commerce or agriculture, and the Inca was a very capable ruler, whereas the Europeans with their bad example had destroyed these well-governed people and made them from a population who did nothing bad into a people who did little or nothing good. It was up to his majesty to do something about this, to cleanse his conscience.

It is an unexpected source for a commentary on the Inca system, and one wonders if Philip II ever heard of the request made by his aged captain. Meanwhile, the looted warehouses stood empty on the mountain ridges where they had been built to take advantage of the ventilation air currents provided. Informal trade networks grew up to replace the Inca system but without the guiding hand of the Inca accountants, who no longer kept track of goods on the *quipus,* the knotted string records. But even with a looser organization the incredible variety of animals and plants that originated in one of the world's most diverse ecosystems continued, and continues, to be exploited.

The recent interest in some Inca crops and the many others that still await discovery in their valleys leads us to hope that this extraordinary people still have many foodstuffs to contribute to the world's diet.

SIXTEEN

The Occupation

The accounts of the conquest speak of the Europeans being greeted by natives coming out of their towns and offering them breadstuffs, fowl, and fruit. Sometimes the food was even left lying by the side of the road, and the donors absented themselves. Many of the peoples of the Americas thought of this as a gesture of peace and friendship, although one cannot help feeling that it was also an unspoken request for the army to take the food and be gone. We read of native women being attached to the European forces to make them the bread of the country, and we read the ecstatic writers who listed all the new products of the New World and made each one sound better than the last. Some are as sweet as if they had been dipped in syrup, they tell us, while others are so fragrant that they perfume entire houses. All this could lead one to believe that the Europeans, very much men of their time as far as religion and world view and everything else went, were unique for their time, or any other time, in having no food prejudices whatsoever. It would appear that they immediately and unhesitatingly accepted the foods of the New World and the way that the New World prepared them.

Appearances are deceiving. The chroniclers listing the products of the New World praised them to the heavens, but they did not demand to be served them for dinner. Many of the military dispatches were for the eyes of Charles V, a notoriously stingy monarch. The Venetian ambassadors to his court commented on the shabby liveries of his servants, shabby because Charles could not bring himself to appropriate money for new ones (Albèri 1859: 74). His own clothing, they said, was more suited to a middling prince than the great emperor he was (Albèri 1859: 342). Given this, even Cortés, a man who had discovered and conquered an enormous realm rich in treasure and population and added it to the possessions of Charles V, found it politic when writing him to stress that his conquest was carried out while living off the country, not relying on expensive European supplies expensively shipped over the Atlantic. It was only when the wave of conquest had rolled off toward the peripheries, and the conquerors had begun to metamorphose into settlers, that a more realistic picture emerges.

The conquerors were given *encomiendas,* groups of Indians who in return for spiritual and physical care from the conquerors rendered tribute and military service. A large part of the tribute was food. The household of Cortés, who by then had been given the title of Marqués del Valle, was in 1533 given weekly fifteen loads of maize, eighty baskets containing twenty tortillas each, ten native fowl, two Castilian fowl, two rabbits, ten quail, three native doves, and fruit, salt, chiles, firewood, and forage. For the elite Europeans native products were acceptable only if they fit into familiar categories like game, fruit, or large birds to be ceremonially served whole. The Europeans soon began agitating to have their tribute in kind changed to tribute in cash, difficult if not impossible for the Indians to obtain. This meant less native food was introduced into European houses, and this lessening of supply was reinforced by the prohibitions against Europeans and blacks in the *tianguiz,* the Indian markets. As the two societies, Indian and European, began ever so slowly to mix, the restrictions on such mixing increased, and many of them were based on matters having to do with food and drink.

The surviving municipal documents, the *Actas del cabildo,* from Mexico City, Santiago in Guatemala, Lima, Cuzco, Arequipa, Ayacucho, and Trujillo in Peru, and Quito, Ecuador, all give us a roughly similar picture of European urban life in the New World in early colonial times. They were nothing if not painstaking, those early city fathers of European America. They concerned themselves with every conceivable facet of city affairs, from the content of the Sunday sermon, to the licensing of taverns and the marital and residential status of the owners thereof, to the interminable complaints about pigs in the streets. The picture of the foodways of early colonial Latin America that emerges from the various *Actas del cabildo* is wholly at odds with the early and complete fusion of food traditions suggested in the first paragraph of this chapter. The *Actas del cabildo* depict one tier of a two-tier society, and the tier that it concerns itself with is almost entirely European, in food as in the rest of its customs.

As far as foodstuffs went, meat was the primary concern of the *cabildo*. The pig, that mainstay of Spanish cuisine, came first. European armies marched accompanied by herds of porkers, although Cortés, on his trek across the base of the Yucatan peninsula to Honduras, kept the pigs four days behind the soldiers to conserve his stock. Gonzalo Pizarro, on his foray to find the land of cinnamon in Peru, went escorted by swine. Pork was the first European meat to have a price set for it in Mexico City. On July 26, 1525, the *cabildo* set the rates that inns could charge: an *arrelde*, about four pounds, of fresh or salt pork or venison cost four gold *reales*, as did a good turkey hen or two fine rabbits (Bejarano 1889). By the next year the price of pork had dropped to a quarter of that asked for the newly available beef and mutton. The concession for supplying meat to the city was auctioned off yearly to the person who promised to sell at the lowest price retail. The auctions were held during Lent, and the contract ran from one Easter to the next. Meat had to be supplied during Lent as well, for the sick and for those who, like soldiers on active duty, were exempt from the requirement to abstain from meat.

The herds of European stock, which rapidly became prodigious in size, presented Indian farmers with new problems. They knew how to protect their crops from native animals and birds, but the larger, more numerous, and more destructive cattle, sheep, horses, and pigs were another matter. It was a constant source of friction, litigation, and dispute between the two populations and another reason for the authorities to physically separate them as far as possible. The Europeans went so far as to accuse the Indians of maliciously planting their crops where they knew they would be destroyed by European livestock.

A domestic animal not mentioned in any *Actas del cabildo* and commonly ignored during discussions of Old World imports to the New World deserves a paragraph here, although it is not generally eaten. The first archbishop of Mexico, Don Fray Juan de Zumárraga, called the attention of Charles V to the good effects which the importation of donkeys would have (García Icazbalceta 1947, 3: 142). Not only were donkeys necessary to provide mules, donkeys and mules being suitable mounts for ecclesiastics like the archbishop, but the greater their numbers, the smaller would be the need for *tamemes,* the Indian porters. The Church and the crown worked in unison to try to discourage the exploitation of this pre-Columbian profession by the Europeans, considering it one of the causes for the precipitate decline of the Indian population.

Bulls and cows were among the more usual livestock. The bulls were necessary for another facet of European life that was an early transplant to the New World. Every festival, either a recurring one like a significant saint's day or the celebration of some unique event, was marked by two events: the *juego de cañas,* a form of joust; and a bullfight. On August 11, 1529, the day of San Ipólito, the patron saint of Mexico City because it was on his day that the final capitulation of the Aztecs took place, was celebrated by a bullfight in which seven bulls were run. Two of the bulls were killed, the meat of the dead bulls going to monasteries and hospitals (Bejarano 1889). On December 31 of the same year a peace signed by France and Spain was the pretext for another bullfight, a *juego de cañas,* and the dispensation of two *arrobas* of white wine, which would add up to between five and seven of our gallons, one *arroba* of red wine, both wines imported from across the Atlantic, and three *arrobas* of candied fruit, which as a dry measure would total about seventy-five pounds of sweetmeats (Bejarano 1889). Caution, however, is in order when interpreting the weights and measures, as well as the coinage, all of which varied between localities.

The presence of cattle meant not only beef on the menu but also the birth of a dairy industry. It got off to an inauspicious start. In 1526, Luis Ponce arrived from Spain to investigate accusations of financial malfeasance brought against Cortés. Before his arrival in Mexico City he was entertained at an inn in Ixtapalapa by an underling of Cortés, and his menu began with lettuces and some *manjar blanco. Manjar blanco* could be made of many ingredients, whiteness being the important feature, but the usual recipe of the time included finely shredded chicken breasts cooked with milk, sugar, and rice flour, a dish served in Turkey today as a dessert and called *tavuk gögsü.* During Lent the chicken and milk were replaced by grated almonds and almond milk. Bernal Díaz said that the next dish was new and novel in those countries (Díaz del Castillo 1982: 564). The dish was *requesones,* made of milk heated with rennet and then drained of the whey, producing a form of cottage cheese. According to Bernal Díaz, Fray Tomás Ortiz, a traveling companion of Luis Ponce, refused the *requesones,* claiming they were poisoned. The official inquest reported Luis Ponce rejecting the *requesones* because he thought that they had an off taste and overindulging in *manjar blanco* (Anon. 1853: 321). Whichever dairy product it was, Luis Ponce died a few days later, giving the enemies of Cortés the opportunity to make the obvious accusations. Fray Tomás died within the month, as did many of his shipmates, and the partisans of Cortés, including Bernal Díaz, said that they had all contracted "sleeping sickness" during their voyage. If this Fray Tomás Ortiz is the same Fray Tomás Ortiz who enumerated the reasons why the Indians were unworthy of liberty that Peter Martyr quotes (Anghera 1912, 2: 274), including the obligatory business about being cannibals and sodomites but also condemning them to slavery because they ate fleas, spiders, and raw worms and had no beards, it would be indeed ironic if he died from the aftereffects of such a very European meal as the one he had that evening in Ixtapalapa.

The dairy industry of Mexico City recovered from this early stumble, and by 1531 the *cabildo* could set a price for cheese. The price for fresh milk, a "necessary provision," the *cabildo* said, was fixed in the following year, with the proviso that the milk be neither sour nor watered. When a price was set by the *cabildo* the sellers were usually admonished to sell by weight or by measure, the former a concept that the Europeans had brought with them. Making and certifying weights, measures, and steelyards was another responsibility of the *cabildo*.

The only foodstuff to escape this European restructuring of trade was one of the highest status pre-Columbian trade goods and the first New World product to make a place for itself on elite European menus. On January 28, 1527, the *cabildo* commanded that nobody sell cacao beans without using a measure sealed with the seal of the city (Bejarano 1889). Every deception that Sahagún listed as being utilized by the cacao trade (Sahagún 1950–1982, 10: 65) must have been brought into play, because by October 1536 the *cabildo* had changed its tune and submitted to the Aztec way of doing things.

> This day the justices and *regidores* said that those who sell cacao in the city have the price set by the thousand beans, and as the people complain that buying said cacao the sellers do not wish to count, or give it counted, but sell by weight, which is injurious because in every thousand they give one or two hundred cacao beans less . . . we command that all those who sell said cacao give it counted and not by weight, so that this deception ceases. (Orozco y Berra 1859: 45)

Let us return, however, to the dairy industry, which at this time had no connection with cacao because both the drink of chocolate with milk and the milk chocolate candy bar had yet to be invented. By December 13, 1549, fresh cheese, aged cheese, milk, cream, and *requesones* (we hope no longer new and novel in the country) were for sale (Espinosa de los Monteros 1862).

The large domesticated animals were to be kept from the Indians. Part of this was for reasons of strategic necessity—the Europeans were afraid of insurrection. They did not wish the Indians to overcome their fear of horses, and even less did they wish to see the Indians riding horses. To diminish Indian familiarity and contact with things Castilian, on May 9, 1527, the *cabildo* prohibited their buying and selling Castilian goods (Bejarano 1889) and on June 12, 1553, it forbade Indians to trade, slaughter, or sell pigs (*Libro del cabildo* n.d.). The only persons allowed to trade in pigs or pork were the European stockraisers, who were required to sell directly to the slaughterhouse.

It was not only the European animals that were to be kept from the Indians; even giving the Indians their meat was controversial. The misunderstandings between the meat-raising and meat-eating residents of the Old World and the less carnivorous inhabitants of the New World are illustrated by an episode that took place in Mexico City in 1555, when a major construction project was planned which was to use Indian laborers (*Libro del cabildo* n.d.: 195).

In pagan times, during the reigns of Motecuhzoma and his predecessors, the *cabildo* said, the precedent had been set for supplying workmen with food and other necessities. The six thousand Indians who were to repair the roads were each to be given a *quartillo* of maize a day for two months, which worked out to a total expenditure of 8,000 *hanegas*, each containing about one and a half of our bushels. The men were also, and this is what summoned a storm of indignation, to be given a pound of meat a day. This proposal affected the Europeans' pocketbooks, a sure way to get a protest. The Indians were to do the work as part of the tribute that they owed, but the maize and the meat would have to be bought either by using a royal subsidy, which was unlikely at the best of times, or from the proceeds of a *sisa,* which was a sales tax paid by the probably European buyer—of meat! No wonder the Spanish court was bombarded with complaints like the following, written in 1561.

Item: whereas the natives of this New Spain used only to eat light things, and lived healthily for many years, and with the coming of the Spaniards, and the cattle they brought with them, they began to eat beef and mutton, and have become sick, weak, and short-lived, and also they have become greatly given to drinking the wine of Castile, on which they get drunk, and being so commit great crimes and enormities, with each other and with their mothers and sisters, and kill and wound each other, there must be a remedy, and we beg His Majesty that in the Indian towns there not be, as there are, butcher shops, and that in the Spanish ones they not sell meat to said Indians, because besides the profit aforesaid meat is sustenance for the Spaniards who are in the habit of eating it, and the supply will not be exhausted as they fear it soon will be, and the same should be commanded for wine, so that the Archbishop of this city could ex-communicate anyone who sells wine to the Indians without interfer-ence from the Audiencia Real, because otherwise no ordinance or penalty is sufficient. (*Libro del cabildo* n.d.: 494)

The controversy had dragged on for five years when the *cabildo* of Mexico City finally received a dispatch from the Spanish court saying that the Indians could eat meat if they wished to and that it would be cruelty to deprive them of it (Espinosa de los Monteros n.d.: 7). The question of alcoholic beverages proved far more intractable.

There is another facet to this controversy. The distaste of the Ameri-can Indians for the fat of European animals is recorded over and over. From the sixteenth century, when the horrors brought by the conquest were listed by the Indians as prisons, and beatings, and basting with lard (Gómez de Orozco 1940: 11), to the twentieth, when a Lacandon Maya spurned a cup of coffee offered him by the Soustelles because he feared there might be grease in it, it is a recurring theme (Soustelle 1937: 35–36). Perhaps there is some sort of genetic difference in fat metabolism between populations of European and American Indian origin, as we know exists among other peoples for the ability to metab-olize alcohol or milk.

The Indians may have found lard repulsive, but it was highly valued by the Europeans newly established in the New World. There were constant disputes with the butchers about the purity of the lard, the price of it, and whether or not the butcher was absconding with fat for his own profit. Tallow was another valuable byproduct of the slaugh-terhouses, and the pricing of wax and tallow candles another responsi-bility for the *cabildo*.

Unlike the highly centralized and professionally handled meat sup-

ply, the other European staple, bread, seems to have been in the hands
of small producers during the early days of the occupation. The first
bread to have a price set on it was "native bread," presumably tortillas, regulated on July 26, 1525 (Bejarano 1889) at the same time that
prices were established for other foodstuffs sold at inns. Two years
later, on May 7, 1527, Antón de Carmona wished to have the monopoly of wheat bread (Bejarano 1889). It does not seem to have been
granted to him, but it was directed that wheat bread should be white,
clean, well-mixed, well-baked, and well-seasoned, without any admix-
ture of barley or oats. It was also suggested that a cloth be stretched
over the kneading area to protect the dough from spiders and dust fall-
ing from the ceiling, and that it be mixed with sweet water coming directly from an aqueduct, not transported by canoe.

Perhaps following the recommendation of Fernández de Oviedo in
his household book for Don Juan, the short-lived son of Ferdinand and
Isabella of Spain, that the bread maker be well known and trustwor-
thy, some households made their own bread (Fernández de Oviedo
1870: 177). The establishment (it can hardly be called a household) of
the first archbishop of Mexico, Juan de Zumárraga, was among them.
The archbishop admitted that as a Franciscan he should cook for himself, but he was too busy baptizing Indians and had an Indian slave to
cook for him and a black slave woman, María, to make his bread. In
his will, written June 2, 1548, he freed them both, and we learn that
the Indian cook, Juan Núñez, was an Indian born in Calcutta (García
Icazbalceta 1947: 287). We can only speculate as to the culinary hybrids produced by Juan Núñez.

Bread was a serious problem for the less prominent. The price of
wheat fluctuated according to the harvest, and the *cabildo* was constantly readjusting the cost of a pound loaf to conform to it. The control over the bread supply was enhanced by the power to assign mill
sites, distribute the water to power the mills, and accept or reject the
millers themselves. Milling was another thing that could not be entrusted to Indians. On July 28, 1531 (Bejarano 1889), the *cabildo* required that a knowledgeable European be on hand at all times when
grain was being ground into flour. Bread making was regarded as a
way of providing poor women with the means to support themselves,
but sometimes the women were unwilling to accept this charity, as the
following extract from the first *Libro del cabildo*, dated Wednesday,
May 5, 1529, shows:

It is said that this city is very poorly provided with bread, and the women who usually make it do not wish to make it, from which much harm is done to the inhabitants, therefore we order and command that an *alcalde* and a *regidor* go and require and order all the married and single women who have been making bread to sell, that from hence forward they make and sell bread at the fixed price, and if anyone says that they have no flour, that they go for it to the house of Antón de Carmona and he will give them flour at four *reales* the *hanega* that they will make into bread, and firewood, and that they come with said bread to said Antón de Carmona, under the penalty that if she who does not make bread is a spinster she will be publicly given one hundred lashes, and if she is married she suffers the same penalty, and she and her husband are imprisoned until they make it. And if they wish to buy wheat said Antón de Carmona will give it to them at one-half peso the *hanega*, and all the bread they make is to be taken out to be sold on the plaza, and if they do not wish to buy the wheat that said Antón de Carmona offers, that he loan each one thirty gold pesos, and they buy the wheat as they use it. (Bejarano 1889: 206)

There is no evidence of any sort of bakers' guild or organization; at least none appear in the orders of march for the Corpus Christi processions, in which the tailors, the smiths, and the carpenters all participated. This lack of concern for the provision of such a vital component of the diet as bread existed in Spain as well. In 1581 the Venetian ambassador Gioan Francesco Morosini informed his superiors in Venice that the people of Spain were fighting for bread, not because of a shortage of grain, but because there was no official competent to assure a steady supply (Albèri 1861: 286).

Another branch of the bakers' profession were the men who baked pies, the *pasteles* and *hojaldías,* which the prince who was to become Philip II consumed in what the Venetians considered "intemperate" amounts (Albèri 1853: 234). The first kind of pie, the *pastel,* usually synonymous with the *empanada,* was baked in either a crust like our pie crust or a bread dough crust, although we never hear of any bread-making woman baking pies. The other kind of pie came wrapped in flaky pastry, *hojaldre.* There seems to have been no difference between the types of fillings the various crusts could contain, but cheating on the quantity and the quality of the fillings must have been incessant, because the *cabildos* constantly inveighed against it. On January 12,

1551, the *cabildo* of Lima, Peru, then called Ciudad de los Reyes, ordered that pies be made only by specialists, in clear sight of the pas-
sersby, and immediately be put into an oven also in plain sight, so as to
eliminate the possibility of any funny business in the back room (Lee
1935). The pie makers of Lima seem to have doubled as medical specialists, because on the same date they were forbidden to administer
sarsaparilla, apply ointments, or cure those sick with buboes (Lee
1935). Alfonso de Villalón of Lima then thought up a better combination of professions and on May 16, 1552, applied for a license to sell
pies, first required of Limeño pie sellers in that year, and also for a license to sell wine, thus setting up what might be the first eat-and-run
establishment in the New World. Having the host serve pies and pour
wine seems more salubrious than having him alternately working
dough and anointing buboes (Lee 1935).

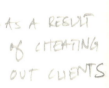
AS A RESULT
of CHEATING
OUT CLIENTS

In Mexico City at least some of the pie makers used materials provided by the customers. Presumably this gave the consumer more con-
fidence in the contents of the finished pie.

> And as some people wish to make pies for sale it shall be understood
> that giving meat and things to make it they charge for making a pie
> of a quail or a chicken a *quartillo* of a silver *real*, and if a larger re-
> spectively, and if it is a large native fowl they can charge for a pie
> containing the whole bird one *real*, and if it is cut up and made into
> more than one pie they cannot charge more than one *real*, and if
> made of Castilian fowl they can charge for a pie containing a hen
> half a *real*, and if the bird is made into several pies they cannot
> charge more than said silver half *real*, all of which is a legally fixed
> price, and must be observed on pain of legal penalty. (*Libro del ca-
> bildo* n.d.: 205)

Meat and fowl were not the only possible fillings for pies. In December 1556 the *cabildo* of Mexico City set the prices on a long list of
foodstuffs, starting with pork lard and beef fat and ending with imported wine, oil, dried fruit, and confections. The prices for three fish
pies are given in the middle of this list. They are called *empanadas*, and
a good bread dough crust is specified. An *empanada* of tuna, presumably imported from the Mediterranean preserved in salt, with proper
spicing and a good crust, was to cost half a silver *real*, as was a pie
filled with Panuco dried fish. A pie with the same quantity of filling,
half a pound, of local lake fish, *pescado de Mestitan,* the name of the

Aztec capital having as many spelling variants as Shakespeare's, cost twice as much. *Manjar blanco* is recorded as having been used as a filling, and small *empanadillas,* possibly filled with sugar and ground almonds as described by Ruperto de Nola (1982), were sold by the confectioners, to whose contributions to the food of early elite colonial Latin America we now turn.

In those days confectionery was not viewed as self-indulgence. Sugar was considered medicine as well as food: it was good for fevers, it was cleansing and digestive, and it prepared the humors for evacuation. It could be used in the form of syrups, but sugar-coated almonds were also good for the sick, and so were confits, sugar-coated anise and coriander seeds (Lobera de Avila 1952). When in 1558 Doña Ana Pizarro of Trujillo, Peru, refused to provide sugar and *confituras,* which could have been either candied fruit or fruit in heavy syrup, it was an antisocial act "considering that at present there are many sick and poor people who need sugar and *confituras* for their illnesses" (*Actas del cabildo* 1969: 287). The *cabildo* felt that they had the right to order Doña Ana to supply the goods, and when she did not, they sent Alonzo Mateos the *alguasil* to her sugar mill at Chicama to get them. Doña Ana had Alonzo Mateos arrested because he had forced the door, but the *cabildo,* because he had done it under their order, set him free. The wrangling continued for months, with sugar and sugar products being brought in from the outside to satisfy the needs of the poor and sick of Trujillo.

The confectioners of Mexico City are first mentioned on May 7, 1527, when they were selling sugar conserves, sugar, and candied almonds (Bejarano 1889). By June 25, 1538, the price was being set on white and muscovado sugar, as well as anise and coriander confits, which cost one and a half silver *reales* a pound. Marzipan, candied citron, and almonds and hazelnuts plain and candied cost two *reales* per pound (Orozco y Berra 1859). On July 3, 1545, there were complaints that the prices of sweets were set too low; no one would sell them to the sick and other people who needed them. The range was impressive, including quinces, peaches, and lemons candied or in syrup, as well as eggplants, carrots, lettuce cores, and something called *calabazate,* unclear in this context whether New World *Cucurbita* or Old World *Lagenaria,* prepared in the same way (Espinosa de los Monteros 1862). The first use of a New World product in confectionery appears at this time, with squash seeds being prepared as confits. Today hulled squash seeds are still being used in Mexico to make pralinelike confections. In the early days of their introduction to the dessert service the *cabildo* warned that the buyer must be apprised that they were purchasing a cheap substitute for almonds, not the real thing.

The importation of Old World fruits and vegetables into the New World was a process that began with the second voyage of Columbus. In other words, hardly had the Europeans discovered all those new things when they began to replace them with the old familiar ones. Five years after the conquest the price was being set in Mexico City on cardoons, members of the cabbage family, lettuces, radishes, broad beans, turnips, and carrots. On June 5, 1528, the *cabildo* discussed the necessity of planting grapes, and because Fernando Damiano had been the first to import plants and cuttings he was given permission to plant them on Chapultepec hill, provided the ground was not worked or inhabited by Indians (Bejarano 1889). Among his many recommendations to root the European settlements more permanently in the soil of the New World, Archbishop Zumárraga was adamant that as many European fruit trees as possible should be planted immediately (García Icazbalceta 1947: 292). When the colonists longed for the old country, he said, what they longed for most was the taste of the old country fruit.

By pack train over the mountains, first from the Atlantic ports and later from the Pacific ones, came ginger, cumin, caraway, and sesame seeds, as well as saffron, cinnamon, cloves, and black pepper. The last four were sold separately, or as a mixture of equal parts by weight. Perhaps this was the spice that stepped up the tuna *empanadas* in Mexico City. Ruperto de Nola, cook to King Ferdinand of Naples in the late fifteenth century whose *Libro de cozina* was published in a Spanish version in 1529, gives several such spice mixtures. Spices for a common sauce consisted of three parts cinnamon, two parts cloves, one part ginger, one part pepper, with the addition of a bit of well-ground coriander seed and a bit of saffron. The spice for peacock sauce, one of the three crowns of culinary art as far as Ruperto de Nola was concerned, was four ounces of cinnamon, one ounce cloves, one ounce ginger, and enough saffron to color (Ruperto de Nola 1982). How were the chile peppers brought as tribute by the Indians used in the Europeans' kitchens? Did they stay in the servants' quarters when confronted by these expensive and status-laden rivals?

All the ingredients for European cuisine were packed in over the mountains. Capers, different varieties of olives and raisins and herrings, prunes, dates, and figs all came this way. Wine and olive oil were imported as well, and the perpetual shortages constantly worried the *cabildo*. The vigor of the European campaign for sobriety among the Indians must have been enhanced when it resulted in more of the limited wine for the Europeans.

The Europeans wanted to have a very selective process of acculturation take place. The Indians might acquire certain profitable arts and skills, but even in these cases some European masters refused to teach them, saying that they would work too cheaply. When the Aztecs were discovered counterfeiting European coins it must have added impetus to the arguments for separate societies, as did the frightening advent of strategic thinking among the conquered, who were recorded as regretting that they had not hamstrung the horses, blown up the powder magazines, and burned the boats Cortés had had built on the lake. Some of the higher ranks of Indian society were co-opted into the European nobility, and the remainder were pushed into a world apart, where as long as the new religion was nominally observed and the tribute forthcoming, they could cultivate their own crops and eat their own foods. From the European missionaries begging for maize tortillas at the doorways of the Indian huts the scene changed to the Indians begging for wheat bread at the gateways of the monasteries. Reading the *Actas del cabildo* one would think that all the achievements of the original inhabitants of the New World had become invisible.

SEVENTEEN

A Final Banquet

For the reader interested in culinary things the Bernal Díaz del Castillo *Historia verdadera* (1982) is focused around two meals. We have read about the first one in the Aztec section of this book, where the Bernal Díaz account of the banquet of Motecuhzoma was quoted at length. Even though the description was written years later it still glows with the excitement, the bedazzlement with things newly discovered, as the two cultures, at that moment equals, encountered each other. The second banquet occurred when the enthusiasm of the discoverers had long since waned. The banquet is a European one, and the history which describes it is no longer one of the world's great adventure stories, but instead a rather wearisome tale of marches and countermarches and political squabbles. Both meals are equally removed from our own food tradition and etiquette, equally outlandish and foreign, although perhaps equivalent in their contributions to our foodways today.

This second banquet, used here because we lack any equally detailed description of a meal from the Maya area or Peru, took place in Mexico City in 1538, where the news had just arrived from Europe that Charles V and his perpetual enemy Francis I had signed yet another peace treaty (Díaz del Castillo 1982: 607–611). The two most prominent men in Mexico, Cortés, the Marqués de Valle, and the Viceroy, Antonio de Mendoza, celebrated the peace in Europe by patching up their own disputes. Bernal Díaz says that such elaborate rejoicings had never been seen before, even in Castile, and attributes their splendor to the impresario, one Luis de León, who claimed to be of patrician Roman lineage. The entertainment he organized went on for days, and Bernal Díaz, who was there, lovingly describes it all. On the first morning the city awoke to find that the great plaza had been transformed into a forest, with real wild animals and birds. Bernal Díaz commends the skill of the Indians in controlling the creatures. There were also groups of savages in the forest, and we are left guessing as to who the savages were, because the Indians are always very clearly labeled as such. The savages commenced to hunt, and others fought among themselves, but that was a mere preface to the appearance of the black king and queen, who came richly dressed on horseback with all their followers. There were hunting disputes with the savages and festivities for the black queen, and that ended the activities for the first day.

On the next day the plaza was transformed into the island of Rhodes, and Cortés played the role of the grand master of the Knights Hospitallers of Saint John of Jerusalem. What this performance meant to the spectators is obscure. The island of Rhodes is off the southwest coast of Turkey and had been the seat of the knights since the time of the Crusades. In 1480, they had repelled a siege by Mohammed II, but in 1522 another siege forced them to withdraw honorably from Rhodes and reestablish themselves on Malta, where they were to deliver a crushing blow to Ottoman forces in 1565. The Ottoman Turks were a constant threat to sixteenth-century Europe, and in fact some of the settlers in the New World worried about the possibility of Turkish raids and attempts at settlement on the new continent.

The show included four ships with masts and sails and working artillery. On their decks were Indians, dressed as Dominican monks on their way from Spain, some busily plucking fowl, while others were fishing. The Turks, all richly dressed, tried to capture the shepherds and their flocks on the island, which resulted in retaliation by the knights, while other Turks attacked the city of Rhodes. The whole thing seems to have been brought to a close by releasing wild bulls to separate the combatants.

The great ladies watching the fray from the windows overlooking the plaza were wearing their crimson and silk and damask, their gold and silver and jewels, while ladies of lesser splendor stood in the corridors. All the ladies were served a collation an hour after Vespers. Marzipan, figures made of a sugar and starch paste, candied citron, almonds, and confits seem to have been served together, and then there was more marzipan, stamped with the gilt or silvered coats of arms of the Marqués or the Viceroy. Unfortunately, Bernal Díaz does not list the native fruits that he says were passed around. The very best wines were provided, as well as mead, spiced wine, and the only dish from the pre-Columbian repertory deemed worthy of such noble company, chocolate with its foamy head. *Suplicaciones* were passed with the drinks. If the *suplicaciones* of 1538 were the same as those of today's dictionaries they were wafers made of flour, egg, and sugar dough without leavening, rolled into thin cylinders. Today such crunchy cylinders arrive thrust into elaborate ice cream desserts. Were they associated with the foamy chocolate, perhaps to help scoop up and consume the delicious foam?

This was just a preface to the two banquets which were the culmination of the celebration, the first hosted by Cortés and the second by the viceroy. All that Bernal Díaz tells us about the first one is that it was very solemn and the courses very copious. He gives a fuller description of the viceroy's banquet, starting with the decor: trees in fruit. Many native birds flew above the trees, and somewhere there was a dummy fountain of Chapultepec, with a chained great tiger, for which read jaguar. There was a figure dressed as a sleeping muleteer, whose wineskins were being drunk out of by four Indians, who were inebriated and gesticulating. They must have been automatons, because Díaz comments on how realistic they were and how men of all social conditions brought their wives to see them.

Bernal Díaz admits that he cannot remember everything that was served at this meal. The first course was two or three different salads, then roasted kids and hams *a la ginovisca,* followed by quail pies and doves, stuffed wattled fowl and chickens, *manjar blanco,* and *pepitoria.* This last was almost certainly not the dish known by that name in Mexico today but a European dish of fowl with their giblets, bound with egg yolk. *Torta real* came next, and chickens, partridges, and quail in *escabeche.* Contemporary *escabeche* consists of meat or fish fried in olive oil and then put into a marinade of vinegar or sour citrus juice for preservation and flavor. Ruperto de Nola (1982) mentions this form of *escabeche* but he also gives another variety, where the object to be preserved, in his case fish, was boiled and then cooled and covered with a sauce of bread soaked in vinegar, ground with nuts and raisins, spiced, and cooked. Ruperto de Nola comments that it eats better cold, but is not bad hot.

A change of tablecloths followed, and a procession of all sorts of foodstuffs which were not eaten. Díaz says that much of the food that preceded the tablecloth change was also not consumed. *Empanadas* of fish, fowl, and game were paraded for show, as well as boiled mutton, beef, pork, turnips, cabbages, and chick-peas. Fruit was put on the table, but Bernal Díaz does not tell us its origin. Then they brought out native fowl with their feet and beaks silvered, large water fowl with gilt beaks, and the heads of pigs, deer, and calves, these last "for splendor," according to our chronicler.

The ladies who dined with the viceroy were far more numerous than those who adorned the banquet of the Marqués del Valle. They washed down the meal with gilt goblets full of mead, wine, water, and spiced wine. After these drinks the grander ladies were presented with larger *empanadas* containing large and small rabbits, all alive, and other *empanadas* filled with live birds. They were all served and opened simultaneously, so that the rabbits hopped out over the tables and the birds fluttered about. Another course covered the tables with olives, cheese, cardoons, and native fruit. The whole business went on from nightfall until two hours after midnight, when some of the ladies protested that they could no longer bear to sit at the table, and others, in anguish, demanded to have the tablecloths removed, even though there were still dishes to come.

Meanwhile, in the patios below, a meal was served to the suites and servants of the three hundred male and two hundred female guests upstairs. For the humblest servitors, the mulattoes and Indians, there were whole young oxen, stuffed with chickens, quails, doves, and cured fat pork and then roasted. We have met this dish before, in Bologna at the coronation of Charles V as Holy Roman Emperor by Pope Clement VII in 1530. There, as in Mexico, it was served to lower-class guests, physically below and outside. In the Old World the stuffing had included that New World exotic the turkey, but in the New World this ingredient seems to have been omitted.

We are told that the excess food, of which there must have been plenty, was carried to all the houses, meaning, of course, European houses, in Mexico City. They received plates and bowls of *manjar blanco* and the pies and *empanadas* that had been paraded around. At some point the marqués was relieved of more than one hundred marks worth of silver, as well as tablecloths, napkins, and knives. The Marqués took his loss as an affirmation of his grandeur, but the Viceroy sent an Indian guard with each of his dishes when the contents were being delivered around town, and lost nothing.

There was more to follow, including bullfights and *juegos de caña*, at one of which the marqués received a wound in his foot. There were

Roasting the ox, Bologna, 1530.
Redrawn by Jean Blackburn, after Paoli 1991: 63.

horseraces and a women's footrace for a prize of gold jewelry. The authorities were so pleased with the whole affair that they had an account of it written and sent to Spain where it was received by the Council of the Indies because Charles V was in Flanders.

From our point of view, more than 450 years later, we find these banquets both similar to and different from that of Motecuhzoma. Different in that the rabbits and birds scurrying and fluttering about the table, the light-fingered guests, invited or not, the vast amount of food displayed for grandeur and not for consumption, and the edgy and uncomfortable ladies all leave one feeling queasy when compared to the description of the gravity, economy, and decorum of Motecuhzoma's banquet. Admittedly this may be because of the ignorance of our witness at the banquet of Motecuhzoma, as it is well known that what seems to the guest to be flawless order may signify disaster to the host. But certainly both these food traditions, the Aztec and the early sixteenth-century European, for which we have surviving detailed accounts of banquets, are equally alien in ingredients, menu, and accompanying ceremonial to the late twentieth-century reader.

Finale

We have concluded our exploration of the principal cuisines of the pre-Columbian New World. It has been a long trail, both in the sense of the time that has elapsed since the ancestors of the American Indians arrived as hunters and gatherers in the New World and started looking for something to eat, and in the geographical extent of our investigations. We have not only traveled through time and horizontal space, we have also traveled vertically from the waters of the oceans to the snowlines of some of the world's highest mountains. Even in inhospitable circumstances we have found the American Indians exploiting just about every microenvironment capable of producing edible matter, as well as developing varieties of edibles to suit the available microenvironments, and in the later stages manipulating the microenvironment as well. That the foodstuffs they domesticated have in many cases spread around the world and become part of the culinary heritage of humanity adds to the honor due to their original discoverers.

The Aztecs, the Maya, and the Inca, the people we have investigated most closely, mainly because the available sources allow us to almost literally open their cooking pots and peer in, were as much the products of millennia of culinary evolution as their Old World conquerors. There may have been differences in things like metal use or the control of the wheel, but in culinary matters the conquering Old World tribe was pretty much on the same level as the conquered New World tribes.

The peoples of the New World and the Old World depended on one, or at most two, staple plant carbohydrate sources. If the crop of the staple plant failed, famine was the result. Any contemporary European ruler could have readily understood and sympathized with the Aztec emperor Motecuhzoma I, during whose reign the Aztec maize crop failed for three years running and his starving subjects had to sell themselves into slavery to survive. There is enough mention of famine and picturing of famine food plants in the Maya prophetic books to convince us that the problem was well known to them. Only among the Inca does this constant threat of medieval life seem to have been done away with by the redistribution system. The accounts of people starving in the streets come from after the European conquest, when the contents of the state warehouses had been dispersed by European greed. It is one more recognition of the achievement of the American Indians in the field of domestication that the more perceptive European agricultural writers of the eighteenth and nineteenth centuries credited the disappearance of widespread and massive famines to the introductions of new crops from the New World.

As the domestication of a plant, staple or not, turns out to be a very slow process of adaptation taking place between plant and propagator, so the adoption of New World food plants by the Old World, and Old World food plants by the New, was, and in some places continues to be, a matter taking centuries. In the vast menu of the 1538 festivities in Mexico City only two New World plant food items were mentioned. Something brushed off as "native fruit" was part of the banquet, and curiously enough it was at the ladies' collation, overlooking the spectacle taking place on the main plaza, that chocolate, a royal drink in the New World that was soon to attain the same status in the Old World, was served.

The slow interpenetration of cuisines, with various foods being accepted in various places for various reasons, was aided by many stimuli, some of them not in the least connected with things culinary. Cheapness was a major one, transportability and storability were others, as well as ease of cultivation. When we complain that the produce in the supermarket is designed by the breeders for just about every purpose save gustatory pleasure we are not discovering anything new.

The decisions which caused the explosive expansion of certain crops had their negative aspects as well. Certain foods were judged cheap and easy to grow, transport, and consume, and others were condemned as unsuitable. Unfortunately these decisions were made in the sixteenth, seventeenth, and eighteenth centuries, when transportation and agricultural practices were, to put it mildly, different from those in use today. Who knows how many cultivars, and entire edible species, have been lost to us because of some decision made in the seventeenth century for reasons that would be utterly irrelevant and ridiculous today. Reading about the foodstuffs of the Aztecs, Maya, Inca, and their European contemporaries, we come across many things which we either do not think of eating today or have simply never heard of. Given modern agricultural and transportation technology, plus the infinitely persuasive power of modern advertising, perhaps we still have a chance to aim for a healthier diversity of foodstuffs, instead of eating more and more of the same fat, soft, sweet things.

Of course it is foolish to blame the past for foodstuffs which are denied us. Part of the problem is ours. Eating habits are very deeply ingrained, a fact which is made evident by the position of apple pie right next to Mom in the litany of sacred objects.

We have shed many food regulations and prejudices, to be sure, but they have almost immediately been replaced by others, based on new criteria but no less binding. Arrest and investigation by the Inquisition may not await us if we eat a piece of meat on the wrong day of the calendar, but it has been replaced by innumerable threats to what we believe to be our health if we eat that same bit of meat. Perhaps human beings cannot confront the monstrous number of decisions that must be made when they are steering a course through the supermarket and as a crutch need to have all the admonitions about health, lifestyle, economy of time and effort, and whatever else the gnomes of advertising have decided will push their buttons for the week.

But even before the outside world's modern persuaders get at us, limits have been set on what we eat. Some of this is done by Western culture—no bugs, thank you very much, even though the Old Testament prohibition explicitly permits grasshoppers, locusts, and their kind. Narrower groups have their customs too, such as the American dislike for leaving the heads on fish. Finally, the family and individual have their laws, be they the exiling of the onion family or the exclusion of liver, tripe, or kidneys. It is probably only our own tribe, which considers itself far more sophisticated than the four tribes that we have been discussing, that can afford such an elaborate proliferation of prohibitions. If one's food supply is liable to be suddenly and drastically curtailed by forces beyond one's control one is not going to add artificial barriers to the all-too-real ones.

In many ways the fifth tribe, ours, is by far the most divergent when compared with the Aztecs, the Maya, the Inca, and their conquerors. We are the only tribe without a carbohydrate staple; we are also the first tribe in the history of our species whose members suffer from surfeit. In no way am I going to recommend a return to the diet of the Aztecs, or that of Paleolithic people, or any other romantic, reconstructed way of feeding. The foodstuffs are not the same, and neither are we. But knowledge of the past will help us to shake the bars of our cage and perhaps expand the perimeters a bit.

It is not a crime or a sin to know about and think about what you are eating. The origin of the bean, or of the potato, should be part of the landscape of everybody's mind, so that eating is not just an automatic process, as exciting and interesting as the fact that the thermostat has just turned the furnace on. If we know something about the history of the things that we consume perhaps we will give them more respect as substances, as well as honoring those who perform the process of making them into something edible. No more hurling the leaf lettuce into the bag, shouting "You can't bruise lettuce" as you do so. No more putting one scoop each of twelve different kinds of ice cream into a bowl and mushing them all together with a spoon, as the late Elvis Presley is reputed to have done.

The history of food is one of the last intellectual frontiers. For years it was considered unworthy of the finer efforts of educated men and women, those same educated men and women who parroted slogans about "eating to live and not living to eat" and made sure that the restaurants in American academic communities were uniformly abominable. It has finally begun to dawn on the public that the food of a country is as legitimate a field of study as its politics or its philosophy, and that the old school of food writing, which might well be called gastro-pornography, is not the only way to approach a cuisine. I hope that this book, one of the first attempts to study the major New World cuisines on a historical and factual basis, will be but the forerunner of other more detailed and more profound studies.

It is instructive to trace the evolution of writing about the food of the New World. In the beginning we have seen it being used as just one more justification for the extermination of the peoples of the New World—those cannibals, consumers of bugs and vermin and raw meat. Then, for centuries, silence, as the Old World appropriated New World achievements, sometimes to the detriment of the Old World when they jettisoned the accompanying New World processing techniques, as we have seen with the nixtamalization of maize. The dictionaries continue to list the words for native American dishes, and they certainly were made and enjoyed in mestizo kitchens and native households, but as with many humble dishes of common folk, the recipes were not written down because it was assumed that everybody who wanted to knew how to cook them anyway. Meanwhile in eighteenth-century Europe there were authors like Robertson and Paw abusing all the productions of the New World even-handedly—both the native land and its inhabitants and products were weaklings, and even those of European ancestry who went there were infected with inferiority. How much they delayed the acceptance of plants like the potato and the tomato we shall never know, as we shall never know how many people starved to death because of their prejudices.

It is not until the nineteenth century that cookbooks appear in Mexico that give recipes for some native dishes that survived the European conquest, and it is only within the past ten years that we have seen flashy books on the regional cuisines of Mexico, for instance, published. Not that a culinary coffee table book is any great sign of progress, but at least they recognize that these dishes are something to be proud of and glorified by elaborately staged photographs.

Today in our country the treatment of pre-Columbian foodstuffs and food has taken two paths. One of them might be described as the American Indian mystique school, where these people are considered to be closer to the soil, nature, the universe, and so forth, possessors of the true diet as well as the true everything else. Yet if you read on about what is supposed to be their diet you find something that no preconquest dweller on this continent would recognize. It sounds much more like a contemporary trendy regimen trying for authentication by attaching itself to the American Indians, without troubling with any research.

The other school, that of the more popular culinary press, does not trouble itself with the facts either. How many times have I read that Motecuhzoma II, of course never called by his proper name, drank five hundred cups of chocolate a day, even though the Bernal Díaz story is available in every library? We are fortunate when the similarity in sounds between *coca* and *cocoa* does not bring the information that chocolate was known and copiously consumed by the Inca of Peru— one more consequence of the deeply ingrained habit of not taking food, and information about it, seriously. Or is this another example of the deplorable tendency to deny the American Indians all their attainments, crediting them instead to Orientals, Europeans, or Africans visiting from across the oceans? I hope enough has been said in the preceding pages to convince the reader of the indigenous American origin of these cuisines and their ingredients.

This book started with the promise that it was going to recount and celebrate the contribution of the New World, its lands and its peoples, to the cuisine of the world. It is to be hoped that it is not an overly Europe-centered account of the food of the Aztecs, the Maya, and the Inca and what happened to it during the first few decades of their coexistence with a fourth tribe, the Europeans. It should show us that not everybody eats the way we do, and that other culinary cultures can provide us not only with actual things to eat, but with food for thought as well. As well as enriching our diet, this encounter could also enrich our minds, and let us hope that this enrichment is but a beginning!

Bibliography

Acosta, José de
1954   *Historia natural y moral de las Indias*. Biblioteca de Autores
            Españoles, vol. 73. Madrid: Atlas.
Actas del cabildo de Trujillo, 1549–1560
1969   Concejo Provincial de Trujillo. Peru: Lima.
Albèri, Eugenio (ed.)
1853   *Relazione degli ambasciatori veneti al senato*, Series 1, vol. 3.
            Florence: Società Editrice Fiorentina.
1859   *Relazione degli ambasciatori veneti al senato*, Series 1, vol. 1.
            Florence: Clio.
1861   *Relazione degli ambasciatori veneti al senato*, Series 1, vol. 5.
            Florence: published by the editor.
Aldrovandi, Ulisse
1963   *Aldrovandi on Chickens*. Norman: University of Oklahoma
            Press.
Allwood, Montagu
n.d.   *English Countryside and Gardens*. Vol. 2. Wivelsfield Green,
            Sussex: published by the author.
Alvarado Tezozomoc, H.
1944   *Crónica mexicana*. Mexico City: Editorial Leyenda.
Anastos, M. V.
1966   "Iconoclasm and Imperial Rule, 717–842." In J. M. Hussey,
            ed., *The Cambridge Medieval History, IV: The Byzantine Em-
            pire, Part 1, Byzantium and Its Neighbors*. Cambridge: Cam-
            bridge University Press.
Anghera, Peter Martyr d'
1912   *De orbe novo*. New York: G. P. Putnam's.

Anon.
n.d.   *Littera mādata della insula de Cuba de Indie.*
Anon.
1853   In *Documentos para la historia de México.* Mexico City: Archivo Mexicano, Vicente García Torres.
Anon.
1870   In *Colección de documentos inéditos relativos al descubrimiento, conquista y colonización de las posesiones españolas en América y Oceania,* vol. 14. Madrid: José María Pérez.
Anon.
1898   *Relaciones de Yucatán.* Colección de documentos inéditos relativos al descubrimiento, conquista y organisación de las antiguas posesiones españolas de Ultramar, Series 2, vol. 2. Madrid.
Anon.
1940   *The Badianus Manuscript.* Baltimore, Md.: Johns Hopkins University Press.
Anon.
1968   *Relación de las costumbres antiguas de los naturales del Pirú.* Biblioteca de Autores Españoles, vol. 209. Madrid: Atlas.
Anon.
1979   *Teatro indígena prehispánico (Rabinal Achí).* Mexico City: UNAM.
Anon. [Juan de Tovar]
1987   *Origen de los mexicanos.* Madrid: Historia 16.
Antuñez de Mayolo, S.
1981   *La nutrición en el antiguo Perú.* Lima: Banco Central de Reserva del Perú.
Arriaga, Pablo José de
1968   *Extirpación de la idolatría del Pirú.* Biblioteca de Autores Españoles, vol. 209. Madrid: Atlas.
Baer, Phillip, and William R. Merrifield
1971   *Two Studies on the Lacandones of Mexico.* Norman: Summer Institute of Linguistics of the University of Oklahoma.
Banks, Joseph
1896   *Journal,* ed. Joseph D. Hooker. London: Macmillan.
Barrera Vásquez, Alfredo
1985   *El libro de los libros de Chilam Balam.* Mexico City: CFE.
Beadle, George W.
1980   "The Ancestry of Corn." *Scientific American* 242, no. 1.
Bejarano, Ignacio (ed.)
1889   *Primer libro de las actas de cabildo de la ciudad de México.* Mexico City: Aguilar e Hijos.

Benzoni, Gerolamo
1962   *La historia del mondo nuovo*. Graz.
Berglund-Brücher, Ollie, and Heinz Brücher
1976   "The South American Wild Bean (*Phaseolus aborigineus* Burk)
            as Ancestor of the Common Bean." *Economic Botany* 30,
            no. 3.
Berlin, Brent
1967   "Categories of Eating in Tzeltal and Navaho." *International
            Journal of American Linguistics* 33, no. 1.
Bernachon, Maurice, and Jean-Jacques Bernachon
1985   *La Passion du chocolat*. Paris: Flammarion.
Bertonio, Ludovico
1879   *Vocabulario de la lengua aymara*. Leipzig: B. G. Teubner.
Betanzos, Juan de
1968   *Suma y narración de los Incas*. Biblioteca de Autores Español-
            oles, vol. 209. Madrid: Atlas.
1987   *Suma y narración de los Incas*. Madrid: Atlas.
Biblioteca Peruana
1968   Primera Serie, Editores Técnicos Asociados, Lima, Peru.
Buc'hoz, Jean Pierre
1787   *Dissertation sur le cacao*. Paris.
Byers, D. S. (ed.)
1964   *The Prehistory of the Tehuacán Valley: Environment and Sub-
            sistence*. Austin: University of Texas Press.
Cabello Valboa, Miguel
1951   *Miscelánea antárctica*. Lima, Peru: Universidad Nacional
            Mayor de San Marcos.
Calancha, Antonio de la
1972   *Crónicas agustinianas del Perú*. Madrid: Consejo Superior de
            Investigaciones Científicos.
1974   *Crónica moralizada*. Crónicas del Perú, Lima, Peru: Edición da
            Ignacio Prado Pastor.
Callen, E. O.
1967   "The First New World Cereal." *American Anthropologist* 32,
            no. 4.
Cantù, Francesca
1979   *Pedro de Cieza de León e il "Descubrimiento y conquista del
            Perú."* Rome: Istituto Storico Italiano per l'età Moderna e
            Contemporanea.
Cárdenas, Juan de
1913   *Primera parte de los problemas y secretos marauillosos de las
            Indias*. Mexico City: Museo Nacional de Arqueología, Histo-
            ria y Etnología.

Carletti, Francesco
1701   *Ragionamenti di Francesco Carletti Fiorentino sopra le cose da lui vedute ne' suoi viaggi.* Firenze: Giuseppe Manni.

Carmack, Robert M., and James L. Mondlock
1983   *El título de Totonicapán.* Mexico City: UNAM.

Cervantes de Salazar, Francisco
1914   *Crónica de Nueva España,* vol. 1. Madrid: Hauser y Menet.
1936   *Crónica de Nueva España,* vol. 2. Mexico City: Museo Nacional de Arqueología, Historia y Etnografía.

Chapman, Jefferson, Robert B. Stewart, and Richard A. Yarnell
1974   "Archaeological Evidence for Precolumbian Introduction of *Portulaca oleracea* and *Mollugo verticillata* into Eastern North America." *Economic Botany* 28, no. 4.

Chittenden, F. J. (ed.)
1974   *The Royal Horticultural Society Dictionary of Gardening.* Oxford.

Cieza de León, P.
n.d.   "La crónica del Perú." In *Crónicas de la conquista del Perú.* Mexico City: Editorial Nueva España.
1967   *El señorio de los Incas.* Lima: Instituto de Estudios Peruanos.

Ciudad Real, Antonio
1976   *Tratado curioso y docto de las grandezas de la Nueva España.* Mexico City: UNAM.

Clavigero [Clavijero], Francisco Saverio
1780   *Storia antica del Messico.* Cesena: Gregorio Biasini.

Cobo, Bernabe
1890–1893   *Historia del nuevo mundo.* Seville: Sociedad de Bibliófilos Andaluces.
1979   *History of the Inca Empire.* Austin: University of Texas Press.

Códice franciscano siglo XVI
1941   Mexico City: Nueva Colección de Documentos Para la Historia de México, Salvador Chavez Hayhoe.

Coe, Michael D.
1973   *The Maya Scribe and His World.* New York: Grolier Club.

Cogolludo, Diego López
1954–1955   *Historia de Yucatán.* Campeche, Mexico: Comisión de Historia.

Colón, Fernando
1749   *La historia de d. Fernando Colon.* Madrid: Historiadores Primitivos de las Indias Occidentales.

Cooper-Clark, James (ed.)
1938   *Codex Mendoza.* London: Waterlow.

Cortés, Hernán
1986   *Letters from Mexico.* New Haven: Yale University Press.
Cushing, F. H.
1920   *Zuñi Breadstuff.* Indian Notes and Monographs, vol. 8. New York: Museum of the American Indian, Heye Foundation.
Dampier, William
1906   *Dampier's Voyages.* London: E. Grant Richards.
Díaz, Juan
1526   "Itinerario de Lisola de Iuchatan." In Ludovico Varthema, *Itinerario de Ludovico de Varthema Bolognese nel Egitto, nella Suria, nella Arabia deserta, e Felice, nella Persia, nella India, a nella Ethyopia.* Venice.
1838   "Itinéraire du voyage de la flotte du roi catholique a l'île de Yucatán." In H. Ternaux-Compans (ed.), *Voyages, relations et mémoires originaux pour servir a l'histoire de la découverte de l'Amérique.* Paris: Arthus Bertrand.
Díaz del Castillo, Bernal
1982   *Historia verdadera de la conquista de la Nueva España.* Madrid: Instituto Gonzalo Fernández de Oviedo.
Diderot, Denis
1779   *Encyclopédie, ou Dictionnaire raisonné des sciences, des arts et des métiers,* 3d ed. Geneva: Pellet.
Dorantes de Carranza, Baltasar
1902   *Sumaria relación de las cosas de la Nueva España.* Mexico City: Museo Nacional.
Dufour, Phillipe
1685   *The Manner of Making Coffee, Tea, and Chocolate.* London: printed for William Crook.
Durán, Diego
1964   *The Aztecs.* New York: Orion Press.
1971   *Book of the Gods and Rites and the Ancient Calendar.* Norman: University of Oklahoma Press.
Earle, Timothy, et al.
1987   *Archaeological Field Research in the Upper Mantaro, Peru, 1982–83: Investigations of Inka Expansion and Exchange.* Monograph 28, Institute of Archaeology. Los Angeles: University of California.
Espinosa de los Monteros, Antonio (ed.)
n.d.   *7° libro de cabildo.* Mexico City: Librería Navarro.
1862   *Quinto libro de actas de la Ciudad de México.* Mexico City: Libreria Navarro.
Esquemeling, John
1684   *Bucaniers of America.* London: William Crook.

Estete, Miguel de
1924 "Noticia del Perú." In Horacio H. Urteaga (ed.), *Historia de los Incas y conquista del Perú.* Colección de Libros y Documentos Referentes a la Historia del Perú, Serie 2, vol. 8. Lima.
Estrada Monroy, Agustín
1979 *El mundo k'ekchi' de la Vera-Paz.* Guatemala: Editorial del Ejército.
Evelyn, John
1818 *Memoirs.* London: Henry Colburn.
Fauvet-Berthelot, Marie-France
1986 "Ethnopréhistoire de la maison Maya." *Etudes Mésoamericaines,* vol. 13. Mexico City.
Fernández de Oviedo, Gonzalo
1870 *Libro de la camara real del principe don Juan.* Madrid: La Sociedad de Bibliófilos Españoles.
1959 *Historia natural y general de las Indias.* Biblioteca de Autores Españoles, vols. 117–121. Madrid: Atlas.
1985 "Della naturale e generale istoria dell'Indie." In Giovanni Battista Ramusio, *Navigazione e Viaggi,* vol. 5. Torino: Einaudi.
Gage, Thomas
1958 *Thomas Gage's Travels in the New World.* Norman: University of Oklahoma Press.
García Icazbalceta, Joaquín
1947 *Don fray Juan de Zumárraga.* Mexico City: Porrúa.
García Pimentel, L. (ed.)
1903 *Memoriales de fray Toribio de Motolinía.* Mexico City: Casa del Editor.
Garcilaso de la Vega, I.
1945 *Comentarios reales de los Incas.* Buenos Aires: Emecé.
Gómez de Orozco, F. (ed.)
1940 *Crónicas de Michoacán.* Mexico City: UNAM.
González Holguín, Diego
1952 *Vocabulario de la lengua general de todo el Perú llamada lengua quichua o del Inca.* Lima: Santa María.
Guaman Poma de Ayala, Felipe
1936 *Nueva corónica y buen gobierno.* Paris: Institut d'Ethnologie.
1980 *El primer nueva corónica y buen gobierno.* Mexico City: Siglo Veintiuno.
Hall, Grant D., Stanley M. Tarka, Jr., W. Jeffrey Hurst, David Stuart, and Richard E. W. Adams
1990 "Cacao Residues in Ancient Maya Vessels from Río Azul, Guatemala." *American Antiquity* 55, no. 1.

Hamblin, Nancy L., and Amadeo M. Rea
1985   "Isla Cozumel Archaeological Avifauna." In Mary Pohl (ed.),
            *Prehistoric Lowland Maya Environment and Subsistence
            Economy.* Peabody Papers no. 77. Cambridge, Mass.
Harner, Michael
1977   "The Ecological Basis for Aztec Sacrifice." *American Ethnolo-
            gist* 4.
Hawkes, J. G.
1967   "The History of the Potato." *Journal of the Royal Horticul-
            tural Society* 92, parts 5, 6, 7, 8.
Heiser, Charles B.
1985   *Of Plants and People.* Norman: University of Oklahoma Press.
Hernández, Francisco
1945   *Antigüedades de la Nueva España.* Mexico City: Pedro
            Robredo.
1959   *Obras completas.* Mexico City: UNAM.
Holmberg, Allan R.
1957   "Lizard Hunts on the North Coast of Peru." *Fieldiana* 36,
            no. 9.
Hosking, F. J.
1948   "Corn Products." *Economic Botany* 2, no. 4.
Ixtlilxochitl, Fernando de Alva
1975   *Obras históricas.* Mexico City: UNAM.
1985   *Historia de la nación chichimeca.* Madrid: Historia 16.
Kalm, Peter
1974   "Description of Maize." *Economic Botany* 28.
Katz, S. H., M. L. Hediger, and L. A. Valleroy
1974   "Traditional Maize Processing Techniques in the New
            World." *Science* 184.
Kempton, J. H., and W. Popenoe
1937   "Teosinte in Guatemala." *Contributions to American Archae-
            ology,* no. 23. Washington, D.C.: Carnegie Institution of
            Washington.
La Fayette, Eugène
1885   *French Family Cook Book.* London: Paris Publishing Co.
Landa, Diego de
1973   *Relación de las cosas de Yucatan.* Mexico City: Porrúa.
Las Casas, Bartolomé de
1958   *Apologética historia.* Biblioteca de Autores Españoles, vols.
            105–106, Madrid: Atlas.
1961   *Historia de las Indias.* Biblioteca de Autores Españoles, vol. 96.
            Madrid: Atlas.

La Torre, Tomás de
1944   *Desde Salamanca, España, hasta Ciudad Real, Chiapas.* Mexico City: Editora Central.
Lee, Bertram T. (ed.)
1935   *Libros de cabildos de Lima, libro cuatro, años 1548–1553.* Lima: Sanmartí y Cia.
Lewis, Dio
1872   *Our Digestion; or, My Jolly Friend's Secret.* Philadelphia and Boston: George Maclean.
Libro del cabildo e ayuntamiento desta ynsine e muy leal ciudad de Tenuxtitan México
n.d.   Mexico City: Librería Navarro.
Lobera de Avila, Luis
1952   *Banquete de nobles caballeros.* (Originally published in 1530.) Madrid: Reimpresiones Bibliográficas.
López de Gomara, F.
1946   *La conquista de Méjico.*
McGee, Harold
1990   *The Curious Cook.* San Francisco: North Point Press.
Mabberley, D. J.
1989   *The Plant-book.* Cambridge, England: Cambridge University Press.
Magalotti, Lorenzo
1924   *Le più belle pagine di Lorenzo Magalotti.* Milano: Fratelli Treves.
Mangelsdorf, Paul C.
1974   *Corn, Its Origin, Evolution and Improvement.* Cambridge, Mass.: Harvard University Press.
Mangelsdorf, Paul C., R. S. MacNeish, and W. C. Galinat
1956   "Archaeological Evidence on the Diffusion and Evolution of Maize in Northeastern Mexico." *Botanical Museum Leaflets,* vol. 17, no. 5. Cambridge, Mass.: Harvard University.
1964   "Domestication of Corn." *Science,* vol. 143.
Marcus, Joyce
1987   "Prehistoric Fishermen in the Kingdom of Huarco." *American Scientist* 75, no. 4 (July–August).
Melhus, Irving E., and I. M. Chamberlain
1953   "A Preliminary Study of Teosinte in Its Region of Origin." *Iowa State College Journal of Science* 28, no. 2.
Mendoza, Antonio de
1864   "Carta al emperador." *Colección de documentos inéditos rela-*

tivos al descubrimiento, conquista y organización de las antiguas posesiones españolas de América y Oceanía, vol. 2. Madrid: Imprenta Española.

Molina, Cristóbal de
1943   "Destrucción del Perú." In *Las crónicas de los Molinas.* Los Pequeños Grandes Libros de Historia Americana, Serie 1, vol. 4. Lima.

Monardes, N.
1925   *Joyfull Newes out of the Newe Founde Worlde.* London: Constable.

Morgan, Lewis Henry
1950   *Montezuma's Dinner: An Essay on the Tribal Society of the North American Indians.* New York: New York Labor News Company.

Morison, Samuel Eliot
1963   *Journals and Other Documents on the Life and Voyages of Christopher Columbus.* New York: Heritage Press.

Mortimer, W. G.
1901   *Peru History of Coca.* New York: J. H. Vail and Co.

Motolinía [Toribio de Benavente]
1903   *Memoriales.* Mexico City: Luis García Pimentel.
1951   *Motolinía's History of the Indians of New Spain.* Washington, D.C.: Academy of American Franciscan History.

Muñoz Camargo, Diego
1981   *Descripción de la Ciudad y Provincia de Tlaxcala de las Indias y del Mar Océano para el buen gobierno y enoblecimiento dellas.* Mexico City: UNAM.

Murrey, Thomas
1884   *Salads and Sauces.* New York: Frederick A. Stokes Company.

Murua, M. de
1962   *Historia general del Perú, origen y descendencia de los Incas.* Madrid: Biblioteca Americana Vetus.

Navajero, Andres [Andrea Navagero]
1879   "Viaje por España." In *Viajes por España.* Madrid: Librería de los Bibliófilos.

Nuttall, Zelia
1930   "Documentary Evidence Concerning Wild Maize in Mexico." *Journal of Heredity* 21, no. 5.

Orozco y Berra, Manuel (ed.)
1859   *Terzer libro de las actas de cabildo.* Mexico City: Librería Navarro.

1880 *Historia antigua y de la conquista de México.* Mexico City: Gonzalo A. Estevo.

Palafox y Mendoza, Juan de
1893 *Virtudes del Indio.* Madrid: Tomás Minuesa de los Ríos.

Paoli, Feliciano
1991 *Il trionfo di Carlo V.* Urbania: Museo Civico.

Pizarro, Pedro
1978 *Relación del descubrimiento y conquista del Perú.* Lima: Pontífica Universidad Católica del Perú.

Popenoe, W.
1919 "Batido and Other Guatemalan Beverages Prepared from Cacao." *American Anthropologist,* n.s. 21.

Porras Barrenechea, Raúl
1959 *Cartas del Perú (1524–1543).* Colección de documentos inéditos para la historia del Perú 3. Lima: Edición de la Sociedad de Bibliófilos peruanos.

1986 *Los cronistas del Perú (1528–1650).* Lima: Banco de Crédito del Perú.

Purseglove, J. W.
1968 *Tropical Crops: Dicotyledons.* Essex, England: Longman, Harlow.

Raynal, Guillaume
1774 *Histoire philosophique et politique.* La Haye: Chez Gosse.

Redi, Francesco
1811 *Opere.* Milano: Classici Italiani.

Remesal, Antonio de
1964 *Historia general de las Indias Occidentales y particular de la governación de Chiapa y Guatemala.* Biblioteca de Autores Españoles, vol. 175. Madrid: Atlas.

Roversi, Giancarlo
1984 "Tra vecchia e nuova cucina." In Aurelio Bassani and Giancarlo Roversi (eds.), *Eminenza, il pranzo è servito.* Bologna: Aniballi Edizione.

Roys, Ralph L.
1931 *The Ethno-Botany of the Maya.* Middle American Research Series Publication no. 2. New Orleans: Tulane.

1933 *The Book of Chilam Balam of Chumayel.* Washington, D.C.: Carnegie Institution of Washington.

Ruiz López, Hipólito
1952 *Relación histórica del viage que hizo a los reynos del Perú y Chile.* Madrid: Real Academia de Ciencias Exactas, Físicas y Naturales.

Ruperto de Nola
1982   *Libro de Cozina.* (Originally published in 1529.) Madrid: Co-
            lección "El Bibliófilo."
Sáenz de Santa María, Carmelo
1963   *Vida y escritos de don Francisco Marroquín.* Anales de la So-
            ciedad de Geografía e Historia, año 36. Guatemala.
Sahagún, Bernardino de
1950–1982   *General History of the Things of New Spain: Florentine Co-
            dex.* Santa Fe, N. M.: School of American Research.
1982   *Historia general de las cosas de Nueva España.* Mexico City:
            Porrúa.
Santacruz Pachacuti Yamqui, Joan de
1968   *Relación de antigüedades deste reyno del Perú.* Biblioteca de
            Autores Españoles, vol. 209. Madrid: Atlas.
Santamaría, F. J.
1959   *Diccionario de mejicanismos.* Mexico City: Porrúa.
Santillan, Fernando de
1879   *Relación del origen, descendencia, política y gobierno de los
            Incas.* Madrid: Ministerio de Fomento.
Scappi, Bartolomeo
1981   *Opera [dell'arte del cucinare],* facsimile of 1570 edition. Vene-
            zia: Arnaldo Forni.
Scholes, France V., and Eleanor B. Adams
1938   *Don Diego Quijada alcalde mayor de Yucatán 1561–1565.*
            Biblioteca Histórica Mexicana de Obras Inéditas, vol. 14.
            Mexico City.
Schultes, Richard E.
1956   "The Genus *Quararibea* in Mexico and the Use of Its Flowers
            as a Spice for Chocolate." *Harvard Botanical Museum Leaflets*
            17, no. 8. Cambridge, Mass.
Serra, Juan de Santa Gertrudis
1970   *Maravillas de la naturaleza.* Bogotá: Biblioteca Banco Popular.
Soustelle, Georgette
1959   "Observations sur la religion des Lacandons du Mexique Mér-
            idional." *Journal de la Société des Américanistes,* n.s. vol. 48.
            Paris.
Soustelle, Jacques
1937   *La Culture matérielle des indiens lacandons.* Paris: Société des
            Américanistes.
Squier, E. George
1877   *Peru: Incidents of Travel and Exploration in the Land of the
            Incas.* New York: Harper Brothers.

Stahl, P. W., and Presley Norton
1987   "Precolumbian Animal Domestication from Salango, Ecua-
          dor." *American Antiquity* 52, no. 2.
Standley, Paul C.
1946   "Food Plants of the Indians of the Guatemalan Highlands."
          Journal of the Arnold Arboretum 27.
Tax, Sol
1950   *Panajachel Field Notes.* Chicago Manuscripts in Middle Amer-
          ican Cultural Anthropology, no. 29.
Tedlock, D.
1985   *Popul Vuh.* New York: Simon and Schuster.
Teresa de Jesús
1959   *Obras completas.* Madrid: Biblioteca de Autores Cristianos.
Thompson, Donald E., and Craig Morris
1985   *Huánuco Pampa.* London: Thames and Hudson.
Torquemada, Juan de
1943   *Monarquía indiana.* Mexico City: Salvador Chávez Hayhoe.
Tozzer, A. M. (ed.)
1941   *Landa's Relación de las cosas de Yucatan.* Papers of the Pea-
          body Museum no. 18. Cambridge, Mass.: Harvard University.
Trujillo, Diego de
1948   *Relación del descubrimiento del reyno del Perú.* Seville: Es-
          cuela de Estudios Hispano-Americanos.
Tudela de la Orden, José
1980   *Códice Tudela.* Ediciones Cultura Hispánica del Instituto de
          Cooperación Iberoamericana. Madrid.
Ulloa, M., and T. Herrera
1986   "Fermented Corn Products of Mexico." *Indigenous Fermented
          Food of Non-Western Origin.* Mycologia Memoir no. 11. Ber-
          lin: J. Cramer.
Valenzuela, Nicolás de
1979   *Conquista del Lacandón y conquista del Chol.* Berlin: Collo-
          quium Verlag.
Velasco, Juan de
1977   *Historia del reino de Quito en la América meridional.* Quito:
          Casa de la Cultura Ecuatoriana.
Vilmorin-Andrieux, M.
1885   *The Vegetable Garden.* London: John Murray.
White, Christine D., and Henry P. Schwarcz
1989   "Ancient Maya Diet: As Inferred from Isotopic and Elemental
          Analysis of Human Bone." *Journal of Archaeological Science*
          16.

Xerez, Francisco de
1988   *La conquista del Perú e provincia del Cusco*. In Giovanni Battista Ramusio, *Navigazioni e viaggi,* vol. 6. Torino: Einaudi.
Xiu, Gaspar Antonio
1986   *Usos y costumbres de los indios de Yucatán*. Mérida: Maldonado Editores.
Yacovleff, E., and F. L. Herrera
1934–1935   "El mundo vegetal de los antiguos Peruanos." *Revista del Museo Nacional* 3, nos. 1–2; 4, no. 1. Lima.
Zanon, Antonio
1982   *Lettere a Fabio Asquini (1762–1769)*. Udine: Ribis.
Zarate, A.
1968   *The Discovery and Conquest of Peru*. London: Penguin.

Index

Boldface page numbers indicate illustrations.

Flesh consumption: Inca, 221,
224–225; Maya, 153–160
Food processing, 7–8, 36
Fowl: Maya, 123–125; New
World varieties, 124
Frogs: Aztec use, 100; Inca use,
177–178; Maya use, 156–157
Fruit: Aztec, 95; European, in
New World, 239; Inca,
186–191; Maya, 165

Gage, Thomas, 51, 157
Game, wild: Aztec consumption,
99; Inca, 176–177, 219
Garcilaso de la Vega, I., 181–182,
185–187, 192–193, 207–208,
219, 221–223
Gardens, botanical, 42
Garlic vine, 159
González Holguín, Diego, 223
Goosefoot, 90. *See also*
Chenopodium
Grapes, in New World, 239
Greens: Aztec, 90, 93–95; and
beans, 163; *chocho,* 182; *epa-
zote,* 181; as food for poor, 28,
220; Inca, 181, 182, 185, 220;
Maya, 153, 154, 164–165; and
posolli, 137; *teosinte,* 12
Gregory XIII, Pope, 55
Grijalva, Juan de, 127–129
Gruel. *See Atolli*
Guacamole, 45. *See also* Avocado
Guadeloupe, island of, 43
Guaman Poma de Ayala, Felipe:
on Inca, 195, 196–198, 201,
219–220
Guanaco: Inca use, 171
Guatemala highlands, 139, 144,
154, 158
Guinea pig: Inca use, 174–175;
Maya use, 127
Guzmán, Juan de, 48

Hamblin, Nancy L., 154
Harner, Michael, 97–99
Hernández, Francisco, 92, 99,
100–101, 114–115, 117–118
Hernández de Córdoba, Francisco,
122–123, 125–126
Hog plum tree, 137
Honey, 137, 148; Maya use,
125–126
Horchata, 40
Huaina Capac, 190, 191, 192,
202, 210–211
Huánuco, Peru, 44, 198; pine-
apples in, 44
Huauhtli, 90. *See also* Amaranth;
Chenopodium
Huehueteotl, 109
Huitlacoche, 94
Human flesh, eating of: Aztec,
97–99; and chiles, 92; Incas
and, 171; Maya, 160; Mote-
cuhzoma and, 74; as test of di-
vinity, 71, 73
Human skulls, as drinking vessels,
208–209

Iguanas, 154
Inca: banquets, 198–200; burial
rituals, 220; clay consumption,
179–180; communal eating,
199–200; drinks, alcoholic,
202–210; and drunkenness, 204,
209; encounter with Europeans,
203; etiquette, 199; and European food, 213–214; flavorings,
225–226; flesh cookery, 225;
food distribution, 196–200;
food gifts, 214; food laws,
196–198; food preservation,
178–179; highland food, 220;
hunting preserves, 176–177;
kitchens, 218, 222; llama rituals, 173; lowland food,